INTRODUCTION TO JAPANESE LAW

INTRODUCTION
TO
JAPANESE LAW

YOSIYUKI NODA

Translated and edited
by
ANTHONY H. ANGELO

UNIVERSITY OF TOKYO PRESS

This book was originally published in 1966 by Librairie
Dalloz in French under the title *Introduction au Droit
Japonais*, vol. XIX of the series Les Systèmes de Droit
Contemporains of the Institut de Droit Comparé de
l'Université de Paris.

English translation © by
UNIVERSITY OF TOKYO PRESS, 1976

UTP 3032-36168-5149
ISBN 0-86008-160-5
Printed in Japan

CONTENTS

CONTENTS

PREFACE

This book, translated and adapted here for English-speaking readers, was orginally published in French in 1966. For more than thirty years, I have taught almost exclusively French law at the Law Faculty of the University of Tokyo. From 1961 to 1963 I was in Paris to extend my knowledge of French law, and during my stay there I had the opportunity to give a course in the Faculty of Law and Economics of the University of Paris aimed at initiating postgraduate students in the elements of Japanese law. After returning to Japan, I rewrote the lectures and added appendices and a chapter relating to the sources of law, and together these were published in a volume entitled *Introduction au droit japonais*. Curiously enough, this introduction to Japanese law is the work of a specialist in French law. Jesus said, "If the blind lead the blind, both shall fall into the ditch" (Matt. 15: 14). Though I do not regard myself as entirely blind in respect to the law of my country, I am nevertheless afraid that I may be a bad guide for my readers. The merit of this book, if any, is that it has till now been the sole manual to give a general survey of Japanese law.[1] Until a better book is written by someone who is well versed in Japanese law, it is my hope that this one will realize its objective.

Several years ago, I received a letter from a foreign lawyer seeking my permission to translate the *Introduction* into English. He wrote in very good French, showing that he possessed a rich

---

[1] My colleague, Junichi Murakami, specialist in German law, has recently published an introduction to Japanese law in German, *Einführung in die Grundlagen des japanischen Rechts* (Darmstadt: Wissenschaftliche Buchgesellschaft, 1974). It is based on lectures he delivered at the Law Faculty of the University of Freiburg i. Br. in 1972 and is thus of nearly the same nature as mine. Readers who read German are invited to consult this excellent work, which is concise but rich in ideas.

knowledge of the French language and would be a suitably qualified translator, should I ever contemplate an English version of
my work. For some time I was hesitant to agree to his proposal.
On reflection, however, I decided to accept the offer, thinking
that however poor the book might be, if it were translated into
one of the world's most widely used languages, it would contri-
bute something to facilitate the study of Japanese law of which
so little was known in the world. I also hoped that this might
also conform to my duty as a comparatist in law. Thus began
the relationship between Mr. Anthony H. Angelo and me.

The structure of the book reflects the audience for which the
original French text was written. For example, almost all of the
illustrations given to facilitate the comprehension of Japanese
law for French readers are taken from French cultural sources.
The foreign law with which I compare Japanese law is limited
almost entirely to French law. The style is on the whole in line
with French taste. Such being the case, a translation following
the original text faithfully would certainly vex English-speaking
readers. Wisely seeking to avoid this difficulty, Mr. Angelo very
freely adapted the text to make it more readable for English-
speaking readers, all the while utilizing fully the French text.
I left the work of adaptation entirely to him. Although I gave
him advice and made suggestions for the translation, the resulting book is his own product rather than a mere translation of
my work. On the whole the composition has been simplified.
The division of chapters has been changed and a large part of
of the text has been rearranged following his scheme, but I find
the rearrangement successful. My original thoughts have not
been distorted in the process.

The English version has a further merit. Ten years have passed
since the publication of the French text. During those years social,
political, economic, and legal conditions have greatly changed
in Japan. In the original text, therefore, we find many facts which
are no longer in conformity with the present situation. Moreover,
the French edition contains a number of incorrect and infelicitous
descriptions and expressions. Efforts have been made to ensure
that this new edition is as correct and up-to-date as possible.

Apart from the changes already mentioned, I should comment

on a fairly significant change, or more exactly, development, which has taken, place in my own thoughts on the subject of this book. When writing the French text I perceived the great importance of the comparative study of civilizations in comparative law. Since that time this perception has been accentuated more and more. Consequently my interest has turned more toward anthropology psychology, linguistics, biology, and history of cultures and ideas than to law as a mechanism of social control.[2] From such a sociocultural point of view, this book should be revised entirely. It goes without saying, however, that so vast and laborious an undertaking cannot be realized within the framework of a translation. In this Preface, I will therefore confine myself to commenting on the subject which I consider the most important from my present standpoint: the problem of Japanese conception of law, treated in Chapter 9, "Japanese and the Law."

In the first place, I wish to draw the attention of readers to the question of national character. As the reader will see, my consideration of that question follows basically the theory of ethnic characters of Paul Griéger, an eminent French scholar. Although I do not mean to abandon his theory entirely, I now think that the national character of the Japanese people might be better explained in another way. It would be easier to appreciate the characteristics of Japanese national character if we consider it as a complex of three character types chosen from the list drawn up by René Le Senne: *nerveux, sentimental,* and *colérique*. Unfortunately, this subject cannot be treated in detail here. I have explained my view on the matter in a paper entitled "Far Eastern Conception of Law," which I contributed to the second volume of the *International Encyclopaedia of Comparative Law*.[3] I hope that it

---

[2] Such a tendency may be perceived in my paper, " Quelques réflexions sur le fondement du droit comparé: Essai d'une recherche anthropologique du fondement du droit comparé," in *Aspets nouveaux de la pensée juridique, Recueil d'études en hommage* à *Marc Ancel*, t. I (Paris: Editions A. Pedone, 1975), p. 23f.

[3] This large-scale publication is to be published under the auspices of the International Association of Legal Science and with the cooperation of legal comparatists and specialists throughout the world. The entire work is expected to consist of seventeen volumes. Although a complete volume is yet to appear, a substantial number of installments, which will be combined to make up a volume, have been published already. Under the direction of the renown comparatist, Professor K. Zweigert, the Max-Planck Institute of Foreign and International Private Law is editing the encyclopaedia.

will be published in the near future, and I would be grateful if the readers take it into account when reading Chapter 9.

Secondly, it may be useful to comment on the mentality of the Japanese. In explaining their mentality, I have said that the Japanese do not like to have recourse to litigation as a means of dispute resolution (see p. 159f). But after the publication of the French edition, there have been many social events which seem to indicate that in this respect a remarkable change may be taking place in the Japanese mentality. Almost everyday the newspapers are full of reports about actions brought to the courts claiming damages for loss caused by public nuisances of all sorts, motorcar accidents, etc. Under such circumstances, is it legitimate for us to leave intact the descriptions given in Chapter 9? The best way of course would have been to drastically modify this section, if possible. But such a modification would exceed the limits of our present scheme, and furthermore it is prudent not to pass hasty judgment on so sudden a change in the mental aspect of a nation. Therefore, as material for the reader's reflection, I will only give my thoughts on the subject.

No one can deny the fact that there has been a sudden recognizable change in the mode of behavior of the Japanese in the field of law in these ten short years. It would almost appear as though Japanese no longer hesitate before resorting to the courts in order to claim their rights. Today, even rural inhabitants, who have till recently been considered the most conservative and the most reluctant to have recourse to judicial remedies, appear, willingly it seems, in court one after another. Without exaggeration we can say that we are now indeed seeing a rush for litigation.[4]

Does this mean a radical change in the national character of the Japanese? I do not think so. But before I justify my opinion, let us define precisely what is meant by *character*. I use this word

[4] We must, however, beware lest we fail to catch the actual meaning of this phenomenon, for the total number of civil cases brought to court has not greatly increased during these ten years. According to judicial statistics, the total number of civil cases brought to various courts was 1,748,344 in 1964 and 1,752,150 in 1973 (*Outline of Civil Trials in Japan*, published by the Japanese Supreme Court in 1975). The rush is more psychological than real. Litigants tend to seek publicity for their causes rather than a settlement by judicial process. This publicity in turn satisfies the general public's interest in sensational issues.

throughout my study in the defintion established by René Le
Senne.[5] He distinguishes two aspects of what is generally called
personality. According to Le Senne, that part which forms the
nucleus of one's personality is character in the strict sense of
the word. "Character," he says, "means the mass of congenital
dispositions which form one's mental skeleton,"[6] while personality
"comprises first the character, but also all the elements acquired
in the course of one's life."[7] Thus, the notion of character is
narrower than that of personality, and character in this sense is
permanent and invariable. The elements composing the biological
base of character might be transmitted by genes. According to
biological theory, genes are extremely difficult to alter, even given
the variation of surrounding circumstances. Therefore, character,
which may also be dominated by the laws of genetics, would
remain immutable for a long time.

So far I have considered only individual character, but national
character, which is a complex of several individual character
types, might *mutatis mutandis* be submitted to nearly the same
biological laws. There are, it is true, some difficulties which warn
us against making hasty conclusions in this matter, but as they
have been dealt with (see p. 160f), I will not repeat myself here.
Be that as it may, if our conclusion is not too far from the truth,
then the national character of the Japanese could not have
changed radically in ten years. I do not deny that Japanese behavior appears very different from that of ten years ago, but in
my opinion, this merely means that their character, invariable
in essence, presents different aspects in expressions and gestures
under different circumstances. I have pointed out that in Japan
we have even known a fashion in ideas (see p. 171). It seems to
me that a sudden rush for litigation arising among people who
until recently were very reluctant to appear in court can mean
nothing but a fashion for litigation. Perhaps their character remains unchanged in spite of its different outward appearance.

I would like to try to find the reason for this mental tendency.

---

[5] René Le Senne, *Traité de caractérologie* (Paris: Presses Universitaires de France,
1963).
[6] Ibid., p. 9.
[7] Ibid., p. 11.

Until recent times, and for over two thousand years, the Japanese have for the most part lived and have been engaged exclusively in an agricultural life involving in particular rice cultivation. This type of work requires all cultivators to do the same thing at the same time following the dictates of seasonal meteorological conditions. Since basically similar weather conditions prevail throughout Japan in each season, it follows that everyone everywhere subconsciously acts in the same way at a given time. This spontaneous uniform set of actions has been repeated regularly generation after generation, and so the habit of behaving simultaneously in the same way has been deeply implanted in the mind of every Japanese. This may be one of the reasons why the Japanese people like to behave uniformly. I hope that this comment will help readers to understand the Japanese mentality.

There are many other points in the text that I would like to comment on or improve, but I must content myself with the the knowledge that what I have done in this book I have done to the best of my ability. Perfection is, after all, not of this world.

In putting down my pen, I wish to express my deepest gratitude to Mr. Angelo for all his kindness in preparing this excellent translation and adaptation. Without his very cordial and enthusiastic efforts, my *Introduction* would not have been available to English-speaking readers. I wish also to thank the editorial staff of the University of Tokyo Press, who took undertook the publication of this book, in particular, to Ms. Nina Raj.

Tokyo
February 1976   Yosiyuki Noda

TRANSLATOR-EDITOR'S NOTE

I wish to record here my sincere thanks to Professor René David of the University of Aix-Marseille for his early support for and continued interest in this translation, to the Japanese Ministry of Education for its financial support for this project, and to the publishers for their methodical preparation of the text and for the efficiency and apparent ease with which they guided it through the publishing process.

Last, but by no means least, I wish to acknowledge the very great assistance I have received from Professor Yosiyuki Noda and to thank him for the inspiration of his example and the privilege of his collaboration.

A need has long been felt for an introductory text to the Japanese legal system in English. It is hoped that this edition will fill that need.

Wellington   Anthony H. Angelo
February 1976

INTRODUCTION TO JAPANESE LAW

INTRODUCTION AND HISTORY

CHAPTER I

INTRODUCTION

THE STUDY OF JAPANESE LAW

Most people are attracted to the study of Japan and its culture because it excites their curiosity. In the case of Japanese law there is, as this book will show, good reason for the study quite apart from the simple satisfaction of curiosity.

One of the most important benefits of comparative law is that it can provide a knowledge of the different patterns of legal thinking current in the world and show that the personal way of thinking that everyone considers without reflection to be that of everybody else is in fact only one of many ways. The comparative study of law reveals, to borrow an expression from Professor David, "the relativity of concepts admitted in different countries."[1]

Although the study of any foreign legal system teaches something about this relativity, the Japanese system provides material which brings out the relativity in an accentuated way. Japan is situated both geographically and historically in a special position. On the one hand it is isolated in the Pacific and, being at some distance from the continent, was free from foreign invasion until 1945. On the other hand the distance from the continent was not so great as to prevent all communication. For these reasons Japan freely adopted ideas and habits from foreign civilizations. The ideas took root in Japanese soil, and cut off from their native cultural surroundings, they have developed and been transformed into something quite different from the original. This pattern is in direct contrast with that of Europe, where nations

---

[1] René David, *Traité élémentaire de droit civil comparé* (Paris: Librairie Générale de Droit et de Jurisprudence, 1950), p. 61.

have been fighting violently for thousands of years and where differing ideas have mixed with and complemented each other to form the basis of a single European type of thought. Though it is possible to speak of Oriental ideas, there is nothing in this conception or in those ideas which can compare with the cohesion found in European thought.

Japanese thought has a further characteristic which results from the policy of isolationism during the two hundred and fifty years which preceded the Meiji era (1868–1912). While European nations were engaged in fierce political and economic competition, Japan was enjoying the idleness of peace. The effects of this isolation are difficult to gauge, but one thing is sure—isolation assured Japanese thought of an excessive accentuation of its natural characteristics and had a great influence on the Japanese conception of law.

As is indicated by the change of the official name of the discipline from comparative legislation to comparative law earlier in this century, this branch of legal study concentrated in its early stages on the parallel study of legislation of different systems. It virtually limited itself to detailing the similarities and differences which existed between the legislative documents of different countries.[2] As research progressed comparatists became more and more conscious of the inadequacy of this method, and the field of investigation has as a result been extended to include case law, juristic writings, and judicial and extra-judicial practices—in short, to law in its entirety. "While it is desirable and right that all lawyers should by their reading try to learn as much about the laws of as many countries as possible and so gain an idea of the variety of concepts used by the lawyers of those countries and expand their own cultural knowledge, it is also necessary that lawyers write only about the laws which they know and understand because they have studied them, and because in particular they understand the social environment in which the law in question operates. It is possible for texts to be written about foreign law if this last condition is not fulfilled, and such compilations may perhaps be used in later

---

[2] Probably due to the influence of European jurists accustomed to thinking of legislation as the only source of law. Cf. David, ibid., p. 10.

studies, but they are not themselves scientific and in most cases will prove to be of more harm than good to the progress of comparative legal studies."[3] The expansion of the field of investigation in a quantitative way is not satisfactory. "In all countries the law stands in a direct relationship to all the other bases of social life. It cannot be understood without a knowledge of the society that it governs, nor can it be understood in ignorance of the modes of behavior, thought, and feeling of the members of that society. The general formulae which are used in the legal world . . . are the most obvious manifestation of this principle. To know a foreign law it is necessary to know the foreign society—the social environment in which the law is applied."[4] The comparative study of law must not be limited to a static or purely structural comparison of diverse legal systems. It must undertake the dynamic or functional comparison of those systems.

> With few exceptions, comparative law in the past limited itself to the study of rules, institutions, and systems from a legal point of view without taking sufficient account of the sociological realities in relation to which the law functions and to which it applies. The study of various rules, institutions, and legal systems, their comparison and the pointing out of similarities and differences in the fields of study is something which can lead us only to the presentation of a superficial framework, so superficial in fact that it is of little value for supplying theoretical consequences or practical directives for future action. It is not enough to know the similarities or the differences. It is necessary also to find the reasons for them. Each positive statement of the law must be explained . . . as a normative crystallization of certain sociological processes. Consequently, when rules are compared, the comparison must be undertaken in terms of the realities which exist behind the rules: as much of the realities which have given rise to the rules as of the present realities to which the rules are applied. . . . Comparative law must not limit itself to the consideration of rules currently in force; but it must, with the aid of socio-legal techniques, examine the degree of relationship or conflict between the rules formerly in force and the present patterns of legal conduct.[5]

[3] Ibid., p. 26.
[4] Ibid., p. 17.
[5] Recasens Siches, "Nuevas perspectivas del derecho comparado," Fourth Centenary issue of the *Revista de la Facultad de Derecho de Mexico* (1953), p. 253.

For those who take this view of comparative law, the development of Japanese law provides material which will enable them to extend their studies both substantially and methodologically.

The relationship between the structure of Japanese law and the reality of the social life to which the law is applied shows itself in a peculiar form. Japan established her modern legal system on French and English models in the first instance, and on the German model at a later stage. The establishment of the modern legal system was a response to an urgent need. Japan had to modernize her entire social system by adopting capitalism, and it is well known how quickly she succeeded, at least superficially, in imitating the European models. Japanese capitalism developed so quickly, in fact, that it reached the monopolistic stage within fifty years. Japan took the shortest possible route to the desired end, and the external modernization of the social framework was carried through without a sufficient mental adaptation by the people to the new social conditions. This is why the great strength of Japan's economy has not been equaled by a modernization of the way of life of the Japanese people. The traditional rules of conduct and the manner of thinking which developed during the long history of the country and which are of a noticeably feudal character will take a long time to change. It follows that the modernized state law has had difficulty in penetrating the actual life of the Japanese people. This has not, however, prevented law and society from acting and reacting upon each other in a very complex way. The ruling class of Japan has tried to maintain its traditional ways as much as possible in spite of its great desire to have the material benefits of the civilization of the West. Nevertheless, it would be ingenuous to think it possible to maintain a perpetual harmony between a morality developed in an entirely feudal environment and the modern social environment. The conflict between the legal structure and the actual life of the people is great, and as a result a great number of difficult and confusing problems, which European societies have not had to deal with in the course of their modernization, have arisen. Isolating and examining these problems is clearly a fruitful field of study for the comparative lawyer.

DIFFICULTIES IN THE STUDY OF JAPANESE LAW

Japanese law is regrettably little known and understood by people outside Japan, principally because of the difficulty of the Japanese language. No study is without its difficulties, but when foreign lawyers wish to study Japanese law in a more detailed way than is done in this book, they necessarily run into difficulties which are, one may say with only slight exaggeration, peculiar to Japanese law.

The difficulty that arises from the structure of the Japanese language appears at first sight to be a problem of a general character, for it is extremely difficult to have an exact knowledge of any foreign language. However, the degree of difficulty varies greatly according to the language that is studied. If the language is one whose structure is not essentially different from that of the student, the difficulty is relatively slight. An example of this would be a European learning another European language. If, on the other hand, the language studied is one whose structure is basically different from that of the language of the student, the difficulties can be almost insurmountable, at least for those who have no special linguistic skill. This, for example, is the usual case when Japanese learn European languages or Europeans learn Japanese. Nevertheless, Europeans experience much more difficulty in learning Japanese than Japanese do in learning a European language. The reason for this is that European languages are, in general terms, more logical and more ordered than Japanese.

The Japanese language had originally no written form. It was only toward the end of the fourth century A.D. that Chinese characters[6] came to be known in Japan, thus making it possible for Japanese to be transcribed by the use of those signs. However, since Chinese characters are ideographs, the Japanese language

---

[6] Writing was known in China from about 1300 B.C.

could not adopt them without modification. The Japanese began to use a great number of Chinese characters, retaining in some cases their original meanings, but not their Chinese pronunciation, to write Japanese words whose meanings were similar to the Chinese, while in other cases retaining both their original Chinese sense and pronunciation to express ideas which had no exact equivalents in Japanese. In this way the Japanese vocabulary was greatly enriched, but at the same time the linguistic structure of Japanese lost its primitive purity. This adaptation of Chinese characters was not in itself sufficient for writing Japanese sentences, because other linguistic elements were needed which had no parallel in the Chinese language, of which the structure is basically different from that of Japanese.[7] The Japanese language had to resolve the problem in its own way. It did this by using the Chinese characters simply as phonetic symbols, without regard to their original meaning. A collection of poems called *Manyoshu*, written in the late Nara period (eighth century A.D.), uses this system, and for this reason the characters used as phonetic symbols are called *manyogana*.[8] Nevertheless, since Chinese characters are of a very complicated composition, they are not suited for use as phonetic symbols and the Japanese were forced to simplify them. This they did in two ways. One way was to break a character down into separate elements and take from it one simple element; the other method was to change the shape of a character completely by rendering it in a less complicated form. From these practices developed two systems of phonetic writing which were perfected after the ninth century.

[7] A Chinese sentence is made up entirely of characters. A Japanese sentence with the same meaning as a Chinese sentence would use the same characters but between each word auxiliary elements would be added.

[8] *Kana* means a phonetic symbol representing a Japanese syllable. In *manyogana* the *k* becomes *g* for euphony. Literally *kana* means false letter as opposed to *mana*, which is a true letter. It was considered that a Chinese character used in its original sense was a true letter, and that a character used simply as a phonetic symbol was a false or provisional letter.

The first system is called *katakana* and the second *hiragana*.[9] The result is that the Japanese language is written by means of a mixture of Chinese characters and two *kana* alphabets used independently or together.

The total number of Chinese characters is considerable. According to one specialist in Chinese history there are as many as 50,000, but the number used in practice is not so great. There are about 9,000 listed in a good dictionary. Of course, not everyone knows all these characters. Moreover, there is no need to know even a half of them to be able to read and write Japanese in a cultured way. Since 1946, the Japanese government has been trying to limit the number of characters used in daily life. At present the limit is set at 1,850, but anyone who wants to read the great Japanese classics would need to know at least 3,000.[10]

A factor that further complicates the matter is that with few exceptions each character has at least two different pronunciations, an original Chinese pronunciation *(kan-on)*[11] and a Japanese pronunciation *(kun)*. Sometimes, however, a character may have five or six different pronunciations and, what is more, a Japanese word may often be written using several different Chinese characters with a range of choice that may be as wide as twelve.[12] In this sort of case each different character would give the word a slightly different shade of meaning.

Another aspect of the problem is that in feudal times when class differences were strictly imposed and observed, the expres-

---

[9] *Kata* means a part or something incomplete ; *hira* means flat or ordinary. *Katakana* is an angular script ; *hiragana* is a flowing script. Each system of *kana* is made up of fifty signs, and each sign, with the exception of those for the sounds *a, e, i, o, u*, can be transcribed into the Roman alphabet by one or two consonants followed by a vowel. The Japanese language does not know the independent use of consonants except the nasal *n*. The signs do not form an alphabet ; rather they form a syllabary.

[10] The reform of the Japanese language by way of rationalization is an urgent but very delicate matter. Strong controversy is aroused by government reform in this area. There is no doubt that teaching in primary and secondary schools is overburdened with studying of the characters ; pupils spend most of their time learning them. Simplification seems very necessary, but conservatives refuse this on grounds of retaining the traditional purity of the language.

[11] There is also *go-on*, another way of pronunciation. The duality comes from the fact that one system is borrowed from the Chinese language of the Han dynasty and the other from the Wu Kingdom of the Six Dynasties period.

[12] E.g., *tadasu*, to make right or correct.

sions used for the same thing varied noticeably according to the social class of the persons concerned. Two persons belonging to different classes did not use the same expression to refer to the same object. For example, one person would use different personal pronouns when referring to himself, depending on the social status of his company. These different modes of expression have survived feudal society and still dominate the Japanese language. This, clearly, is one of the most troublesome areas. There are for instance about ten personal pronouns that are used by a man to refer to himself, and the greater number of these ten are not those used by women. Although there is currently a move toward uniformity of usage, there is still a long way to go and, of course, this state of affairs is not limited to pronouns. Professor Kawashima lists five ways in the case of men, and six in the case of women, of asking: "Have you read the newspaper?"[13]

From all this it can be concluded that the Japanese language is very complicated. Further, it is more suited to the expression of emotion than logical argument. It is capable of expressing every subtle shade of feeling,[14] but is quite unsuited to expressing the logical relationship between objective things. It is a language of poetry, not of science. G. Bousquet who was in Japan from 1872 to 1874 as legal adviser to the Japanese government wrote: "[The Japanese language], even when spoken by a highly cultured person, cannot formulate all inflections of thought, nor can it reproduce the complicated terminology of the sciences.... Will it ever be possible to teach or learn philosophy, psychology, or transcendental mathematics in this language which is so resistant to analysis, stubborn of construction, and filled with words but lacking in abstract terms?"[15] In its present state the

[13] Takeyoshi Kawashima, *Hoshakaigaku ni okeru ho no sonzai kozo* [Structure of Law from the Viewpoint of Sociology of Law] (Tokyo: Nippon Hyoronsha, 1950), p. 72. The variation in each case depends on the degree of respect shown toward the person addressed.

[14] E.g., Japanese has many different verbs to express the feeling of love: *aisuru* (general), *koisuru* (to love a person of the other sex), *suku* (not limited to love for human beings), *mederu, itsukushimu, ito-oshimu*, etc.

[15] Gustave Bousquet, *Le Japon de nos jours* (1877), Vol. II, p. 220. "Their vocabulary," he says, "rich in more or less noble words to represent objects or feelings is essentially realist in nature, but at the same time is lacking in abstract terms and words for general or metaphysical ideas." (Vol. I, p. 329.)

Japanese language has changed a little, but its basic character remains almost the same as in earlier times.

The characteristics of the Japanese language are closely related to the character type of the Japanese people. As will be seen later, the Japanese belong to a character type that is predominantly emotive. According to linguistic psychology, human thought is determined structurally by the language which is used to represent it. Without this, whatever is conceived by the human mind could not be stabilized in thought.[16] If this is correct, the Japanese manner of thinking is dependent on the structure of the Japanese language, and since law is a product of thought, there must be an inseparable relationship between law and language. This leads by logical necessity to the following conclusion. Without an adequate knowledge of the Japanese language, a knowledge of Japanese law in its true form is almost unattainable.

The difficulties of the language have not been emphasized to discourage those who are interested in studying Japanese law, but to warn them against making a superficial study. With advance knowledge the difficulties likely to be met during research can be encountered and overcome more successfully.

Apart from the difficulties of the language, there is also the problem resulting from the double structure of Japanese society. Japanese capitalism caught up with that of advanced countries in an extremely short period of time, but it has been impossible to accomplish in less than one century what has been achieved in Western countries during more than four. Naturally, many things have been neglected in reaching the goal that Japanese capitalism set for itself—the modernization of the state structure on a capitalistic base. In the international political situation, as it related to Japan in the Meiji era, modernization, or simply Europeanization of the state structure, was imperative if Japan wished to be recognized as an equal by its European counterparts. Yet, the social structure has in large degree, either purposely or out of necessity, been left intact. Many relics of the past, and of

[16] Ferdinand de Saussure, *Cours de linguistique générale* (Paris: Payot, 1915), p. 155. See also Jean Stoetzel, *La psychologie sociale* (Paris: Flammarion, 1963), p. 130f. What Stoetzel says about Chinese can be said equally of the Japanese language.

the feudal period in particular, have been preserved.[17] Japanese society has passed directly from the state of feudalism to that of capitalism without knowing anything of the intermediate stage which Gurvitch calls that of "society giving way to the development of capitalism." In European countries in which capitalism developed gradually, feudalism broke down equally gradually to prepare for modern society. It was a long, slow process. When Gurvitch's "liberal democratic society making way for competitive capitalism"[18] appeared, what remained of the feudal state had all but been swept away. By contrast, Japan has from the beginning of its modernization been confronted with both two stages at the same time. Thus, the double structure of Japanese society has arisen. That is to say, in Japanese society today a state transitional between feudalism and capitalism exists side by side with that of an already well advanced capitalism. And these two aspects are interrelated in a very complex manner. Japanese society has within it at one and the same time problems that stem from vast capitalistic development and others that relate to a social evolution still geared to the birth of capitalism. It is possible to speak of an excess of liberal competition on the one hand, while on the other to say that the true meaning of liberty is not known.[19] Indeed, only since World War II have individual dignity and liberty become real problems for the Japanese people. The reality of Japanese law would be misunderstood if only one side of this double structure was considered.

It is difficult to appreciate the reality of this double structure since it does not follow from the fact of its existence that two clearly distinguished sections—a socially advanced section and a more retarded section—can be seen in Japanese society. Certainly, from the macroscopic point of view it could be said that the

[17] This is a question of degree. Each society evolves without losing continuity with its past, but in the normal course of evolution the new elements gradually take the place of the preceding ones, leaving them to settle at the basis of historical knowledge. In the case of any sudden change in a society the old elements are as much alive as the new. The more that these old elements are localized in underdeveloped regions, the greater the complexity with which they mix in with the modern morality.

[18] Georges Gurvitch, *Problèmes de sociologie du droit*, in *Traité de sociologie*, ed. Georges Gurvitch, Vol. 2 (Paris: Presses Universitaires de France, 1960), p. 202.

[19] The party that calls itself the Liberal Democratic Party is dominated by an ultra-traditionalist mentality, and it is the Socialist Party which often finds itself advocating liberal individualism though even its outlook is somewhat feudal.

urban areas are more advanced than the rural ones, but from the microscopic point of view it could be said even of urban dwellers that the manner of thought and behavior of former times is still retained to some degree.

The type of fiction by which all groups in society are modeled on the family is still alive in all segments of Japanese society and prevents any radical change in social life. For instance, in the most modern industrial enterprises, relations between employers and employees are dominated, if not by the principle, at least by the sentiment of a hierarchical order of a feudal nature. Even between employees such a ranking often exists. Stoetzel, a French sociologist, who conducted an inquiry into the attitudes of post-war Japanese youth in 1952, has described these different social relationships in the following terms: "[The] relationships of sub-ordination and superiority are complex, and the notion which characterizes this structure is that of a hierarchy. ... The hierarchy is evident in many aspects of modern Japanese life."[20] He also mentions "the transposition of a patriarchal system into the professional and economic field." "Whatever the size of an enterprise, be it big or small, the workers in it form small family-like groups, in a system known by the name of *oyabun-kobun*, that is to say 'quasi-father and quasi-son.' The *oyabun* is likely to be an older worker, probably an overseer, who takes the young workers and the new employees, under his protection and as-sumes the role of father toward them. This system is most fre-quently found in mines. The *oyabun* helps the *kobun* in his work, draws his attention to the traditions[21] which are honored in the mine, helps him in his private life, and sometimes chooses a wife for him. Frequently the *oyabun* declares that he loves his *kobun* more than his own children. The *kobun* in turn show their ap-preciation to the *oyabun* in the feeling that they express toward him. They call him *ototsan* [*otosan*=father] and his wife *okkasan* [*okasan*=mother] and take care of him and of her in their old age."[22] This description is perhaps reminiscent of the *com-*

[20] Jean Stoetzel, *Jeunesse sans chrysanthème ni sabre: Etudes sur les attitudes de la jeunesse japonaise d'après guerre* (Paris: UNESCO–Plon, 1953), p. 53.
[21] Often of a superstitious nature.
[22] Stoetzel, *Jeunesse sans chrysanthème ni sabre*, pp. 54–55.

pagnonnage of France of earlier times and, to a certain extent, of the paternalism of the modern state.

Social reform in Japan was pushed forward under the patronage of the Allied Occupation Force at the beginning of its period of control, but the speed of the reform slowed down increasingly rapidly with the change in policies determined by the international situation and the strong backing of the ultra-conservative government of Japan. Since the conclusion of the peace treaty in San Francisco in 1951 a noticeable move back toward the past can be observed in many quarters. A large number of politicians who were excluded as war criminals have returned to the political world where they now occupy important positions. Tutored in the old ideas and thoroughly convinced of their value, these people are trying to orient the course of history in a backward-looking direction. It can be said of them as it was of certain royalists at the time of the Restoration of 1814 in France that they have "learned nothing and forgotten nothing." They believe that the errors of what they consider the excess of democratization and of modernization must be corrected. They claim that the reforms carried out under the direction of the U.S. Army were in most cases not in conformity with the traditional morality of the country, and this view arouses the sympathy of most of the older generation. Sustained by these traditionalists, recent governments with the same tendency have implemented policies aimed at counter-reform. The revision of the present constitution, called by them the "McArthur Constitution" or the "Constitution, made in U.S.A.," is on the agenda, and many laws promulgated during the Occupation have been amended in a reactionary manner.

In these circumstances the modernization of the social structure will meet with resistance from the traditionalists for a long time, and the double structure of Japanese society will continue to exist as before. As Dean Okochi, a specialist in labor problems, said:

> It was not till after the Second World War that the Japanese working class was emancipated from the personal servitude to which it had been submitted under the military regime and it is

only now that it enjoys the 'liberty' necessary for working as a modern-day labor force. But what made this possible was the primitive policy of the Occupation Forces which imposed the evolution from outside, or rather encouraged it from above. Even that, however, was not enough to totally suppress the peculiarly Japanese conditions that were undesirable and that weighed against the interests of the working class. Certainly the right to association granted them by the trade union law, and work conditions assuring them a life 'worthy of human beings' have been guaranteed by the law on conditions of work, and the possibility of work contracts analogous to slavery has been abolished by the law on the stabilization of the professions. . . . The establishment of these new workers' laws was not sufficient to eliminate conditions fatal to improvement, such as low salaries, the factors which have restricted the right of association, and that manner of thinking of former times which is characteristic of the working class . . . , in a word, the whole semi-feudal set-up which enclosed the life of the worker. . . . The fact must not be overlooked that the 'democratization' or modernization of work relations which saw prosperous days at the beginning of the Occupation has encountered many obstacles, and workers' laws which originally meant 'democratization' for Japan have been subjected to modification under the pretext of editing out excesses.[23]

Such then is the double structure of Japanese society, but a false picture of Japanese law would be given if no effort were made to see the other side of the coin, that is, the gradual breaking down of the old ideas. The process has already begun. From the beginning of modernization in Japanese society the movement seems to have been gaining momentum among the younger generation. Even now this group is ignorant of a great portion of the traditional morality, although the national character that favored its formation remains unchanged in them. Stoetzel says that Japanese youths do not fully understand the meaning of the notion of *giri*.[24] *Giri*, as will be explained more fully later, means those very important rules of conduct which regulate the social life of the Japanese people. This code of behavior exercises a great influence on the older people, but young people seem no longer

---

[23] Kazuo Okochi, " Rodo" [Labor], in *Gendai nippon shoshi* [A Short History of Contemporary Japan], ed. Tadao Yanaihara, Vol. 2 (Tokyo: Misuzu, 1952), p. 111f.
[24] Stoetzel, *Jeunesse sans chrysanthème ni sabre*, p. 193.

to care about it. Another factor of the same kind is mentioned by Stoetzel in speaking of the problem of citizen participation in political life:

> Japanese on the whole think that citizens must be able to comment on public affairs. In general, the percentage of citizens who express this opinion is in all age groups less high in the country and . . . one often finds in the country regions the opinion expressed that it is better to leave the government to look after policy matters without interference, but in all cases the younger the subject questioned, the more frequently is the idea expressed that it is better to express one's opinions as much as possible.[25]

It is wise, therefore, since it is difficult even for Japanese to understand Japanese law, never to forget that Japan is in the process of changing and that Japanese society has a complex and unstable structure.

[25] Ibid., p. 151.

CHAPTER II

HISTORY OF JAPANESE LAW TO 1868

It is not known exactly how long Japan has been inhabited.
The most recent archaeological excavations show that paleolithic
man inhabited the Japanese islands.[1] Where these first Japanese
ancestors came from and when they arrived in Japan is uncer-
tain, but it is assumed that they had been there for some thousands of years. Of their social life very little is known.
The first written data on Japan are to be found in Chinese books.
According to chronicles of the Han Dynasty, Japanese society
was, in about the first century A.D., divided into a hundred or so
separate clans that fought among themselves.[2] Toward the second
century these clans were grouping themselves in thirty or so
regions. At the beginning of the third century the groups were
united under the power of Queen Himiko of the state of Yamatai.[3] From these facts can be seen the birth of the Japanese state,
although state organization was very feeble at that time. Professor Ishii, the Japanese legal historian, claims that Himiko was

[1] Although no skeletons of paleolithic man have been found, a few pieces of
human bone and stone tools have been found which archaeologists say are of the
paleolithic age. It is thought that the islands of Japan were at that time linked to
the Asian continent.
[2] Japan is mentioned for the first time in a Chinese book called *Chronicle of the
Former Han Dynasty* written about the end of the first century A.D.
[3] It is a historical fact that there was in the fourth century a dynasty known by
the name Yamato ruling in the region of Yamato, which is the area of the cities
of Nara and Kyoto. But there is great controversy among historians about whether
the state Yamatai was the origin of the Yamato dynasty. Some historians claim
that the Yamatai state was situated on the island of Kyushu, the southern island
of Japan. This is, however, only an assumption which finds no basis in direct historical
sources. The southern region was the center of ancient civilization at the beginning
of Japanese history because Chinese culture came to Japan through Korea. It is
thought, therefore, that the dynasty of Himiko was established somewhere in Kyushu.
A Chinese book of the end of the third century describes the dynasty in some detail.
Yamato was the old name of Japan; perhaps it originated in the word Yamatai.

the ancestor of the imperial family, and this is what the Chinese documents, particularly the description of *San-kuo Chih* (History of the Three Kingdoms), lead one to believe. There is however a great difference between this thesis and the tradition handed down in *Kojiki*[4] and *Nihonshoki*,[5] the first historical books produced in Japan. According to them, the foundation of Japan dates back to the year 660 B.C., when the emperor Jimmu ascended the throne. These books were written at the beginning of the eighth century, at a time when national sentiment was blossoming. In order to boast of the antiquity of the foundation of the Japanese state it was thought necessary to date its origin as far back as possible, without too much concern for historical accuracy. The tradition may not therefore fit the facts, but the matter is far from clear and historians are divided on the answers.

The historical survey that follows is based on the hypothesis that Himiko unified Japan at the beginning of the third century A.D.; it will proceed from that time and work through until 1868, the year of the Meiji Restoration. The history of Japanese law shows quite a different aspect after that date and will be dealt with in a separate chapter.

FIRST ERA: EARLY SOCIETY

From the third to the fourth centuries the social life of Japan came under strong religious influence. Law at that stage was not

---

[4]   *Kojiki*, the *Records of Ancient Matters*, is the oldest historical document extant. It was written by Ono Yasumaro in 712 on imperial order. The book is in three parts and contains the history of Japan from its origin until the reign of Empress Suiko (554[?]–628). The greater part of the book deals with myths and legends handed down by word of mouth from generation to generation, and it is written in old Japanese. For these reasons it is a treasure house of the language, religion, and customs of ancient Japan.

[5]   *Nihonshoki*, *Chronicles of Japan*, is another very old historical document. It was written in 720 on the direction of an imperial prince called Toneri. The book is divided into thirty volumes and contains the history of the period from the first emperor, Jimmu, to the empress Jito (645[?]–702). It is written in Chinese, which was until about the end of the nineteenth century the learned language of the Far East, as Latin was for Europe, and the style of writing follows the pattern of the chronicles of the Chinese dynasties. The bulk of the book deals with legend rather than history.

distinguished from other social rules, and in particular was not distinguished from religious rules. According to the *San-kuo Chih*, Himiko was considered a pontiff and governed the cult of ancestors.[6] Traditional Japanese religion considers ancestors as gods; hence Himiko served the gods and the foundation of her political power was religious. Through prayer she knew the will of the ancestor gods and pronounced oracles which were law. As evidence of this, the old Japanese words describing political matters are very closely linked to religion. For example, "to govern" was *shiroshimesu* or *shirasu*. Both these words mean "to know" (*shiru*), and the main object of politics consisted in knowing the will of the gods. Politics in Japanese is *matsurigoto*, which means religious cult; law is called *nori* and *noru*, the verbal form of *nori*, means "to declare." Thus, law was the will of the gods as declared by the person interceding between the gods and the people. The person interceding was almost always a woman, and it could even be said that in this first era the "woman-king" was the rule rather than the exception. The fact that the most important divinity in Shinto is the goddess Amaterasu[7] strengthens this opinion. It is interesting to note, however, that Himiko did not herself execute the will of the gods, although she declared it. It was her brother who undertook the execution of the divine will. Himiko therefore reigned but did not govern. This fundamental principle was observed for a long time with only a few exceptions.

The governmental institutions of the era were not influenced in any way by foreign civilization and in them is reflected the manner of thinking that is peculiar to the Japanese people. For example, the old-time Japanese considered delicts as blemishes or blots that the gods detested but that could be cleansed by religious ceremonial.[8] Condemned persons had to present offerings to the gods. The priest said prayers for purification, and sometimes there was a washing of the bodies of condemned per-

[6] "Himiko served the gods and exercised a charismatic influence over the whole nation. She was elderly and she had never married. Her younger brother helped her rule." *San-kuo Chih*.

[7] *Amaterasu*, literally, she who lights up the heaven.

[8] The essential part of Shintoism is the *harai*, that is, the solemn act by which the priest banishes evil. It is a kind of sweeping away of ills.

sons. Delicts came under the notion of *tsumi*, which dealt at the same time with illness and plagues.[9] People's manner of thought was non-rigorous and simple, and they were by nature optimists. The *San-kuo Chih* shows us that Japanese morals were very strong and that there were few crimes or trials.

SECOND ERA: THE REGIME OF RITSU-RYO

During the preceding era the imperial power had become more and more laicized and was continually being threatened with overthrow by the powerful clans. Partisans of the imperial family sought to stabilize the situation by concentrating all state powers in the government of the emperor. This method was also necessitated by the external political situation. There was a highly centralized government in China, and in order to defend itself against possible invasion the national cohesion of Japan became a matter of great importance. By the beginning of the seventh century, Japan had a state organization of a centralized type along the lines of the Chinese model. The task of centralization was a difficult one because the powerful clans resisted it, but from the Taika Reform[10] of 646, the basis of the imperial government was gradually strengthened, and a strongly centralized and bureaucratic state emerged. The emperor governed personally, following the model of the despotic Chinese emperor, and all the Chinese political institutions were transplanted to Japanese soil.

Similarly, in the field of law several codes drawn up on the model of the Chinese ones were promulgated and put into practice. This legal system is called the system of *ritsu-ryo* because the codes were made up of two parts, the *ritsu* and the *ryo*. *Ritsu* is a body of penal rules and *ryo* a body of admonitory rules. The laws had a strong moral character, closely linked to the Confucian doctrine according to which the *ritsu-ryo* had as its mission either the encouraging of people to do good or the

---

[9] This word *tsumi* corresponds to the modern word "sin," and sin for the old-time Japanese was simply a stain that could be got rid of by cleaning.

[10] *Taika* means great reform.

punishing of them for doing wrong. The aim of the laws was to educate ignorant men and lead them toward the Confucian ideal.[11] Since the education of the people was under the control of public officials, rules of administrative law occupied a very important place in the system of *ritsu-ryo*. The criminal laws that made up the *ritsu* were also important, but there were few rules of civil law.[12]

During this era several *ritsu-ryo* codes were promulgated and all fairly faithfully imitated the codes of T'ang,[13] the powerful Chinese dynasty of the time. The language used in these Japanese codes was Chinese, with the result that it is difficult for present-day jurists who have no special knowledge of the history of Japanese law to understand them. The *ritsu* is a replica of the Chinese *ritsu* except that the punishments prescribed were mitigated in the Japanese code. The *ryo* on the other hand is very much simplified, for account was taken of the customs and social conditions peculiar to Japan. Of these codes that known as the *Taiho Ritsu-ryo*, promulgated in the first year of the Taiho era (701), is the most famous, but regrettably it is no longer extant. The one of which the greatest part is still extant is the *Yoro Ritsu-ryo*. It was promulgated in the second year of Yoro (718) and came into force thirty-nine years later. In this code the *ritsu* is divided into twelve books and the *ryo* into thirty. The code was amended and complemented by particularized laws (*kyaku*), and rules (*shiki*)[14] were promulgated to facilitate its application.

Since the aim of the codes was the education of the people, it was necessary that they be made known, and so a faculty of law

---

[11] For a concise description of the Confucian theory of law see David, *Traité élementaire de droit civil comparé*, p. 377f.

[12] The development of Roman law, the forebear of all Western law, shows that in the West the task of law is to resolve disputes. It is inseparably linked with procedure, the wellspring of the law. The aim of law in the Far East is rather to prevent disputes. Confucius said: "If I judge a dispute I cannot do other than what others do, but what I sincerely want is to do my best to see that there is no dispute."

[13] It is to be noted that the most important part of the Chinese codification is criminal law. Nida Noboru, famed historian of Chinese law, points out that the Chinese codification attached the greatest importance to the organization of the state power and to criminal law, while the codification of Justinian concentrated its efforts on private law.

[14] The body of law as a whole was called *ritsu-ryo kyaku-shiki*.

known as *myo-bo-do*[15] was set up in the *daigaku*[16] under the control of the Ministry of *Shikibu* (the ministry with responsibility for the examination and education of public officials). The *daigaku* had about 400 students and was the national administrative college set up to educate state functionaries. Apart from it there were provincial schools called *kokugaku*, which had the same aim. It is said that legal knowledge was very much respected throughout this era, a phenomenon exceptional in Japanese history.[17] Studies on the *ritsu-ryo* were carried out with great zeal and many commentaries were published. Among them are two important books that are still extant: *Ryo-no-gige* (Commentary on the Ryo) and *Ryo-no-shuge* (Collection of Theories on the Ryo). The first is an official commentary on the *Yoro Ryo*. It was drawn up by twelve scholars and published with the force of law in 833.[18] The second is a private collection of doctrinal writings on the *ryo* drawn up about the beginning of the tenth century by Koremune Naomoto, a doctor of *myo-bo*, and is said to contain a comparative study of the Japanese and Chinese codes.

The system of *ritsu-ryo* did not stay in favor for long. The cultural milieu of Japan differed considerably from that of China, which made it difficult for the laws to be assimilated. Most of the provisions soon fell into disuse, and around the legislative texts more and more usages of an administrative or judicial nature developed, with the result that the basic text soon became obscure or was forgotten. Though the *ritsu* admitted capital punishment, there is no case of an execution in the three and a half centuries between 810 and 1156. However it must not be forgotten that these laws were never formally abrogated and some of them were even applied after the 1868 Restoration.

[15] *Myo-bo-do* means literally "the way of clarification of the law," hence legal training.

[16] *Daigaku* means big school. Those who taught at the *daigaku* were called *hakase*. These two terms are still used today. All Japanese universities have the title *daigaku*, and *hakase* corresponds to "doctor." The notion of *daigaku* has no connotation of *universitas*. All colleges of the highest rank have this title whether they are state-run or not. There are also *daigaku* that specialize in one branch of knowledge only.

[17] Since law was not closely related to procedure, it was not judicial practice, but administrative practice, which developed the law. Even at this period when legal science was prospering, there was no legal profession. This reflects the essentially non-procedural nature of Japanese law.

[18] For this reason this is a commentary only in form. Basically it is a code.

By means of the *ritsu-ryo* system the imperial government succeeded in concentrating all state powers in its hands. The political powers of the big clans were closely related to the ownership of land, and these powers they lost to the imperial government. The legal and political position of the emperor came very close to that of the Chinese *tenshi*,[19] who was a despotic monarch. In order to imbue his powers with religious authority the cult of the emperor was invented. He was held to be a living god (*akitsukami*). At the beginning of the Taika Reform, the emperor proclaimed, in accordance with the Confucian ideal, that all land and all persons were in direct submission to imperial authority. Public offices and land were from that time distributed by the imperial government according to the rules of the *ritsu-ryo*. A certain amount of land, as determined by a law which distinguished several categories of persons, was given for life to every person of six or more years of age. This was an agrarian system with socialistic tendencies, but the main aim was to assure the state of its taxes. As far as public offices were concerned they appear to have been open to everyone, but in practice those who were given high offices belonged almost exclusively to the noble class.

The Confucian ideal was quickly neglected. In the ninth century a definite tendency toward appropriation of public offices and land can be seen. The estates obtained by means of usurpation, hoarding, and accepting offers of those who wanted to submit themselves to the patronage of the strong grew little by little and were known as *sho* or *shoen*.[20] Though illegal and aimed solely at increasing wealth, private property of this kind gradually acquired an official character, and its owner (*honjo*) was given immunities. He was exempt from taxes and had the right to prevent the provincial governors (*kokushi*) from entering his *sho* to collect tax. This law was negative in effect at the beginning but was later accompanied by prerogatives in the legislative, administrative, and jurisdictional fields exercised within the framework of the *sho*.

[19] *Tenshi*, literally, child of heaven.
[20] See the excellent explanation by Fr. Joüon des Longrais in *L'Est et l'Ouest: Institutions du Japon et de l'Occident comparées* (Tokyo and Paris: Maison Franco-Japonaise and Institut de Recherches d'Histoire Etrangère, 1958), p. 32.

Parallel to this development a military class was emerging. Under the *ritsu-ryo* system the army was composed of professional officers and soldiers recruited from among the people.[21] Military service was considered an unpleasant duty because the soldiers were obliged to provide arms and supplies at their own cost and because the officers used the soldiers as their servants. As a result, the system was suppressed at the end of the eighth century and replaced by an army consisting of members of the powerful families from the provinces. For this reason the powerful provincial families came to form a new social class—the samurai.

With the weakening of the central government the military class increased its power in the provinces. The Taira (or *Heike*) and Minamoto (or *Genji*) clans became particularly important. In the twelfth century the Taira succeeded in gaining political control in the imperial government, and its head, Kiyomori, was named *dajo-daijin* (prime minister). But the Taira clan was soon defeated by the Genji clan, and in 1185 the head of the Genji, Yoritomo, set up a military government at Kamakura, a town near Tokyo. The emperor continued to reign, but he no longer ruled.

This form of military government lasted till 1868. From the legal viewpoint, the change meant that the centralized *ritsu-ryo* system gave way to feudalism. This feudal system developed in two separate stages, dual feudalism and unitary feudalism.[22]

THIRD ERA: DUAL FEUDALISM

The feudal regime of this era is characterized by a dualist nature, a mixed regime of feudalism and *sho*. Under it the *sho* continued to exist but were used as the economic basis of the feudal system. All Japan was not immediately subjected to feudalism. It was only the domain of the *bushi*[23] that it governed. The domains of the *kuge* (courtiers of the imperial court) and of

---

[21] Ibid., p. 195f.
[22] Joüon des Longrais divides the historical development of Japanese feudalism into four phases. Ibid., p. 108f.
[23] *Bushi, buke,* and *mononofu* are synonyms, meaning samurai.

the *honjo* remained from the earlier systems, though the influence of the *bushi* was felt more and more.

This era is divided into the Kamakura period, during which the central government (*Bakufu*) of the *bushi* was established at Kamakura, and the Muromachi or Ashikaga period, during which the Bakufu dominated by the Ashikaga military clan was set up in 1338 at Muromachi, a suburb of Kyoto. Between these two periods there was the short-lived Kemmu restoration of the emperor in 1334.

After the victory of Yoritomo over the Taira clan, all the *bushi* came under Yoritomo, and a hierarchical order was established with Yoritomo at the top. In this order the inferior owed his superior a duty of devoted service and the latter gave the former some benefits by way of reward. The bond of vassalage had a marked familial character, and each group of *bushi* linked by a blood relationship constituted a coherent unit directed by its head (*katoku*). The head had the right and the duty to receive obedience from the members of his group. When the Bakufu wished to call the *bushi* together, it had only to give the order to the clan heads.

The bond of vassalage was constituted by a contract in the broad sense between the suzerain and his vassal, but its content was not given precision by agreement between the parties.[24] The vassal owed his overlord an absolute duty of fidelity but had no legal right to ask for the fulfillment of the overlord's duties.[25] Thus the suzerain's duty was not a legal one, though the vassal was bound legally in his duties toward his lord. In this characteristic, it is said, is the essential difference between vassalage in Japanese feudalism and Western feudalism.[26]

[24] Jouon des Longrais emphasizes, "a great lack of detail in the relationship between lord and vassals, and the almost complete impossibility of systematically classifying their reciprocal duties under the heading of rights and duties as we are accustomed to do in relation to Western feudalism." *L'Est et l'Ouest*, p. 147.

[25] "The Japanese vassal was never known to claim the exercise of his legal rights against his overlord, because litigation between lord and vassal was prohibited. In relation to his overlord the vassal was without any recourse at all, just like a child as regards his father. . . . Japanese feudalism retains its purity and is quick to see in the chicanery so common among Western lords an outlook incompatible with feudal loyalty," Jouon des Longrais, ibid., pp. 147–148.

[26] "In Japanese feudalism the obligations of the parties had none of the characteristics of the European feudal contract," Jouon des Longrais, ibid., p. 144.

The benefices the lord gave his vassals in reward for their services were of a varied nature[27] and had the general name of *on* or *go-on*,[28] while the act by which the lord deigned to grant a benefice to his vassal was called *onkyu*.[29] The system of *onkyu* has many points of similarity with the *beneficium* of European feudalism, and it is possible without too great a degree of inaccuracy to translate *onkyu* as *beneficium*. The *onkyu* is literally an act of beneficence on the part of the lord that he was in no way legally bound to perform because by law the vassal could not demand it of him. In practice, however, the lord could not wait for the performance of a suitable act of service by one of his vassals before distributing him due benefice, and the vassals themselves were not slow in seeking the *go-on* from their lord.

The link of *onkyu* was originally created in connection with the *sho*. The lord of a *sho* gave benefices to a person who owed him services and duties, whether of a military or non-military type. Most frequently it was land which was the object of the *onkyu*, but as time went on the masters of *sho* more and more frequently appointed their servants to positions which obliged the servants to conduct the business of the *sho*, and the master simply received land revenue from it. Such an appointment was called *shiki*,[30] and as this sort of office was always accompanied by certain rights of enjoyment over the land of a *sho*, the word *shiki* came to represent the right of enjoyment itself.

After his victory over the Taira clan, Yoritomo confiscated all the land that had belonged to that family and distributed it to his vassals. He then required that the imperial court appoint him as chief *jito*, which meant that he could send his vassals to each *sho* in his capacity as *jito* and allow them to enjoy the *shiki* corresponding to his office. The *jito*, an officer of the *sho*, was also the official of the Bakufu who had responsibility for police and judicial activities in the *sho* to which he was sent and, as Joüon des Longrais says, "It was by this means that Yoritomo could place *jito*, who were warriors, even on manors (*sho*) that

---

[27] See Joüon des Longrais, ibid., pp. 122f.

[28] *On* means grace, and *go* is a prefix of respect.

[29] *Kyu* means act of performance. *Onkyu* is used today in the sense of old-age pension.

[30] An old form of *shoku*, which means office or duty.

did not belong to him. Once in this position these new military officials quickly took on a leading role."[31] Many very violent conflicts arose concerning the rights given to the *bushi* and those of the masters of the *sho*. Moreover, the *jito* frequently usurped the *sho* by using their military and political influence. In spite of the efforts of the Bakufu to find a balance between the interests of the two parties, the rights of the *bushi* increasingly exceeded those of the lords of the manors, and in the last half of the era under discussion the *sho* regime had largely come to an end. The development was hastened by the promulgation of a law by the Muromachi Bakufu called *Hanzei-ho* (law on the payment of half), under which each lord of a manor was ordered to set aside half his taxes from the *sho* for the *bushi* for military provisions.

Apart from the feudal dualism there was pluralism on the legal side, too, and the coexistence of the following three systems can be seen:

1. *Kuge-ho*.[32] At the end of the *ritsu-ryo* era the administrative and judicial customs constituted a system of customary law based on the *ritsu-ryo*. The *ritsu-ryo* itself continued to apply even in this period in the field reserved to imperial authority. During the Kamakura era the *kuge-ho* was still in theory common law, but in practice it was increasingly being limited in application and had little importance in the Muromachi period. The imperial court often promulgated laws, but they were mostly of a moral character. They aimed at encouraging a moderate way of life and exhorted people to improve their morals. It is to be noted, however, that the opinions of jurists who gave solutions to problems posed by the government authorities according to the rules of *ritsu-ryo*, constituted an important source of customary law.

2. *Honjo-ho*. The customary law that applied to all the private manors was called *honjo-ho*. It varied greatly in content from region to region, but it is possible to distinguish the custom peculiar to a given *sho*, that common to the region, and that common to the whole country. The *honjo-ho* was a variant of *ritsu-ryo*.

3. *Buke-ho*. The moral rules or customs peculiar to the *bushi*

---

[31] Joüon des Longrais, *L'Est et l'Ouest*, pp. 129–130.

[32] *Kuge* here means the imperial court, and *ho* means law or statute.

class formed gradually with the class. They were called *bushido*,[33] the body of rules of conduct for *bushi*, and can be likened to a code of chivalry. Based on them to a certain extent and supported by the *honjo-ho* for the rest, this third system was established to regulate relationships between the *bushi*. It was mainly a customary system but contains some written law which was known at the time as *shikimoku* or *shikijo*.[34] The most important of these written laws was that promulgated in 1232 and called *Goseibai-shikimoku*, or *Joei-shikimoku*.[35] The object of this law, according to the draftsman, was to inform the public of the nature of the law of Bakufu so that the administration of justice would be impartial.[36] This law contained only fifty-one articles, but its influence on the laws that followed was very great. The code was, of course, applicable only to the *bushi* class, and was based on reason rather than positive legal principles.[37]

Generally the law of the era is of a customary nature, and morality occupies an important place in it.[38] The law of the *buke* in particular is distinguished from others in this respect. The system of morality of the *bushido* rests in Confucianism but, in contrast to the moral concepts of the preceding era when Chinese

[33]   Literally, the way of the *bushi*.

[34]   *Shiki* is the abbreviation of *hoshiki*, which means legislative formulae. *Moku* or *jo* are both abbreviations of *jomoku*, which means provisions.

[35]   *Seibai* can mean several things: general policy, administrative, or judicial decisions and criminal penalties. According to one historical document this code was promulgated to prevent underhand dealings, and judges were required to solve disputes in accordance with its rules. From this it should be understood that according to the traditional conception of law its purpose was rather to prevent social conflict than to determine which of the parties to a dispute was right. Law existed first for the rulers; the protection of the interests of the governed was only a reflection of the realization of the aims of the rulers. The reason why this code is also called *Joei-shikimoku* is because it was promulgated in the first year of the Joei era, 1232.

[36]   This declaration of the draftsman must not, however, be taken too seriously. According to a recent study of Japanese law of the middle ages, at that time even the courts were not fully aware of all the statutes in force. It was the duty of the parties to the case to prove the existence of the law they wished applied. The Bakufu did not have any real interest in informing the public of legislation nor in conserving or systematizing legislation. Because of this it is not unusual to find contradictory judgments relating to the same question.

[37]   The draftsman of the code was Hojo Yasutoki, head of the Kamakura Bakufu, who himself said that the rules that it contained are only based on reason (*jori*).

[38]   A recent study by two legal historians affirms: "The court of the Kamakura Bakufu applied nothing comparable to modern law whether it be of a legislative, customary, or judicial nature." According to this study the legal system was dominated by emotional rather than moral factors.

ideas were followed blindly, the *bushido* was formed in a spontaneous manner in the daily life of the *bushi*. However, it must not be forgotten that the Kamakura period was one in which Japanese Buddhism flourished. Buddhism had spread throughout Japan in the preceding era under state patronage, and its influence had been limited to the nobility. In the Kamakura period Buddhism penetrated into the daily life of the people, and its influence was very great on the *bushi*.

FOURTH ERA: UNITARY FEUDALISM

The power of the Kamakura Bakufu shifted in the fourteenth century to the Bakufu of Muromachi (1338–1573). The dualist nature of the social structure remained intact under the Muromachi reign, but as the power of the Bakufu weakened, the *sho* regime broke down rapidly. In place of the owners of the *sho* and the public officials appointed by the Bakufu or by the imperial court for the administration of the *sho*, there arose local lords who banished others in order to seize political power over the conquered lands. The *sho* disappeared one by one, and by about the end of the fifteenth century small independent states were emerging here and there. The ruler of each such state or province was called *sengoku daimyo* (lord of the period of the private wars) by historians. These *sengoku daimyo* fought among themselves, each seeking to gain political power over the whole of Japan, and at the end of a long period of violence and after the short-lived hegemony of Hideyoshi, Tokugawa Ieyasu succeeded in 1603 in establishing a solidly based unitary feudal regime. Thanks to the skillful political handling of Ieyasu and to the form of politics known as *sakoku* (closure of the country) this period, known as the Tokugawa or Edo period, lasted until 1868.

The new regime was purely feudal; all of Japan was *bushi*-dominated. The head of the central government, still known as the Bakufu, was just one of the *daimyo*, who was the strongest and greatest of them and had the title of *shogun* (generalissimo). He had the greatest domain, *tenryo* (literally, the heavenly domain), which he governed directly, and all the other land was divided into fiefs among the big and small *daimyo* and the direct vassals of the shogun who were not *daimyo*. Even the imperial court was under the shogun's surveillance, but the emperor remained the symbol of national unity. All *bushi* were attached by a bond of vassalage to their immediate superiors.[39] The vassals of the shogun were the *daimyo*, *hatamoto*, and *gokenin*.[40] The rest of the *bushi* were vavasors as far as the shogun was concerned. In order to maintain the hierarchical order as long as possible the Bakufu took very strict measures, which it enforced pitilessly,[41] and adopted Confucianism as the official ideology in order to use it as moral support for the hierarchical order that existed. The Bakufu tried to convince the people that the established order was an immutable natural order. The result was that authoritarian ideology was deeply rooted in the heart of the nation. Japanese society at that time was characterized by a rigid and extremely detailed system of superiority and subordination in all social relationships. Not only was the bond of vassalage dominated by this principle but so too were the relationships between master and servant, parent and child, husband and wife, and among persons outside the *bushi* class.

The classes making up society[42] were the *kuge* (nobles of the imperial court), the *buke*, the clergy (Buddhist and Shinto), the commoners, and pariahs. The court nobles were not bound by any bond of vassalage to the shogun, but they were under the strict control of the Bakufu. Commoners were divided into three categories, which were, in order of their social standing, peasants, artisans, and merchants. The peasants had the highest status among the commoners, but they had extremely heavy burdens to bear in the form of levies and service. They were therefore obliged to live extremely frugally and to work from dawn to dusk. A book published in 1720 said that the peasants were treat-

---

[39]   This bond became less a family one and more an individual one at this time.

[40]   For the distinction between these three vassals cf. Yosiyuki Noda, "*Le Japon*," in *Histoire universelle*, Vol. 3, ed. Emile G. Léonard (Paris: Gallimard, 1958), p. 1515f.

[41]   What Montesquieu says in *The Spirit of the Laws* about the severity of punishments in Japan at the time is, in spite of its errors, partly true. Cf. Book VI, ch. 13, and Book XIV, ch. 15.

[42]   In the Edo period the following schematic formula was often used to designate the social order: *shi* (abbreviation of *bushi*), *no* (peasant), *ko* (artisan), *sho* (merchant). Edo, the capital of that time, is now called Tokyo.

ed by a pitiless government like domestic animals and were borne down by heavy taxes and demanding service. Further they were not allowed to change their place of residence or their occupation. They were almost serfs. In a word the peasants, 80 percent of the population, were persons of abject condition. Another book published anonymously in 1815 describes their misery in the following manner:

> In order to supplement their meager diet they earned some money, using any leisure time they had by working as day laborers or performing other manual tasks. But even this was not enough to enable them to live comfortably. Thus they knew no rest for their body or their mind. They were not allowed to look after a relative who was kept in bed by illness nor were they able to provide him with medicines. The whole family suffered in summer from fleas and mosquitoes and in the winter from the cold because they had no heating. They did weaving but since they had to pay the price of materials in advance they were at the mercy of the merchants who exploited them on any number of pretexts, and so they made no profit. For this reason farmers are called *mizunomi-byakusho* [peasants who only drink water], but they could not even get enough water.

The *chonin*, or city dwellers, were no better off. They were involved in artisan's work and in commerce, but they were allowed to do so only by the grace of the *bushi*, and many restrictions were imposed on them to prevent them from exceeding their *bungen*. This word *bungen* is very important in understanding the hierarchical order. Literally it means the line of demarcation. Each social level is separated from the others by an impenetrable barrier; each individual belongs from birth to a given social status which imposes on him a manner of life adapted to that status. As Stoetzel says, "It was forbidden to change class. Class distinctions were rigidly maintained and moral, social, and customary practices appropriate to each class were carefully codified."[43] A regulation put out by the Tokugawa government directed to the peasants stated:

1. It is henceforth forbidden for the head of the village and

[43] Stoetzel, *Jeunesse sans chrysanthème ni sabre*, p. 49.

any peasant to build a house out of proportion to their status.
2. As far as clothes are concerned the village chief, his wife, and
his children can wear silk or cotton, but the peasants can wear
only cotton, and they may not use other materials even for the
collar or the belt.
3. It is forbidden for a village chief or any peasants to dye
their clothes violet or red. They can use all other colors but
without pattern.
4. As far as food is concerned everyone must eat cereals other
than rice. Rice can be eaten only on special occasions.

This hierarchical morality was strongly inculcated in all persons of the era. A book published in 1721 instructed peasants
that "everything which is above is called heaven and all that is
below earth. The heaven is high and noble, the earth is low and
humble. Peasants are destined to the earth. Therefore it is their
heaven-ordained duty to busy themselves with agriculture and
remain very humble." Another book counseled merchants:
"Never, never desire the *bungen* that does not suit your rank.
However intelligent you may be, you cannot attain a higher rank
by your intelligence or talent, for our fate is determined by
heaven from birth." Besides this the arrogance of the *bushi* was
almost quixotic. They despised the lower classes only because
they were not *bushi* and disdained commerce in particular, as the
following extract from a letter written by a high Bakufu official
at the beginning of the nineteenth century shows: "There is a
custom among the barbarians to deliberate day and night on
commercial dealings, and, even in a letter embellished with the
royal seal and addressed to a foreigner, to mention openly an
interest in commerce without feeling shame. This is a custom of
the barbarians, but it is nonetheless detestable." Another book of
the period shares this opinion of commerce: "In the barbarian
countries of the West the kings and generals are all a type of rich
merchant and have no cares for their honor or for honesty. There
is no distinction between knights and merchants because distinguished persons sail the world to do business with strangers.
They have no feeling of shame." Fukuzawa Yukichi, a brilliant
liberal of the Meiji era, recounts an interesting fact in this connection. As a boy he studied under a private teacher who taught

him arithmetic. Fukuzawa's father, who was a samurai, found this unworthy of his son and withdrew him from the school, saying, "It is unpardonable that you should teach my young boy arithmetic."

Such was the social order of the Edo period. As for the law of the period, it was not unified and custom was dominant in every domain. Each *han*, that is to say, each of the territories that had been divided up among the *daimyo* into fiefs, enjoyed political and legal autonomy and had its own law. The law of Bakufu applied in principle only in the area governed directly by the shogun. Nevertheless, since the Bakufu exhorted each *han* to follow the model of the shogunate law and as each of the *han* willingly did so, the laws of the *han* came to resemble those of the shogunate. Diversity of laws did, however, continue to exist until the Restoration of 1868, and Voltaire's statement that, when traveling in France one changed customs as often as horses, very aptly described the situation in Japan too. This system, which is called *baku-han taisei* by Japanese historians, was made up of two elements: a strong central power and autonomous *han*, which, though always different from it, gradually came to govern in a manner similar to the central power.

Alongside customary law, legislation (*hatto*) was promulgated by the Bakufu[44] and by each of the *han*. This legislation dealt mostly with matters concerning the feudal regime. In 1742 a very important code was drawn up. It was called *Kujikata Osadamegaki* (Written Rules of Procedure) and was commonly known as *Osadamegaki-hyakkajo* (The Hundred Written Rules). This code has one hundred and three articles and is divided into two volumes. Volume I contains eighty-one regulations of various sorts, and volume II rules relating to both criminal and civil procedure. The civil law dispositions are not numerous and although called a code it is not so much a code as a series of directives addressed to judicial authorities. The text could only be

---

[44] The public law codes *buke sho-hatto* (the general status code of the *buke*) and *kuge sho-hatto* (general status code of the *kuge*) of 1615, in particular, should be noted.

consulted by the three *bugyo*,[45] the top magistrates of the three important Bakufu courts.

Apart from these codes, several official collections of Bakufu law were made. Five collections of penal judgments, of which the first four are still extant, were also made. On the civil side there was a collection of judgments in forty-five volumes, of which only two volumes have survived. The jurisdictional setup of the period was very complicated, but the judgments collected all concern the *Hyojo-sho*[46] jurisdiction of the central government.

The law of the period was strongly influenced by Confucianism, and in this respect it resembles the *ritsu-ryo* system. There was a basic difference between the two systems. Under the *ritsu-ryo* system the object was to control and educate the people in order to make them cognizant of the law for the purposes of maintaining public security and assuring the receipt of revenues. The government of the Edo period, on the other hand, wanted to attain the same objects by constraining the people to obey silently like domestic animals. The more ignorant and docile the people were, the easier it seemed for the Bakufu to realize its political objective. This attitude is expressed very clearly in the Tokugawa political motto: "Let the people know nothing, but make them obey." Under such conditions it was quite natural that the rights of individuals were not respected. Everything useful and necessary according to Bakufu politics was justified by reasons of state, and there was no possible way of criticizing the government. The government imposed its will pitilessly on the people, menacing with, and even executing, inordinately severe punishments for disobedience.

In a book written by a famous Confucianist of the time there appears the following dictum: "According to the old theory, you must not censure the rulers of the country in which you live. If

---

[45] The *bugyo* was a top official of the Bakufu whose job was not limited to legal matters. There were several categories of *bugyo* but the following three were the most important: the *jisha-bugyo*, who controlled religious business; the *machi-bugyo*, who were responsible for the municipal business of Edo, the capital; and the *kanjo-bugyo*, who controlled public finances.

[46] The *Hyojo-sho* was the department which dealt with matters concerning two parties whose business was within the competence of different *bugyo*. This was not an appeal system, so the *Hyojo-sho* was not a jurisdiction superior to the *bugyo*.

you do not occupy a position which gives you competence, you must not criticize state policy. It is contrary to loyalty and fidelity that an inferior should criticize his superior." In the accusation against Oshio Heihachiro, who provoked an insurrection because he felt sorry for the plight of the populace, one reads: "The accused did wrong to criticize policy because he was only a man of humble origin." Yoshida Shoin, one of the precursors of the Meiji Restoration, was condemned to capital punishment for a similar reason: "Whereas the accused who is only a person of low rank was wrong to have criticized important state policies . . . ." Furthermore, the imposition of penalties was not submitted to a procedure that guaranteed the dignity of the individual against the caprice of the judges. Since the confession of the guilty party was frequently the only means of proof, torture was officially admitted, and the legitimacy of its use to obtain a confession was not even questioned for a long time. It was Gustave Boissonade, when he arrived in Japan in 1873, who advised the government to abolish it.

From what has just been said it is clear that the law for most Japanese meant little else than the means of constraint used by the authorities to achieve government purposes. Powerless before the government might, the people could only obey, but because they were not convinced they developed a complex (*menju-fukuhai*) which became part of their psychological make-up.[47]

In the Edo period doctrinal writings developed very little. There was no special law school corresponding to the faculty of law instituted in the *daigaku* under the *ritsu-ryo* regime, there was no class of professional lawyer such as formed early in French and English history, and judicial offices were not distinguished from other public offices. The *bugyo*, who enjoyed an important position in the field of justice, was a public official whose competence covered all public matters within his territorial jurisdiction, just like a bailiff of the French middle ages. He was therefore far from being comparable to the *Conseillers au Parlement* in pre-Revolutionary France. There were no barristers, no notaries, and no *ministère public*, and in the plays of the era there is

---

[47] *Menju-fukuhai* means that one obeys one's superior outwardly but rebels against him inwardly.

nothing comparable to the advocates and notaries who often played an important part in Western dramas.

This state of affairs continued almost unchanged for two hundred years and contributed greatly to the formation of the Japanese conception of law. Isolated and confined to their small islands and forced to put up with wretched living conditions, the Japanese people quickly lost all sense of initiative. A quotation from a book of the period speaking about the immobility of the peasants represents accurately the mentality of the nation during that time: "They did not easily accept new ideas. Imbued with the moral outlook and the customary practices of their province, they refused to consider other manners of behavior. They obstinately maintained their traditional agricultural methods in everything from the setting out of the rice paddies to the sowing of seeds. They did not wish to change the known pattern for a better method even if it was found to be suitable." The Japanese outlook was dominated by one concern—personal security. "Don't get involved" was the sad maxim of the greater part of the population. Even at the beginning of the following era, Fukuzawa was able to write:

> The Japanese people are so concerned with their own security that they have no desire to distinguish between the closed circle of their personal life and public life. All political business is left to the government. Millions of men with millions of different attitudes withdraw into themselves. Outside his home the Japanese feels at a loss and has no interest in anyone else. Since this is so, no one would consider the repairing of a community well, and the repair of public roads was even further from his thoughts. Seeing a dead person in the street the Japanese moves away as quickly as possible, and he turns away when he sees dog excrement in his path. This happens because everyone is trying to avoid what is called *kakariai*, being implicated in embarassing matters. In such circumstances how could it be hoped that important matters would be discussed in public? Habits followed for so long have come to be rooted deep in the life of the Japanese of today.[48]

[48]   Yukichi Fukuzawa, *Bummeiron no gairyaku* [Outline of the Theory of Civilization] (Tokyo: Iwanami Shoten, 1969), pp. 101–102.

What is the real importance of the old Japanese law to the modern law of Japan? As will be seen, the modern state law has no connection with the former Japanese law. The modern law considers itself rather as an heir of Western law. It is only rarely that studies of the former Japanese law are used to interpret the law currently in force. In France the works of Domat and Pothier are indispensable for civil lawyers, but in Japan there is nothing comparable. An eminent Japanese student of Romano-Germanic law, Harada, in his work *Genealogical Study of the Japanese Civil Code*, makes it clear that all the articles of the Japanese Civil Code had their origin in modern Western law or in Roman law and not in early Japanese law. It could therefore be said that the history of Japanese law is, for the present at least, a luxury.

All this does not mean, however, that early Japanese law has no place in an extensive or profound study of contemporary law. There may be a marked difference between the modern and the old law at the level of state law, but at the level of living law there was no break in continuity. The latter evolved spontaneously and unconsciously. Historical continuity interrupted in the conscious continues in the subconscious, and this subconscious factor plays an important role in the social life of the Japanese people today. It surprises non-Japanese to see that in the studies of jurisprudence in Japan no mention is made of Japanese legal thought, although there is a detailed analysis of Western ideas from Socrates to Geny. The relationship between the old and the new law is one that has not yet been fully studied, and the historical study of Japanese legal thought itself is still a virgin field.

CHAPTER III

RECEPTION OF WESTERN LAW

THE PROCESS OF RECEPTION

In 1853 Commodore Matthew Calbraith Perry of the United States Navy arrived in Japan to present to the Tokugawa government a letter from President Fillmore to the Japanese emperor, asking Japan to open its doors freely to foreigners once more. Perry was escorted by four warships. Though the tone of the letter was courteous, it left no doubt of the real intention of the United States, and the Bakufu was thrown into great confusion. Already a small number of Japanese had seen the reopening of Japan to the outside world as a necessity and had launched an impassioned campaign to propagate their ideas at the risk of losing their lives.[1]

The Bakufu finally took account of the fact that it was no longer possible to maintain its policy of *sakoku* and decided to reestablish relations with foreign countries. In 1858, the fifth year of the era of Ansei, Japan concluded commercial treaties with the United States, England, France, Russia, and the Netherlands, but in its ignorance of international law it accepted unfavorable conditions. These treaties, concluded as they were on the basis of an inequality of bargaining power, could not but hurt the pride of the Japanese people, and the Meiji government which succeeded the Bakufu was obliged to try to do away with them.

The Bakufu had, even before the arrival of Perry, begun to become unsettled, and the change it then made in its policy was decisive for its fall. In the end, after violent political and military campaigns between the partisans of the imperial court, who sought to strike down the Bakufu by means of the imperial authority,

[1]   E.g., Yoshida Shoin.

and those who sustained the Bakufu, the imperialists won. They were a group made up mostly of *bushi* of the lower class of the four great *han* of the southwest: Satsuma, Choshu, Tosa, and Hizen. In 1867 the last shogun handed back his political powers to the emperor, and the system of military government that had lasted for seven hundred years came to an end. A new page in Japanese history began with the era of Meiji.

This revolution is called Meiji Ishin, and *ishin* means literally "here are new things."[2] From the beginning the new government had to grapple with a critical problem—what could be done to maintain the independence of the state against the imperialistic forces of the West? Were there other ways besides adopting capitalism? No better means could be found for preserving its independence, so the new government set to modernizing the social and political organization of the country on the principles of modern capitalism. This of course called for a restructuring of the legal system, but the reform of the law was an urgent necessity anyway, as the Meiji government wanted to obtain the revision of the treaties of Ansei and the other parties to the treaties demanded the modernization of the Japanese legal system as a condition precedent to that revision. The Japanese government did not have time to allow the law to be created spontaneously in response to the needs arising from the gradual transformation of the social structure to a capitalist society. The pressure was to concentrate on providing a new legal system whatever the social state of Japan might be.

The best way to obtain this result as quickly as possible was of course to follow the example of the advanced capitalist countries, which at that time were France and England. Japan chose the legislation of France as its guide because the Common Law

[2] It is a matter of dispute whether this historical event can be called a revolution. It all depends on the definition of revolution. According to the *Vocabulaire juridique* of Henri Capitant a revolution is "a popular movement of reasonable size which aims at overthrowing the rulers of a state by force and changing the organization of that state without observing the legal requirements previously laid down." The Japanese political reform had all the elements required by this definition with the exception of "popular movement." Since the Meiji Ishin brought about a change of the subjects of political power only within the same privileged class, it could not be qualified as a revolution. It is perhaps better to speak of restoration rather than revolution, though this movement, which was not in itself a popular one, did constitute an anticipation of the will of the people.

system appeared too complicated, whereas France had the five Napoleonic codes. Moreover the French codes had already been the inspiration for many countries that were modernizing their societies. From 1869 the Japanese government showed a great interest in the translation of the French codes. One of the members of the first imperial government, Soejima Taneomi, in that very year ordered Mitsukuri Rinsho, an intellectual with a good knowledge of French, to translate the Penal Code. Mitsukuri finished a section of his translation before the end of the year and the minister of justice, Eto Shimpei, who read the translation, was greatly impressed. So impressed in fact that he rather hastily conceived the idea of also having the French Civil Code translated and applied as Japanese law, and he thereupon ordered Mitsukuri to translate the Civil Code and all the other Napoleonic codes as quickly as possible. When he gave the order to Mitsukuri, Eto is reported to have said: "Translate those codes as quickly as you can and don't worry too much about any errors you may make." Mitsukuri worked diligently and accomplished his task in less than five years.

At the end of the period the Bakufu realized the necessity of having information on things foreign and created an institute for the study and teaching of European culture (*yogaku*). The main topic for study in this institute was European languages; among them Dutch was originally considered the most important because the Netherlands was the only European country which had permission to trade with Japan through the period of the *sakoku* policy. Mitsukuri had begun by studying Dutch. He learned quickly and was soon an assistant teacher at the institute. It did not take him very long to see how important French was, and he busied himself with learning it too. He had no particular knowledge of law, but all the learned men of the *yogaku* were encyclopaedists, and were regarded as omniscient. With this background Mitsukuri undertook the task of translating the French codes. It is easy to imagine the difficulties that he must have encountered in completing his task—he did not have the use of a good French-Japanese dictionary or the assistance or advice of any French lawyer. It is therefore surprising to know that the greater part of the current Japanese legal terminology was invented, or at least suggested, by him. Even the two basic words "right" (*kenri*) and "obligation" (*gimu*) are attributed to Mitsukuri.[3] He was like an architect who had to begin by making his own bricks. One result is that his translations are highly defective to the eyes of modern jurists, though they were of invaluable assistance to the legal men of the time. As a judge of the Japanese Supreme Court said much later, "these translated codes were like a light shining suddenly through the dark night," and the judges of the time found in them the only legal bases on which they could properly base their decisions.[4] Although none of the translated codes was applied in Japan as Eto had wished, these translations were the first step to the reception of Western law. Eto gave up the idea of applying the civil code in a translated form, but he did not give up the idea of having a Japanese civil code as soon as possible. He immediately undertook to draw up a Japanese civil code and set up a committee for the purpose, with himself as president, and proceeded with zeal on a draft based on the French Civil Code.

[3]   A biography of Mitsukuri gives us some idea of his extraordinary efforts: "At the time of his translation legal science was still in its formative stages and Rinsho had no knowledge of it anyway. He had no commentary, no dictionary, and no lawyer with whom to consult. He had great difficulty in understanding difficult passages in the French texts, and as he found many ideas in them which did not exist in the traditional Japanese conception of law, he was greatly embarrassed by the lack of words with which to translate the French. He sought advice from Sinological experts, but they were unable to advise him on adequate terms. He therefore had to invent the terminology himself, but his words were not readily accepted because they were not Japanese. Words such as *kenri* and *gimu* were borrowed from Chinese words which he found in the Chinese translation of an English text of International Law! Almost all the other legal terms, such as *dosan* (moveables), *fudosan* (immoveables), *sosai* (compensation), and *mihitsujoken* (condition subsequent), were invented by Rinsho after much difficult research." Fumihiko Otsuki, *Mitsukuri Rinsho Kun den* [Biography of Mitsukuri Rinsho] (Tokyo: Maruzen, 1907), pp. 88–100 passim.

[4]   Although it cannot be conclusively proved that the judicial decisions of the first years of the Meiji era were based on the Japanese translations of the French codes, there is good reason to presume that this was the case. The following expressions are found in the reasoning of numerous decisions: "It is obvious according to the general principles of law . . ."; "According to the nature of things . . ."; "For the reason that . . ."; "Equity requires that . . ." There is little doubt that the judges of the time in fact relied on the rules applicable in the French codes under the guise of general principles. Boissonade said: "The civil law judges of Japan, deprived of the sources of their ancient law, are most of the time unable to rely on fixed and certain customs, and are obliged to resolve their difficulties according to the principles of natural law which they find formulated in foreign codes which form a sort of common law of the West." Gustave Boissonade, *Projet de code civil de l'Empire du Japon* (Tokyo, 1882–1889), Vol. I, p. XXIV.

After the dramatic death of Eto in 1874 by capital punishment for a political crime, the drafting work was continued under the direction of the new minister of justice, Oki Takato. In 1878 a draft civil code in three books and 1,820 articles was completed, but it was not adopted because of its too faithful imitation of the French code.

The need to modernize the law was not limited to the field of civil law, but it was in the drafting work related to the civil code that the difficulties inherent in Europeanization of the law were most felt by the draftsmen. The government therefore decided to call in French jurists to help. In 1872 Georges Bousquet, advocate at the Paris Court of Appeal, came to Japan as legal adviser to the imperial government. He stayed four years and spent his time principally in educating Japanese lawyers at a special school of French law which was established on his advice in the Ministry of Justice.[5] In 1873 Gustave Boissonade, professor at the Faculty of Law in Paris, was invited by the Japanese government to take on the task of improving the legal system,[6] and he stayed in Japan for twenty years at the wish of the Japanese. He performed a great service, not only for the law and in the education of lawyers, but also in the political field.

Boissonade began his legislative work by drafting a penal code and a criminal procedure code. He finished both in 1877 in their French form, and they were then translated into Japanese for discussion and modification by the legislature.[7] The codes were adopted and promulgated in 1880 and came into force in 1882. They were the first modern codes to be applied in Japan. Until

[5] The Japanese translation of the course that he gave at this school of law is still extant. Bousquet participated in the drafting work for the civil code project and also suggested a section of the project which he drafted himself. After his return to France, he published a very interesting in-depth study on Japan, (*Le Japon de nos jours*, 2 vols.), which is essential reading for all those who are interested in Japanese history of the period.

[6] Concerning Boissonade, see Yosiyuki Noda, "Gustave Boissonade, comparatiste ignoré," published in *Problèmes contemporains de droit comparé*, ed. Naojiro Sugiyama, a collection of comparative law studies commemorating the tenth anniversary of the foundation of the Japanese Institute of Comparative Law (1962), Vol. II, p. 235f.

[7] The legislature was not as yet the Imperial Diet. The most important legislative organ before the creation of the Diet was the *Genroin* (Senate). Legislative bills were in principle discussed by this body, but the government could promulgate law without prior discussion in the *Genroin*.

then the Meiji government had formulated some rules relating to crimes, but it had publicized them only in the Chinese manner as directives to public officials.[8] The Japanese people as a whole had no knowledge of the principle of legality in crime and punishment until the codes drawn up by Boissonade were promulgated. The penal code remained in force until 1908, and the criminal procedure code until 1890.

In 1879 Boissonade proceeded with the task of drafting a civil code. He took charge of drafting the bill only insofar as it related to property law. Family and succession law were to be left to Japanese draftsmen because these subjects were closely related to the traditional mores of the country, though the influence of Boissonade was very great on those parts of the draft also. Boissonade based his draft on the French Civil Code, but he used comparative methods in its elaboration. He worked tirelessly, studying the case law and theory of French civil law, trying as far as possible to harmonize it with legislative, judicial, and doctrinal developments in other countries. Of his method of work, Boissonade said: "Doubtless what Japan adopts should not be French law purely and simply. I want your government to adopt our laws only to the extent that they have been proved good by the experience of three-quarters of a century. I will use every effort to incorporate in the draft the improvements that time has shown necessary and particularly those improvements that other Western jurisdictions have adopted in their wisdom and justified by their experience."[9] Thus inspired, he drew up the text and a commentary[10] on the draft civil code in French. "The drafting of the civil code was finished in April, 1889. It has thus taken us ten years although we had the temerity to

---

[8]   More precisely, the government promulgated three penal codes between 1868 and 1873. The first code was officially known as the Provisional Criminal Code. The last two were applied concurrently until the promulgation of the Criminal Code of Boissonade. The third code amended and complemented the second without abrogating it. The influence of the French code, though slight, can already be seen in the third code. Though the last two codes were published by the government, the preamble to them declared: "All public officers are commanded to observe the rules of this code."

[9]   Gustave Boissonade, "Ecole de droit de Jedo," *Revue de Legislation* (1874), p. 511.

[10]   The text and commentary have come down to us in Boissonode's monumental work, "*Projet de code civil de l'Empire du Japon*, 5 vols.

believe that five years would be sufficient."[11] The draft was translated into Japanese as it was drawn up. Then the translated portions were discussed and modified by the legislature.[12]

In 1889 part of the draft drawn up by Boissonade was adopted. It contained the book on "Property," the greater part of the book on "Methods of Acquiring Property," the book on "Securities Guaranteeing Obligations," and the book on "Modes of Proof." In 1891 the other part, that was entrusted to the Japanese drafts-men, was completed. It included a book on "Persons" and a part of the book on "Methods of Acquiring Property" dealing with "Succession." Together the two parts formed a single code which was promulgated in 1891, to come into force on 1 January, 1894. The code was not just a copy of the French code but followed a plan very similar to that of the Napoleonic Code, even though it was composed of five books instead of three. Unfortunately it did not come into force as envisaged. From 1889 there were indica-tions of a movement hostile to the future application of the code. Lawyers divided into two camps and a violent debate, which has been compared with that which arose in Germany between Savigny and Thibaut concerning the need there for a code, arose between the partisans of the immediate enforcement of the code and those who favored a postponement. Articles, mono-graphs, and manifestoes were published and distributed for and against the Boissonade code. Postponement was demanded be-cause the Boissonade code did not sufficiently take account of the traditional customs and morality of the Japanese people. One of the most conservative of the jurists, Hozumi Yatsuka, professor of constitutional law at the Imperial University in Tokyo, went so far as to state that once the civil code came into force, loyalty to the emperor and filial piety would be at an end. The reasoning of the partisans of postponement was ill-founded, because the part of the code strictly relating to moral traditions had been drawn up by Japanese and took account of those traditions. Further-more, it had been modified to a great extent by the committee and by the senate in order to adapt it even more to Japanese

[11] Ibid., Vol. I, p. VIII.
[12] The drafts were first discussed by the civil code drafting committee, then by the *Genroin*, and finally were debated in the Privy Council.

tradition.[13] The political situation, however, favored the adversaries of the Boissonade code, and in 1892 the Imperial Diet, which had begun to function as a legislative body in 1890, voted for the postponement of the civil code.

This failure of the Boissonade code is usually explained as the result of opposition between the school of French law and the school of English law.[14] Outwardly this would appear to be so, but there is possibly a more important reason, a political rather than a legal one.[15] The postponement of the code was only a manifestation of the general decline in influence of French culture.

The 1868 Restoration was brought about by *bushi* of the lower class. They had occupied a lowly place in the feudal hierarchy, though they had nevertheless belonged to the privileged class. Their ideology had never been bourgeois, but they wanted a capitalist society. For this reason the government born

[13]   For example, the first draft provided that a minor, man or woman, could not marry without the consent of the parents, but the Senate changed this provision to provide that every man and woman of no matter what age had to obtain the consent of parents to marry. The new civil code of 1898, which purported to be in conformity with the wishes of the partisans of postponement, demanded parental consent only for a man under 30 and a woman under 25. Boissonade himself said: "He [the French lawyer with responsibility for drawing up the draft of the civil code, i.e., Boissonade] submitted his work [text and commentary], bit by bit to the Japanese committee. The latter, having had it translated by those members who knew French and French law, sought to reconcile the new law with the old and often sought amendments for this reason, or else they made the changes themselves when the author was unable to accept them. This is to say that in spite of his reluctance, plurality of heirs was abandoned in favor of the maintenance of rights of seniority of the kind known under the former regime, with an absolute character as regards both moveable and immoveable goods and a generality of persons, such as had never existed in any European country." Boissonade, "Les anciennes coutumes du Japon et le nouveau code civil, à l'occasion d'une double publication de M. John Henry Wigmore," *Revue française du Japon* (1894), p. 12.

[14]   English law was taught along with French law from the beginning of the Meiji era. The center of instruction was the Law Faculty of Tokyo University for English law, and the school of French law in the Ministry of Justice for French law. Besides these two schools there were several others which specialized either in French law or in English law. The students of the two different systems naturally formed groups of differing legal outlooks.

[15]   It is worth recalling what P. Koschaker said: "Foreign law is not received because it is considered the best. What makes a legal system suitable for reception is rather a question of force [*eine Machtfrage*]. Reception relates on the intellectual and cultural plane, at least, to the extent to which the law benefits from a position of strength: Whether this strength still exists at the time in question, or whether there is a vivid recollection of it and the civilization it represents at the time in question, is an important political question." *Europa und das römische Recht* (München: Verlag C.H. Beck, 1947), p. 138.

of the Restoration, which was made up largely of these *bushi* of the lower rank, did not want the development of a bourgeois society. Instead they favored the formation of an absolutist state, but at the beginning the government was extremely weak. This government had succeeded somehow or other in bringing the *han* under the imperial power, but it was by no means certain that it could take strength from this situation in the immediate future. It was therefore obliged to seek the voluntary collaboration of the former *han* until it had consolidated its position. It was forced to appear democratic and even appeared to respect public opinion and to encourage discussions in public. One of the five articles of the imperial declaration promulgated at the beginning of 1868 says: "It is desirable to convoke public gatherings as often as possible for the purpose of discussing all important problems." And in the same year it proclaimed the fundamental principles of government in which the principle of the separation of powers was announced. In this milieu liberal ideas from the West quickly spread among the Japanese. In the first years of the Meiji era the works of Mill, Bentham, Montesquieu, de Tocqueville, and even Rousseau, to mention only the leading names, were well known.[16] People even discussed French and English philosophy.[17] Consequently it was quite natural that the legal ideas of France and England should also be received and that French law along with English law should have exercised a considerable influence on Japanese law.[18]

Inspired by liberal ideas, a political movement called the *Jiyu Minken Undo* (the liberal movement for human rights) started about 1880. It was supported by a large part of the populace, and it succeeded in getting the government to agree to the creation

[16] From 1871 to 1877 translations of Mill's essay, *On Liberty, Representative Government, Political Economy*, and *Utilitarianism* appeared; in 1873, *Theory of Legislation* by Bentham was translated into Japanese; a complete translation of *L'esprit des lois* was made in 1875; Rousseau was well known by the partisans of the *Jiyu Minken*, and his *Social Contract* had been translated into Japanese by 1882.

[17] ". . . the first two decades of the Emperor Meiji's reign saw a Japan to all appearances intoxicated with the strong wine of Western thought, techniques, and customs." Richard Storry, *A History of Modern Japan* (Penguin, 1960), p. 107.

[18] Numerous French legal texts were translated in the first years of the Meiji era. From 1870 to 1889 there appeared translations of the works of Laferrière, Demolombe, Batbie, Accolas, Faustin-Hélie, Mourlon, Ortolan, Bélime, Boistel, and Baudry-Lacantinerie among others.

of a national assembly. The movement was liberal in appearance
only, for most of its supporters were discontented former *bushi*
who had been excluded from political power. The government
took steps against the movement both by oppressing it and by
corrupting its leaders. The oppression was extremely violent
and the leaders were easily corrupted, so the liberal camp did
not last long.

Also about this time the government was beginning to feel
strong enough to show its hand. Even in 1881, when it had
submitted to the pressure of the liberal movement, it had secretly
decided to draw up a constitution following the Prussian model
to prepare for the opening of the national assembly which had
been promised to the liberals. According to its idea the new
constitution was to be granted by the emperor to his subjects, and
for this reason the absolutist character of the Prussian Empire
was more attractive to the Japanese statesmen than was the
French Republic.

From 1881 on the absolutist character of government policy
became more accentuated, and this political tendency was reflected at the legal level too. The decline in the influence of French
law was only one of its aspects. Another aspect was the increasingly important role that German law was playing in the Japanese
legal world.[19] Seen in this context the failure of the Boissonade
code becomes more comprehensible, and it is significant that the
year in which the first attack was made against the code was
also the year of the promulgation of the absolutist constitution.

In 1893 a council for codification studies was set up, and
within the framework of this council a law-drafting commission
was appointed for the civil code. It consisted of three persons,
Hozumi Nobushige, Tomi Masaakira, and Ume Kenkiro, all of
whom were professors in the Faculty of Law at the Imperial
University of Tokyo. Tomi and Ume had done their legal
studies in the Law Faculty of Lyons and both had obtained their
doctorates in law there. The commission was formally charged
with the revision of the Boissonade code, but basically its job was
to draw up a new code. The three commissioners proceeded to
their work by dividing the labor. All the topics of the code were

[19]   It is no accident that the translation of German works began about 1888.

shared among them, each choosing those topics in which he believed himself most knowledgeable.

Many foreign systems were consulted in this work, but particular reference was made to the two drafts of the B.G.B. (the German Civil Code). The commission had decided to give up the scheme of the French Civil Code and substitute it with that of the B.G.B. The code was divided into five books. The first three, the general part, the book on real rights and the book on obligations, were completed in 1895, and voted by the Diet and promulgated in 1896. The other two books, on family law and succession, were then drawn up with great prudence because the draftsmen had to avoid being in a position where they would be subject to criticism for not having taken proper account of traditional morality. The last two books were finished in 1898 and approved by the Diet, and the complete new Civil Code came into force on 16 July 1898.

How much did the new code differ from the Boissonade code? Those who had favored postponement of the Boissonade code wanted to believe that it differed substantially, and looking at form alone it could indeed be thought to be entirely different, for the method followed in its construction was German; but when the content is considered the story is different. The three draftsmen adopted many of the solutions given in the drafts of the German Civil Code, but they also retained many of the provisions drafted by Boissonade. What is more they sometimes accepted solutions other than those found in either the German or Boissonade codes. The new code was therefore somewhat eclectic. Articles 415–422, relating to damages for the non-performance of obligations, may be taken by way of example. Of these eight articles six were drafted on the basis of the articles of the code drafted by Boissonade supplemented by a study of the solutions provided in other European codes, such as the German, Swiss, Austrian, and Dutch. Sometimes the draftsmen of the new code were more faithful to the Code Napoleon than Boissonade himself. Article 420, relating to penal clauses, does not allow the court to increase or diminish the sum agreed upon between the parties. This is what the French Civil Code provides in article 1,152. Yet, in his code, Boissonade had admitted the possibility of the sum being reduced. This example in itself is insufficient to give a total view of the new Civil Code, but it does serve to show that it was not a faithful imitation of the B.G.B.

The tendencies of the three draftsmen were as follows: Hozumi, *primus inter pares*, had been educated in English law but had also studied at the University of Berlin.[20] Ume and Tomi had been trained in French law. Tomi, who had not studied in Germany, thought that the German Civil Code was better than the French. Ume represented the French law school in Japan, although he too had studied in Berlin; he had been the most ardent of those supporting the immediate implementation of the Boissonade code. At the French Civil Code centenary celebrations in 1904 at the Faculty of Law at the Imperial University of Tokyo, Ume, who was presiding, stressed the influence of French law on the new Japanese Civil Code:

> Professor Boissonade, who was invited to come to Japan, finished his drafts of the Penal Code and Criminal Procedure Code first. Then he began drawing up a civil code. This code was completed and promulgated in 1890. It was in form a little different from the French Civil Code but its content was based entirely on the French Civil Code, with account having been taken of the modifications made to it by legal theory and case law. This code never came into force. The code that replaces it and that resembles the German Civil Code in form has often wrongly been believed to follow exclusively the pattern of the German code. In truth, however, it does not. The new code is based on the French code and other codes of French origin at least as much as it is on the German code.

The legislator devoted his main efforts to the drafting of the Civil Code, but other laws were produced too.

The drafting of the Commercial Code was carried out along with that of the Civil Code. The person in charge was a German jurist, H. Roesler. He began his work in 1881 with a study of the commercial laws of all civilized countries. Although he was

---

[20] He was therefore familiar with German law. Hozumi was very interested in legal philosophy, and his legal ideas took an evolutionist tendency under Spencer's influence. His thinking on the civil code can be found in his English work: *Lectures on the New Japanese Civil Code as Materials for the Study of Comparative Jurisprudence*, 2nd ed., (Tokyo: Maruzen, 1912).

German his draft is based principally on the French Commercial Code. Roesler ended his work in 1884. His draft was discussed in the legislative commission created under the minister of justice in 1887, and in 1890 the Commercial Code was promulgated to come into force from 1 January, 1891. However, apart from the articles on companies and bankruptcy, for which there was a great economic need, its coming into force was postponed just as was that of the Civil Code. In 1893, in the interim period, a commission to revise the Commercial Code was appointed to the council for codification studies. This body drew up a new draft in two and a half years. The Diet voted the new Commercial Code in 1899 and it came into force on 16 June of the same year. This new code followed the German system with the subject matter allocated as follows: Book I, General Part; Book II, Commercial Companies; Book III, Commercial Acts; Book IV, Bills of Exchange; and Book V, Maritime Commerce. Book IV was abrogated in 1933 and replaced by two special laws relating to bills of exchange and cheques, which were necessitated by the accession of Japan to the Geneva Conventions on those topics; Books I and II were entirely redrafted in 1938.

In the field of judicial organization and civil procedure the influence of French law was at first very great. From the early Meiji era, Eto Shimpei was much concerned with the improvement of the judicial system and followed the French model, though in his time the separation of powers had not been implemented because the Ministry of Justice was also the Supreme Court. In 1875 a Supreme Court of an autonomous nature, called the *Daishinin* (court of superior hearings), was constituted, and beneath it were structured inferior tribunals of various types. The special school of French law created in the Ministry of Justice in 1872 was training judges; English law was being taught in the Tokyo University Law Faculty; and the special school of French law where Bousquet and Boissonade taught was annexed as a French law section to the Faculty of Law of Tokyo University in 1885. In the first years of the Meiji era a very large number of the judges were trained according to French law, and prior to the coming into force of the Japanese codes the judges decided most cases according to French or English law.

In 1904 sixteen of the twenty-nine judges of the Supreme Court were law graduates who had specialized in French law. After the promulgation of the Constitution, however, the influence of German law gradually extended to the field of judicial organization. In 1887 the government entrusted Otto Rudolph, a German jurist, with the task of drawing up the law on the organization of the courts. Rudolph drafted a bill on the model of the German law of 1877 but he also collaborated with other foreign jurists, notably Roesler, Albert Mosse, also Germans, Boissonade, and Kirkwood, an Englishman. The bill was discussed by a commission, became law in 1890, and governed the judicial and court system until the radical reform of the judicial organization after World War II. The statute was called the Law on Court Organization, but it also dealt with the ministère public.

The evolution of the law of civil procedure was almost the same as that on judicial organization. At the beginning of the Meiji era many civil procedure laws were established on the French model,[21] but it is very doubtful whether the judicial officers of the time completely understood them. A Ministry of Justice memorandum addressed to judges in 1872 places on record that "Since the judicial service aims at protecting the rights of the people . . . , judges must handle litigants with care. However, it is said that there are some judges who confuse civil and criminal cases and submit civil litigants to birching or whipping. This is absurd, and judges are required henceforth to avoid any repetition of this sort of thing." It should also be pointed out that at this time conciliation in the manner of the preceding era was greatly encouraged, with the result that the judges had the conciliation of litigants as their main task. There was no desire to give a definitive solution to cases according to the law.[22]

The modernization of the legal system demanded the perfect-

---

[21]   In the law of 17 July, 1873, relating to civil procedural forms, many provisions are reminiscent of those in the French code. For instance, a plaintiff had to go to a scrivener to have procedural documents drawn up. The function of this scrivener was incompatible with that of the *daigennin* (barrister), and the office was therefore perhaps created on the model of that of the *avoué*. Moreover, the number of words which may appear on each line of a page of a deed drawn up by the scrivener is laid down in the law. No such tradition had previously existed in Japan, so once again the limitation seems to have been imported from France.
[22]   This is still a very strong tendency today.

ing of procedural law as well. So, in 1884 a German jurist, Techow, was asked to draw up a draft civil procedure code based on the German law of 1877. This Code of Civil Procedure was promulgated in 1890 and came into force the following year.[23] In contrast to the Civil Code, which is an eclectic work combining the French and German principles, the Code of Civil Procedure follows the German system almost exactly. There was a failure, however, to harmonize it with the Civil Code, so that in many cases there is a significant gap between the solution given in each.[24]

At the time when the movement of *Jiyu Minken* was flourishing, a great desire for a constitution was expressed among the Japanese. Numerous private projects for a constitution with varying political standpoints were published, and the greater number of the draftsmen saw that the constitution should be, if not an agreement emanating from the social will of the people, at least an agreement between the emperor and the people, and that a constituent assembly was required for this purpose. The government had other ideas; it had no intention of taking the wishes of the nation into account. After the repression of the liberal movement it secretly began the drafting of a constitution of its own. In 1882 Ito Hirobumi, one of the highest officials in the imperial government, left for Europe to study European constitutions. He concentrated his studies on constitutions of the German type and was strongly influenced by German constitutionalists such as Gneist and Stein. Ito returned to Japan in 1883, and the drafting of the constitution probably started in 1886. Three high officials faithful to Ito were chosen as his assistants, and one of them, Inoue Kowashi, was given prime responsibility for the drafting of the text. He worked with the assistance of advice from the two Germans, Roesler and Mosse, who were both known to be great admirers of the Prussian Constitution of 1850. It is natural, therefore, that the draft drawn up by Inoue bears the visible

[23] Since the date for coming into force of the Civil Code was 1898, the procedural rules were applied earlier than those of substance!

[24] For instance, the equivalent of the French *contrainte* is employed in differing senses in the two codes: article 414, paragraph 2, of the Civil Code uses it to mean *contrainte directe*, while article 734 of the Civil Procedure Code uses it in the sense of *contrainte indirecte*.

imprint of the Prussian Constitution. In 1888 the draft was completed and submitted to a specially set up private council for consideration. Ito thought that the draft of the constitution should be discussed not in any constituent assembly representing the nation but before a body composed of the great men of the state.[25] On 11 February, 1889 (legend has it that the emperor Jimmu ascended the throne on 11 February), the Constitution was solemnly granted by the emperor to his subjects. On that day the emperor informed his ancestors of the Constitution, and deigned to issue an imperial rescript in imposing style to impress upon his subjects the grandeur of the constitutional empire. He said in the rescript that he proclaimed this great charter as an intangible and everlasting gift to all his present and future subjects.

The Constitution was a work of compromise between the idea of divine law and constitutionalism, but the powers of the emperor were nevertheless undeniably great under it. Article 4 provided that the emperor was the head of the state and that he combined in his person all the governmental powers. The Imperial Diet was only an organ for collaboration with the emperor. The laws were made with its consent (article 37), but the legislative power was exercised by the emperor (article 5). The powers of the Diet were extremely limited. For example, the government could bring back the budget of the preceding year if the new year's budget was not voted on in the required time (article 71). This measure in itself considerably weakened the power of the Diet to control the government. What is more a very extensive controlling power was reserved to the emperor. He could promulgate several types of regulatory measures, such as urgent measures and independent measures (articles 8 and 9), without the intervention of the Diet. Urgent measures were issued during the period when the Diet was not sitting and could be abrogated if disapproved of by the Diet. Independent measures were those that sought to maintain public security or to increase national well-being. Neither could derogate from statutes, but they nevertheless limited the legislative power of the

[25] This privy council, which was never a constitutional organ, continued to play an important role in the absolutist government even after the promulgation of the Constitution.

Diet. Another point to note is the independence of the military. It was not the Constitution itself which formally provided for this, but under the constitutional regime the former practices continued. It consisted in placing the military power beyond the control of the civil ministers and in permitting the army and navy chiefs to deal directly with the emperor. This absurd custom favored military despotism and finally led Japan to catastrophe.

In spite of its absolutist character, the 1889 Constitution did permit the democratization of government, and a democratic political tendency did develop during this period of evolution of constitutional life in Japan. After World War I a liberal democratic movement grew in all sectors of national life. In the field of legal theory this tendency was represented by Minobe Tatsukichi, professor of constitutional law at the Faculty of Law of the Imperial University of Tokyo, and Yoshino Sakuzo, professor of political science of the same faculty. Unfortunately the democrats were forced to retract under the pressures of the military. In sum, what was assured by the Constitution was, as Professor Oka, one of the most eminent historians of Japanese politics, points out, only apparent constitutionalism.

In the field of administrative law the evolution was very complicated. In the first years of the Meiji era the political and administrative organization was modified frequently. Initially the *ritsu-ryo* system was reinstated, but slowly the influences of French and English law were felt in this field too. In 1871 the *han* regime was suppressed and the country was divided into *ken* (prefectures). The reform reverted to an old model, but even at this time some European influence could be traced in the law. About 1885 the central and local administration was perfected along Prussian lines. In 1885 the cabinet (*naikaku*) system of government was established, and in 1888 a law on *communes* and in 1890 a law on *départements* was promulgated. The operation of the Japanese administration before World War I was characterized by its bureaucratic, centralized, and police-state tendencies.

Japan made great efforts to modernize its legal system on the model of the advanced countries, and it is not an exaggeration to say that the modernization can be analyzed as a Europeanization or Westernization of Japan. It has been shown that the basic structure of the Japanese legal system was formed mainly by German and French law, but, as has also been shown, the rules of these Western laws were not always properly understood by the Japanese draftsmen. In one piece of legislation rules borrowed from both French and German law could be found. The draftsmen were short of time and often combined rules superficially without harmonizing them at a conceptual level. The reception was not a direct one. It was the result of a complex process of referring from one body of law to the other.

REAL SIGNIFICANCE OF THE RECEPTION

Although Japan succeeded in faithfully and skillfully imitating the French and German legal systems, its own culture could not help but give an original character to the system that was received. The rapid Europeanization was limited to the field of state law, which dealt with only a very small section of Japanese society. Further, it must not be forgotten that the modernized law was put into operation by men whose outlook was determined by a peculiar set of geographical and historical factors. As Koschaker said, "No legislator could avoid leaving some area for the application of indigenous law, and even if he envisaged an en bloc reception it is doubtful that he could even then completely exclude indigenous law. For though the law can be changed from one day to the next, the men to whom it is applied and those who have to apply it in the future cannot be changed this way."[26] Japan was destined to remain a long time subject to social rules that were quite foreign to the received law.

The modern codes predicated a bourgeois society in which every individual is presumed free and equal with everyone else, in which all legal relationships constitutive of rights and obligations are formed by the individuals themselves, and where legal relationships are created by the exercise of the individual's free will. This is of course an ideal which no real society fully attains, though it is true that any modern society worthy of the name does attain the ideal to a greater or lesser degree. There was no

[26] Koschaker, *Europa und das römische Recht*, p. 145.

important difference between the archetypal society on which the French Civil Code was based and the society to which it applied, which is why the school of exegesis was able to dominate French legal thought till the end of the nineteenth century. Japanese society, on the other hand, retained an essentially archaic morality from the preceding period after the reception of Western law. There was a great gap between the society presumed by the modern-style codes and that which existed almost independently of them. Japanese society had no knowledge of ideas of right and duty before the reception, and so the school of *Begriffs-jurisprudenz* prospered in Japan after the promulgation of the codes. Japanese jurists did not concern themselves with the actual life of the people because this life followed rules of quite a different kind from those of state law. Even the people did not want the state law to be interpreted for their benefit, so that judges contented themselves with giving logical coherence to their decisions without trying to convince the parties. A former professor commenting on the judicial practice of the prewar judges said, "A good judge was considered to be the one who disposed of contrary arguments by saying that they were ill-founded in as few words as possible. The judge's merit was in his being able to formulate his decisions in an extremely laconic manner and in his having some knowledge of the German language."

Why was Japanese society able to continue in this way for such a long time in spite of the rapid progress of modern capitalism? The development of capitalism in Japan was dominated from the beginning by political rather than economic considerations. The Meiji Restoration of 1868 was not brought about by the bourgeoisie. The lower ranking samurai, who were the main engineers of the political reform, had absolutely no intention of abandoning the feudal principles which they considered constituted a morality far superior to the European. They understood that they could not preserve Japan's independence without recourse to the material means that the Western powers controlled, but they believed that it was possible to adopt the material civilization of Europe and to harmonize it with Oriental morality. Even the most progressive intellectuals toward the end of the Edo period expressed this idea, and their motto was "Western techniques, Oriental morality." As a consequence the Meiji government intended to modernize Japan only to the extent necessary to make it an equal of the great powers of the world. It was necessary to be wealthy and strong; thus the basic principle of government was embodied in the motto *fukoku kyohei* (rich country and strong military).

The adoption of capitalism proceeded not just from the economic point of view but also from the political and military points of view. From its inception Japanese capitalism was encircled by a martial halo, but being in its infancy it was weak both bodily and spiritually. It did not have enough energy to grow healthily. The initial accumulation of capital was insufficient, there was no spirit of liberalism, and free competition was unknown. All the modern industrial enterprises were promoted by the government and then given by way of concession to individuals subject to the diligent protection of the state. The Japanese bourgeoisie was nurtured by the government, and was, in a sense, the favorite daughter of absolutism. There was neither liberalism nor individualism in its spirit. What a difference between that and the *Geist des Kapitalismus* of which Max Weber speaks. The Japanese never thought that the state could be a necessary evil. They did not even realize that the state could be founded on social contract, and it is perhaps in this that their chauvinism lies.

The historical conditions were obviously favorable to the survival of the former morality, but there is yet another factor that prevented the breakdown of the previous structuring of Japanese society. Japanese capitalism was unable to make use of sophisticated machines in its early stages, so it had to resort to the labor of women and children. The rural population was therefore partially absorbed by industry, but even when the great industrial enterprises needed workers, those who had originally come from the country returned to the country in periods of unemployment. The result was that the rural areas were an asylum for the unemployed and sheltered a very large number of inhabitants living in conditions little better than those of the preceding era. Agricultural exploitation was maintained usually by the labor of the members of each peasant family, and the mechanization of agriculture was retarded by this abundance of manpower. Naturally, the tempo of life remained static and society changed little.[27] As a result Japanese capitalism, prospering as it did at the expense of the peasants and workers, was unable to find any worthwhile internal market and was obliged to seek an outlet for its goods in external markets, which helped to accentuate its militaristic character.

The government for its part profited one hundred percent from the situation and tried to reinforce the outlook of the people through the national education system. In 1890 an imperial rescript was issued defining the fundamental principles of public education. These principles rested on Confucianism and emphasized loyalty to the emperor and filial piety as cardinal virtues. The state was conceived as a large family in which a hierarchical order was operative. At the top of the hierarchy was the emperor, the compassionate father of the nation. He was a divine man, literally an incarnate divinity. Not only was he omnipotent but he was himself the source of morality. On all national festivals a solemn ceremony took place in all schools for the cult of the emperor. All those present had to give adoration to the imperial image and then in an impressive voice the principal of the school would read the Imperial Rescript on Education. Thus the whole nation was indoctrinated from childhood with the idea that Japan was a holy country guarded by godly ancestors and the emperor himself and could never be conquered by its enemies. This sacred and mystical character of the Japanese state was called *kokutai* (the form of the state) and the slightest fault committed against *kokutai* was severely punished as a crime of *lèse-majesté*. The old customs were linked to *kokutai* and criticism of them, even of a purely scientific nature, was severely repressed as a dangerous idea.[28]

[27] This state of affairs continues today in the backward areas of Japan. R. Guillain, Tokyo correspondent of *Le Monde*, published very interesting articles on this subject in *Le Monde*, 27–30 December, 1962.

[28] This is the sole reason why scientific historical studies ran into almost insurmountable difficulties in the prewar period. All critical research incompatible with the traditional myths was severely repressed. Many excellent historians were put out of jobs because they studied Japanese history from a critical viewpoint. It is only since the war that the history of ancient Japan is being clearly established.

After World War I jurists had begun a critical and sociological study of law, and also a very lively movement toward democracy was growing among a large section of the populace. This tendency coincided with the movement for social rights in Europe, but in Japan it was nothing more than the beginning of true liberalism and democracy. The dominant class feared this development, and in 1925 it had a law, which is well known in Japan for its severity, voted by the Diet. This was the *chian-iji-ho*, the law on the maintenance of the public security. The first article provided: "Those who have associated to reform the *kokutai* or to deny the private property regime as well as those who have knowingly cooperated with them, will be punished by imprisonment with or without hard labor for a term not exceeding ten years." This law was used, with the assistance of the police and the special secret police, *tokubetsu koto keisatsu*,[29] to repress progressive ideas.[30] Originally it was used to repress communist activities, but in the end it was used to stifle any idea that could, in the eyes of the ruling class, constitute the slightest danger to the existing political regime.

Such was the cultural milieu in which the reception of Western laws was undertaken. It is easy to see what a great gulf existed between the social structure presupposed by the received legal system and that which operated in Japan. Rationalism, which is the soul of modern law, was for the Japanese only a beautiful borrowed garment which hid a traditional psychology imbued with mystic sentimentalism. The *homo juridicus* on which modern law was based was a man who thought mathematically and logically and had no concern for the delicacy of the subtle nuances of concrete life. Those who were not used to the abstraction of objective things were embarrased by a fashion of thought which admitted only two colors, black and white. The Japanese, a man of poetry, had great difficulty adapting to legal rationalism, but eventually he began to understand this law which guaranteed him his liberty and personal dignity.

[29] Also called *tokko*.
[30] A very large number of intellectuals were victims of the *tokko* because of their progressive ideas.

GOVERNMENT AND THE LAW

CHAPTER IV

THE *TENNO* REGIME

The Japanese emperor (*tenno*)[1] is quite different from the head of other countries. It is in fact doubtful whether, strictly speaking, the tenno is part of the executive, and that is why he is dealt with in a chapter apart.

The tenno was under the former regime considered, as the word itself indicates, an incarnate divinity. All his governmental powers were presumed to be derived from the very nature of his divinity, which he shared with his divine ancestors. But from the moment of the unconditional surrender in 1945, when Japan was subjected to the conditions imposed by the Allies as declared in the Potsdam Declaration, the situation changed completely. According to this declaration, the form of government of Japan had to be determined by the Japanese people, and from that moment the old tenno regime disappeared. On 1 January, 1946, the tenno himself stated in an imperial rescript that he was deprived of his divine character. Consequently, although the title tenno is still used as in the former period, the nature of the institution is entirely different.[2]

Under the new Constitution the essential function of the tenno consists in being the symbol of the Japanese state. Article 1 of the Constitution says, "The emperor shall be the symbol of the state and of the unity of the people. His position is determined by the general will of the people in whom resides sovereign power." A symbolic characteristic attaches to nearly all mon-

[1] The word, which until now has been translated as emperor, is in Japanese, *tenno* (heavenly prince), and from now on this term will be used instead of emperor to point up the special nature of this organ of state.
[2] Sometimes the use of the term tenno regime (*tennosei*) is limited to the old type regime but it is also current to use the term in a broader sense.

archs, and the tenno of the old regime were no exception to this, but when they possessed all governmental powers their role as national symbol masked that of omnipotent dictator. The new Constitution did not endow the tenno with any attribute that preceding tenno did not have, but his role as state symbol comes out much more clearly today because he has lost his quality of dictator. According to Miyasawa, article 1 only serves to emphasize that the tenno no longer enjoys any power or role other than that of symbol.[3] Indeed the tenno can only perform acts known as state acts (*kokujikoi*), and these are limitatively enumerated in article 4 of the Constitution; the tenno has no governmental attribution. The expression "state acts" is a bad choice because it is susceptible of misunderstanding. Literally it could mean act concerning government, but article 4 of the Constitution excludes all governmental acts from the notion of state acts. Therefore state acts must be understood as acts which are outside the field of determination by state will. In other words the tenno can perform only those acts which serve to give a ritual and outward form to acts which have already been decided by the competent state organs. There is absolutely no way the tenno himself can determine the state will.

By comparison with the all-powerful position of the tenno under the Meiji Constitution, the attributes of the tenno under the present Constitution are of a very limited nature. They are enumerated in articles 6 and 7 of the Constitution:

1. Appointing of the prime minister after he has been elected by Parliament.

2. Appointing of the chief judge of the Supreme Court on the advice of the cabinet.

[3] Takayanagi Kenzo who was, until recent times, president of the Commission for Constitutional Research says: "In feudal Japan the emperor was in theory considered to be the head of the state, but his political power was weaker and of a more nominal nature than that of the European kings . . .; even after the Meiji Restoration the symbolic importance of the emperor was greater for the unity of the nation than his sovereign political powers. . . . Seen from this point of view the rules relating to the tenno in the new constitution are not as revolutionary as they might appear to be to ardent supporters of the theory of *kokutai*." "A Century of Innovations: The Development of Japanese Law, 1868–1961," in *Law in Japan*, ed., Arthur von Mehren (Cambridge: Harvard University Press, 1963), pp. 5, 13. It is my view, however, that the political powers of the tenno under the old regime were much more important than his symbolic role.

3. Promulgation of amendments of the Constitution, legislation, decrees, and treaties.

4. Convocation of Parliament.

5. Dissolution of the House of Representatives.[4]

6. Calling of a general election for members of Parliament.

7. Attestation of the nomination and dismissal of ministers and other public officials as provided by law as well as of the powers and credentials of ambassadors and ministers.

8. Attestation of general or special amnesty, the exercise of the prerogative of mercy, the commutation of punishments, and restoration of civil rights.[5]

9. Granting of state honors.

10. Attestation of instruments of ratification and other diplomatic documents as provided by law.

11. Receiving of foreign ambassadors and ministers.

12. Performance of certain state ceremonies.

[4] The tenno can only declare the House of Representatives dissolved when this has already been decided by the government, but since dissolution is a very important political act certain public lawyers doubt whether it is desirable to permit the tenno to take part in it even at a formal level.

[5] Japanese law does not know the distinction between pardon and amnesty. Every act by which the effects of a penal conviction are partially or totally suppressed is referred to by the general term *onsha* (*on* means favor, and *sha* means pardon). *Onsha* includes the five things listed in the text and is covered by a special law of 28 March, 1947, which sets out the topic as follows:

1. General pardon (*taisha*, literally, big pardon) is determined by *seirei* (decree), which specifies the categories of offenses to which it relates (article 2). It has the following effects:
   (a) for those who have been convicted, the conviction lapses;
   (b) for those not yet convicted, the prosecution is discontinued (article 3).
2. Special pardon (*tokusha*) is directed to specific individuals who have been convicted (article 4). It has the effect of annulling the conviction (article 5).
3. Commutation of penalty (*genkei*) is established by *seirei* which specify the offenses or penalties for the benefit of either convicted persons in general or specified persons (article 6). Penalties are commuted by this measure (article 7).
4. Exoneration from the execution of the penalty (*keino shikko no menjo*) works for the benefit of specified individuals who have been convicted (article 8) and exempts them from suffering the penalty.
5. Rehabilitation (*fukken*) is a measure taken to reinstate those who have been deprived of an attribute of their status or those who have had one of the attributes of status suspended as a result of a criminal conviction. The conditions are determined by *seirei* (article 9).

As can be seen *onsha* is granted by the government, and there have been grave fears about the abuse the government has made of this institution. For example, when Japan joined the United Nations in December, 1956, the government pardoned a large number of convicted persons who had broken the electoral laws.

For the tenno to be able to validly perform all these state acts he has to act according to the advice of and with the approval of cabinet.[6] That is to say, he cannot even exercise these functions except in accordance with a previously reached decision of the cabinet. What the Constitution requires is that the tenno do nothing by his own power. Consequently, if the nature of an act is determined by one competent state organ, for example by Parliament, the advice and approval of cabinet are no longer necessary for the act.[7] Those acts the tenno is permitted by the Constitution to perform are all nominal. They add nothing to the content of state acts determined by other state organs, but they adorn them with a mystical and irrational type of authority, which if humans were perfectly rational would have no purpose.

Some declare that the tenno is a monarch, while others compare his role with that of the king or queen in England. But Miyasawa has doubts about this. According to him, the notion of monarch is very vague. In his view the common traits of every monarchy that has existed up till now are that (a) it is an organ comprised of one person, (b) who has an important part of the government power, or at least an important part of the executive power, (c) who represents the state abroad, (d) who has a status peculiar to himself, which is in some way different from that of the ordinary people, and is in most cases hereditary,[8] (e) whose position is imbued with a charismatic authority, and (f) who fills the role of state symbol. The present tenno system has characteristics (a), (d), (e) and (f), but lacks (b) and (c). Of these six traits of a monarchy those that the tenno possesses are those of a mystic and sentimental character, while the two that it does not have are rather more legal in nature. If importance is attached to the last two points, the tenno is not a monarch. However, for those who consider the other points as the essential ones, the tenno is a monarch.

The legal position of the tenno under the new Constitution is unique. He is neither to be compared with an ordinary monarch

---

[6]   Article 3 of the Constitution.

[7]   There are, however, some constitutionalists who even in this case say the advice and approval of the government is required.

[8]   Article 2 of the Constitution provides that the imperial throne is hereditary, and succession to it is determined according to the Code on the Imperial Family.

or a president of the republican system, nor can he be said to be the head of state[9] as it is not he but the cabinet who represents the Japanese state in foreign affairs. Miyasawa says that the tenno neither governs nor reigns, he only stands as a symbol of the nation.[10] It is an institution born of the efforts made to harmonize a long monarchic tradition with the requirements of a modern democratic republic. For this reason it is not quite accurate to translate tenno as emperor. Indeed Japan is no longer an empire. Instead of the former title of *Dai Nippon Teikoku* (Great Japanese Empire), the official title under the Meiji Constitution, the present Constitution adopts the more modest *Nippon Koku* (State of Japan). In Capitant's *Vocabulaire Juridique* the notion of empire is defined as "a form of government having as its head a monarchical authority of a more or less absolute nature." According to this definition present-day Japan is obviously not an empire, but may it not be a republic? Miyasawa seems to think it is. A republic according to the definition of the *Vocabulaire Juridique* is a state whose head is elected and whose position is not hereditary. The tenno is neither elected (his position is hereditary) nor is he the head of state, so the notion of republic may be compatible with that of tenno.

In terms of social function it can be affirmed from the macroscopic point of view that the tenno regime does truly fill the role

---

[9] Certain people claim, however, that he must be considered as head of state even under the present Constitution. According to them the tenno represents Japan as far as foreign countries are concerned.

[10] Those favoring revision of the present Constitution criticize the notion of symbol on the grounds of ambiguity of meaning, but the Constitution does clearly provide that the tenno fulfill the function of national figurehead by accomplishing certain state activities. Kiyomiya, one of the best known constitutional lawyers in Japan, is against revision and maintains that activities in relation to state matters must be distinguished from symbolic acts. According to him the tenno's activities can be classed as follows:

    1. Public acts:
      (a) State activities set out in the Constitution.
      (b) Symbolic acts which are not set out in the Constitution but whose validity is accepted, e.g., when the tenno participates in a function organized by a foreign country. This activity does not come within item 12 listed in the text, according to Kiyomiya. The performance of functions in terms of the Constitution only covers cases where the tenno presides.
    2. Private acts.
Kiyomiya thinks that state acts are fulfilled by the tenno as an organ of the state, while his symbolic functions are foreign to his quality as state organ. But is not the tenno a state organ whose sole function is to symbolize the state?

of state symbol. Feelings of respect toward the tenno are deeply rooted in the hearts of most Japanese people. This attitude is quite natural in the older generations because they were taught the mystical ideas of the Imperial Rescript on Education in an exact way. They have a vague feeling about the compassionate nature of the tenno without sometimes being able to find any reason for their feelings. This attitude is very similar to the traditional religious attitude of the Japanese. An old poem says:

> Although I do not know in whose presence I am
>   in this temple,
> A feeling of compassion overcomes me and I cry.[11]

This type of reaction can be observed even in the younger generation. On the basis of the results of an inquiry Stoetzel concludes that even among the young people much of the traditional devotion to the emperor is still alive. "Although," he writes, "the young people seem to show a rather greater independence of spirit than their elders, they remain very much attached to the idea of the emperor, and even more attached to the notion of the imperial system, to symbols, to memories, traditions and to the values that they represent."[12]

From a microscopic point of view the situation is quite different. The regime has been the object of criticism so strong that there is a reactionary tendency which wants to profit from the attitude of those favoring the tenno in order to restore the former regime. The present regime is neither monarchic nor republican, but it can be interpreted either in a monarchic or in a republican sense, and there is great tension between these two poles. The conservatives want to strengthen the monarchic character of the Constitution, while the progressive group wants simply to achieve a democratic republican system. The former have nostalgic feelings for the privileged way of life they enjoyed under the empire, and they attribute all the glory of the preceding era to the virtue of the regime of divine law. The latter, on

---

[11] This sentimental attitude is ingrained in the Japanese national character.
[12] Stoetzel, *Jeunesse sans chrysanthème ni sabre*, pp. 157, 162.

the other hand, see the viciousness of political measures taken by the absolutist government before World War II as a result of the tenno system. For them no modifying of the old regime would achieve democracy. On this point an interesting inquiry on political views was conducted in 1959 among those attending the Legal Training and Research Institute. The result showed that 123 out of 167 opposed the tenno regime in one group and 153 out of 266 in a second group. This result would lead one to conclude that most people who are used to thinking in a rational way have no sympathy for the tenno system. However, most Japanese find themselves in a position somewhere between the two extremes, and this situation will probably not change for a long time.

CHAPTER V

THE LEGISLATURE

PARLIAMENT

The Constitution formally declares that Parliament is the sole
law-making organ of the nation (article 41).[1] Legislation is therefore in principle monopolized by Parliament. Under the Meiji
Constitution the legislative power was reserved in large measure
to the government, but the new Constitution does not admit
that. The legislative power of the government is limited to the
issue of regulations relating to the application of a law or exercised by delegation in legislation, though there are some
exceptions to this principle. For example, each House of Parliament can make its own rules and the Supreme Court can make
certain regulations without any legislative delegation.[2]

Parliament is also, according to article 41, the supreme organ
of state power. The meaning of this provision is not entirely clear,
because of course the will of Parliament is not supreme, as the
laws which it promulgates are subject to control for constitutionality by the courts. What article 41 does mean is that Parliament is the most important of the state organs because it represents the nation. In contrast with the Imperial Diet, which was
simply an organ of collaboration with the tenno, Parliament
possesses very great power. It is qualified to decide the general
will of the people without recourse to any other state organ.

[1] The body which exercises the legislative power of the state is the *kokkai*. The
present Constitution has rejected the Meiji title of *teikoku gikai* because *teikoku* means
empire. *Kokkai* is sometimes translated as Diet, but this word was also used in the
Meiji Constitution and evokes for Japanese the idea of the political assembly of the
Holy Empire. To avoid confusion therefore, *kokkai* will be translated as Parliament.
The word diet comes from medieval Latin *dieta*, which is the translation of the German word *tag*; *tag* means both day and assembly.
[2] Articles 58 and 77 of the Constitution.

Parliament is made up of two chambers, the House of Representatives (*Shugiin*) and the House of Councillors (*Sangiin*).[3] This bicameralism is not perfect.[4] The House of Representatives has much greater power than the House of Councillors, as its will carries the day in the case of an irreconcilable difference of opinion between the two Houses.[5]

The Constitution provides that both Houses should be made up of elected members who represent the whole nation (article 43) and lays down certain basic rules for the elections:

1. All important matters relating to elections must be determined by legislation (articles 44 and 47).

2. No discrimination on the basis of race, creed, sex, social status, family origin, education, property, or income is permitted in respect of voting and eligibility for office (article 44).

3. Every adult has the right to vote (article 15).

4. Secrecy of ballot is guaranteed (article 15).

More detailed rules relating to elections are provided by the law on election to public offices of 15 April, 1950.[6] Article 4 sets the number of seats for the House of Representatives at 466.[7] An elector must have reached the age of majority, which is twenty, and have been domiciled for three months in the commune in which he votes (article 9). Even when these conditions have been fulfilled the elector cannot exercise his right to vote unless he is on the electoral list drawn up on 15 September of each year.

The system of electoral districts adopted is that of the "medium constituency." By this the number of seats in each district is between three and five. This is a kind of grand constituency—a constituency where the number of seats that can be held is plural. Japan is divided into 123 constituencies, and the number of seats is calculated on the basis of the population in each constituency. The law provides that the list of the number of seats for each

---

[3] Article 42 of the Constitution.

[4] The Imperial Diet had adopted perfect bicameralism. Miyasawa calls the present-day bicameralism lame bicameralism.

[5] E.g., articles 59, 60, 61, and 67 of the Constitution.

[6] This statute has 273 articles and is applicable to all elections of public officials. It codified about twenty preexisting electoral laws.

[7] In reality the number is now 491 because seats have been added by a special law which has left article 4 unchanged.

constituency should be modified every five years according to the results of the most recent census, but in fact no modification has been made to the constituency lists since 1950. It follows that there is, as in other countries, a considerable disproportion in many constituencies between the number of seats and the number of inhabitants. The result is overrepresentation and underrepresentation. For example the worth of a vote in the Tokyo constituency is equal to only a third that of a vote in a neighboring prefecture.[8] For the conservative party, of course, it is desirable that overrepresentation be maintained in the rural regions, the stronghold of conservative ideas.

An elected representative must be Japanese and at least twenty-five years of age.[9]

The present law adopts the system of uninominal polling in each constituency. Each elector votes for a single candidate with the result that the majority of the electors sometimes fails to monopolize all the seats of a constituency. It remains possible for the minority to have itself represented. The system, then, is a minority one and has been favored by the Japanese since 1900. Those who have obtained a majority relative to the number of votes cast are elected up to the number of seats that are available in each constituency, provided that each has a number of votes equal to at least a quarter of the total of all the votes cast divided by the number of seats available for that constituency (article 95

---

[8] In 1962 a law student brought an action seeking to annul the election of councillors that had taken place in a district of Tokyo because the value of a vote in that district was only a quarter that of a vote in the district of Tottori. This was contrary to article 14 of the Constitution which guarantees citizens equality before the law. The Supreme Court dismissed the application by a judgment of 5 February, 1964. One of the reasons for the decision was: "As far as the number of seats available in each constituency is concerned, it is Parliament which has to determine this and it can do so freely unless its decision brings about an excessive inequality among electors. Therefore, the mere fact that the number of seats available is not well distributed in relation to the population of each constituency is insufficient reason to justify the annulation of an election on the basis of inequality under article 14 of the Constitution." This judgment leaves many points in doubt; for example, what degree of disproportion amounts to excessive inequality? Most public lawyers are unwilling to accept it as good law.

[9] There is also electoral unworthiness. Those condemned to certain penalties laid down by law and interdicted persons are excluded from the electorate and from eligibility. (Cf. articles 10 and 11 of the electoral law.)

of the electoral law).[10] Electors must, with certain exceptions, present themselves personally at the polling booth on election day (article 44 of the electoral law). After the necessary preliminaries the elector goes into a booth and writes the name of one candidate on the voting slip that he has been given. He then puts the slip into the ballot box.

Councillors too are elected directly by the people. Indirect election is not forbidden by the Constitution, but it has never in fact been used.

If the same mode of voting were adopted for the two Houses, the composition of the House of Councillors would reflect a political tendency almost identical to that of the House of Representatives. In order to establish some difference between the two a curious method of voting has been devised. The difference is in the constituency. The 1950 law on elections provides a dualist system. There are two types of constituency. One is called the national constituency, the whole country being a single constituency; the other is called the local constituency, each prefecture being one constituency.

The total number of seats for councillors is 252. Of these 152 are for the local constituencies and 100 for the national constituency. In relation to the local constituencies the number of seats available in each constituency varies, according to the prefecture, from two to eight. In practice, between one and four councillors in each local constituency and fifty in the national constituency are voted for in every election. Because the term of election is six years, half the number of members in the House are renewed every three years.[11] This is a monster constituency with uninominal voting,[12] and in such a system candidates who are promoted by organized groups, such as workers unions,

---

[10]　For an illustration of this system, imagine a constituency for which the number of seats is four. Six candidates offer themselves and the number of votes cast is 100,000. The candidates obtained votes as follows: A, 30,000; B, 25,000; C, 20,000; D, 15,000; E, 8,000; and F, 2,000. The quotient is 100,000:4=25,000. To be elected a candidate must gain at least a quarter of this figure, i.e., 6,250 votes. The result is that candidates A, B, C, and D are elected. If candidates A and B belong to party *A* and candidates C and D belong to party *B*, the minority of the electors who supported party *B* are represented. In a majority system the minority would not have a representative where the spread of votes was as in this example.

[11]　Article 46 of the Constitution.

[12]　Each elector has to choose one person from among two hundred candidates.

bureaucrats, religious bodies, or candidates who are well known by the whole nation, like a film star, find themselves in a privileged position. The defects of the system are the subject of much discussion, but a plan for a better system has not yet been worked out.

The conditions required of a person to be an elector are the same as those for elections for the House of Representatives. The conditions of eligibility are also the same in the two Houses, except that a councillor must be at least thirty years old (article 10 of the election law). The mode of voting for councillors is the same as for representatives. The elector votes at the same time for one candidate from his local constituency and for another from the national constituency. In two-seat local constituencies a majority system operates because only one seat is to be filled at each election. In the other local constituencies and in the national constituency the Japanese-style minority system operates. The manner of deciding the elected candidates is identical to that for representatives, save that the minimum number of votes to be obtained is one-eighth of the number arrived at by dividing the total number of votes cast by the number of seats available in the case of a national constituency and one-sixth in the case of a local constituency (article 95 of the election law).

It is impossible to give a detailed description here of how elections actually operate in Japan, but the following are some characteristic points. In general, Japanese do not have a personal political opinion. Very often the voter votes for a candidate who has given him *go-on*, or else he votes for a candidate on the advice of his *oyabun* to whom he is linked by *giri*. Leading citizens frequently dictate the way the vote of the populace, over which they exercise their influence, will be cast and a great number of voters are corrupted.

The sentimental characteristics of the Japanese play a very important role in elections. For example, a candidate who has often failed in earlier elections attracts the sympathy of electors, particularly of women voters. It frequently happens also that a woman who replaces her husband who died during his candidature obtains sympathy votes. There are again many women who vote according to the advice of their husbands. This does not mean that they agree with their husbands on matters of politics; they often just do not have an opinion of their own. Even among young people indifference to political matters is widespread. Stoetzel remarked that young Japanese do not appear to show any great interest in the internal politics of their country.[13] According to the results of an inquiry carried out in 1958, the proportion of persons abstaining in relation to the number of voters is almost the same among those in the age group 20–24 as among people in their sixties. However, the proportion of voters in relationship to electors is generally quite high. Eleven general elections have taken place from 1947 to 1972, and the number voting was from 67.95 percent to 76.99 percent of the number on the electoral rolls. For councillors there have been eight ordinary elections from 1950 to 1971, and the proportion of voters was from 58.7 percent to 72.1 percent. Finally, the proportion of voters is higher among men than among women, though this is a difference that is disappearing.

Each member of Parliament represents the whole nation (article 43 of the Constitution); he cannot be bound by any imperative mandate. Representatives are elected for four years, and councillors for six years.[14] Needless to say, in the case of dissolution of the House of Representatives the length of the representatives' mandate is reduced by the appropriate amount because they lose their status of representatives by the dissolution. Every member of Parliament also enjoys certain immunities[15] under the Constitution and receives an allowance that cannot be less than the best salary for state officers in the general category,[16] plus various other payments that go with their office. The amount paid to members is determined by Parliament itself, and it is often criticized for increasing members' allowances in an arbitrary manner.[17]

[13] Stoetzel, *Jeunesse sans chrysanthème ni sabre*, p. 147.

[14] Articles 45 and 46 of the Constitution.

[15] Cf. articles 50 and 51.

[16] Article 49 of the Constitution; article 35 of the law on Parliament.

[17] The salary of parliamentarians is at present calculated as follows: the presidents of the two Houses receive a sum equal to that of the prime minister, i.e., ¥1,050,000 per month. The other members receive ¥520,000. Besides this every member of Parliament receives an expense allowance of ¥230,000 a month. In order to understand the relatively high sum involved this should be compared with that received by a professor at a national university, which at best is ¥242,900 a month.

Article 58 of the Constitution provides that each House elect its own president and officers (*yakuin*).[18] According to Miyasawa the term *yakuin* is ambiguous and has to be interpreted in a broad sense, and should include all persons employed by Parliament. But the law on Parliament uses the term to mean only senior officials. According to article 16 of this law the notion of *yakuin* includes the president, the vice-president, the acting president, the chairmen of permanent committees, and the general secretary. Of these officials only the general secretary is chosen from outside Parliament. In this sense then, *yakuin* corresponds almost exactly to *bureau parlementaire* of French law. Where the post of president or vice-president or of both is vacant when Parliament is convened, they must be elected at the beginning of the session (article 6 of the law on Parliament). The mandate of the *yakuin* has a duration coinciding with that of the parliamentary mandate. Should neither the president nor the vice-president be available to act in a given case, an acting president is elected to perform the president's functions.

THE STRUCTURE OF PARLIAMENT

Article 58 of the Constitution provides that each House establish its own rules for governing its meetings, proceedings, and internal discipline. In Japanese law important matters relating to Parliament have, since the Meiji Constitution, been determined by the law on Parliament. The field left for regulation by each House is therefore limited. Nevertheless, apart from the law on Parliament which has 133 articles, there are the regulations of the House of Representatives, 258 articles, and regulations for the House of Councillors, 253 articles. The regulations made by each House are rules of law of a class inferior to the Constitution and statutes.

As in most parliamentary systems Japan has a series of committees whose job is to prepare business for discussions in the plenary sessions. These committees are not mentioned in the Constitution but are regulated by the law on Parliament. Two

[18] *Yaku* means duty or responsibility, and *in* means personnel.

sorts of committees are provided for—permanent committees
and special committees. There are sixteen permanent committees for each House (article 41), and, of those sixteen, twelve
are more or less directly linked to the ministries. Every member
of Parliament must be a member of at least one permanent committee (article 42). The members of each permanent committee
or of each special committee are nominated in relation to the
proportional representation in Parliament of each political grouping (article 46). The chairmen are elected from among the members of each committee (article 25), and the posts of chairman
are shared according to the proportional representation of the
political groups. At the present time they are monopolized in
the House of Representatives by the government party. The committees deal only with business submitted to them during the
current session, and in principle they cannot act outside the
current session (article 47). Each committee has the right to
present bills which relate to the matters within its competence
(article 50B).

A committee may hold public hearings when it is dealing with
important business of a general nature, so that those who have a
direct interest in or special knowledge of the matter can be
heard. Public hearings are obligatory for the general budget and
for bills relating to taxes (article 51).

The system of public hearings was borrowed from the United
States, but it cannot be said to function very well in Japan as
Parliament has unfortunately taken little account of what it
should have learned from these hearings. Thus, the system of permanent committees has been vigorously criticized. Each committee is too closely linked, it is said, to a corresponding ministry.
The impression given is that the committee represents the interests of the ministry in Parliament, and this seriously affects
the committee's value from the national point of view. However,
under present conditions where Parliament is subject to a very
complicated set of machinery, it would be difficult to concentrate
the discussion of all business into plenary sessions.

Japanese law does not permit a permanent Parliament. Parliament, with a few exceptions, can act only during a set period
called a session (*kaiki*). Matters that are not settled before the

end of one session cannot properly be discussed in the following session. Thus the principle of discontinuity of sessions is accepted (article 68 of the law on Parliament). The Constitution provides for three sorts of sessions: ordinary sessions, extraordinary sessions, and special sessions. There must be one ordinary session each year (article 52 of the Constitution). No date is prescribed for it, but under article 2 of the law on Parliament an ordinary session should usually open in December.[19] Extraordinary sessions are called when the need arises outside of the ordinary session (article 53 of the Constitution). Special sessions are like extraordinary sessions, but they are called in the thirty days[20] after a general election following the dissolution of the House of Representatives (article 54 of the Constitution).[21]

Parliament is always convoked by the tenno whatever the type of session (article 7 of the Constitution). It is the government which decides on the calling of Parliament, but when a quarter of all the members of one of the Houses demands the calling of Parliament, the cabinet must call an extraordinary session (article 53 of the Constitution). This right of calling Parliament to an extraordinary session is admitted in order to protect the right of minority parties, and the government is therefore supposed to answer the call as quickly as possible, though it has not always done so in practice.

The length of a session is not determined by the Constitution but by the law on Parliament. The length of an ordinary session is 150 days (article 10) unless the mandate of the members of Parliament has expired. The duration of extraordinary and special sessions is determined by a decision taken in agreement between the two Houses (article 11). In the case of disagreement or failing a decision of the House of Councillors, the will of the House of Representatives takes precedence (article 13). The

[19] It is the government which decides the date of opening according to this principle, but the tenno performs the ritual of the opening.

[20] In private law, if a period of time is expressed in days, the first day is not included (article 140 of the Civil Code); in public law there is a custom, dating from the Meiji era, of counting the first day in the period.

[21] If the date for the opening of a special session of Parliament coincides with that of the opening of an ordinary session, the Parliament can be called at the same time, both for the ordinary and for special session (article 2b of the law on Parliament).

length of each session can be extended by a decision taken by agreement between the two Houses. However, an ordinary session can be extended only once and extraordinary and special sessions only twice (article 12).

The Constitution does not provide for emergency laws, such as those by which the government provided for matters of urgency outside the session of the Diet under the former regime. The result is that it is now necessary to call Parliament to sesssion in every case. If such a convocation is necessary while the House of Representatives is dissolved, the House of Councillors in an emergency meeting must act in the name of Parliament (article 54). It is the cabinet which calls the House of Councillors to this meeting. Measures taken by such a meeting are valid as the will of Parliament, but they have a provisional character and will fail if they do not obtain the approval of the House of Representatives within ten days after the opening of the following session (article 54).

The Constitution, the law on Parliament, and the rules of the two Houses provide detailed provisions on debating procedure, and only a summary appraisal of the subject will be given here. The first thing to note is that the lack of democratic experience of the members of Parliament tends to prevent them from following the rules properly, and this results in some extraordinary scenes more worthy of a circus than of a debating chamber. Frequently what takes place is emotive rather than rational parliamentarianism.

For the opening of debates and the taking of decisions in plenary sessions, the presence of a third of all members is required in each House.[22] In committee sessions the presence of a half plus one of the members is necessary.[23] The validity of debates and decisions which do not fulfill this condition as to quorum is decided by the House itself, and no court has jurisdiction in the matter.

Plenary sessions are, in principle, public, but a House can sit

---

[22] Article 56 of the Constitution. All members, in this context, means all members who are in office at the time of the session and not the legal number of the members.
[23] Article 49 of the law on Parliament.

in secret meeting if a majority of two-thirds of the members present decide to do so (article 57 of the Constitution). The minutes of the sessions must, subject to exceptions in the case of non-public sessions, be published and available to the public. Committee sessions are not covered by the principle of publicity and only parliamentarians can attend them without the permission of the chairman of the committee concerned. In practice, however, reporters are usually admitted.

In Parliament all decisions are taken by majority vote, though the nature of the majority varies according to the case. In plenary sessions a simple majority is required, that is, a half plus one of the members present (article 56 of the Constitution), but the Constitution sometimes requires a majority of at least two-thirds of the members present (articles 57, 58, 59, and 96). In committee sessions all that is required is a simple majority of the members present (article 50 of the law on Parliament). The chairman does not have a deliberative vote, but in the case of a division he has a casting vote. Constitutional usage established under the Meiji Constitution was that the chairman could not participate in the voting as a member of Parliament, and that practice is still followed.

There are three forms of voting used in Japan. The first is sitting and standing voting, the second is by ballot, and the third is vote by way of non-opposition. In the case of ballot voting, those supporting a project put a white ballot into the ballot-box, and those opposed to it put in a blue ballot. Where a project is submitted to vote by way of non-opposition, the chairman asks those present if anyone opposes it; if he affirms that there is no opposition the project is declared adopted, but if a member opposes the project, resort must be had to another voting method.

FUNCTIONS OF PARLIAMENT

Parliament is considered by the Constitution as the sole legislative organ of the state. This does not mean that its functions are limited to the making of laws, for beyond that it fulfills functions relating to many things, such as finance and diplomacy. Only the legislative and financial functions of Parliament will be reviewed here.

All rules of law established by Parliament are called *horitsu*. Japanese legal terminology does not make a distinction between legislation and law, and the word *horitsu*[24] is also used in the sense of law, as in *horitsugaku*, science of law. The domain of *horitsu* is unlimited. Although each House and the Supreme Court can promulgate rules in certain areas without delegation by law, these matters are not reserved to the regulatory power of those organs, and there is nothing to prevent Parliament from derogating by way of legislation from the rules established by these other bodies.

The initiative for legislation rests concurrently with members of Parliament and the cabinet.[25] If a member of Parliament wishes to present a proposal for a law it must be supported by a specified number of members of the House to which the promoter belongs. When the proposal relates to financial measures the number required is greater (article 56 of the law on Parliament). Originally no such restriction existed, but abuse of the procedure by members who wished to please their electors made modification necessary in 1955. The law on Parliament provides that any committee can present proposals of laws in the field within its competence (article 50B). A governmental bill is presented to Parliament by the prime minister in the name of cabinet.[26] Governmental initiative is much more frequent than parliamentary initiative. In 1959 the total number of bills adopted in the ordinary session was 183, and of these the government presented 161. In 1960 the proportion was 125 out of 140.[27]

Examination of bills is governed by general laws relating to parliamentary debate. In principle, bills become law when they have been adopted by the two Houses (article 59 of the Con-

---

[24] A parliamentary bill is *horitsu-an*. The fact that the notion of legislation is not clearly distinguished from that of law is a sign that parliamentary sovereignty is not well established in Japan.

[25] The Constitution does not deal with this.

[26] Article 5 of the law on the cabinet.

[27] In both cases more than 80 percent of the bills had been sponsored by the government.

stitution), but the Constitution admits some exceptions to this rule. When the House of Councillors has rejected or modified a bill adopted by the House of Representatives, the bill becomes law if the House of Representatives passes it again with a majority of two-thirds of the members present (article 59 of the Constitution). In such a case the will of the House of Representatives alone suffices to make law. The House of Representatives can, instead of deciding alone, call for a meeting of the joint committee of the two Houses (*ryoin kyogikai*) (article 59 of the Constitution). The role of the joint committee is not limited to legislation. It can be convoked by either House at any time when there is disagreement between them. In principle if one of the Houses demands a meeting of the joint committee the other cannot refuse, but where a bill is concerned the House of Representatives can reject the request of the other House (article 88 of the law on Parliament). The joint committee is composed of twenty members, half elected by each House (article 89 of the law on Parliament), and its quorum is two-thirds of the membership. It draws up a compromise text that is first submitted to the House which called the meeting of the joint committee but that cannot be amended (article 93 of the law on Parliament). When the joint committee fails to draw up a compromise text, or when the text drawn up is not accepted by both Houses, the vote of the House of Representatives alone suffices to make law under article 59 of the Constitution.

When the House of Councillors has not voted a bill within sixty days of receiving it from the other House, the bill can be regarded as rejected by the House of Councillors (article 59 of the Constitution).[28] Therefore, the situation can again arise where the will of the lower House alone becomes law, by application of article 59 of the Constitution.

All laws must be signed by the competent minister and the prime minister.[29] Japanese law provides for no formality for the

[28] According to Miyasawa, for this to happen, the House of Representatives must expressly state that it regards the bill as rejected. If the lower house did do this, the conditions required by article 59(2) would be fulfilled.

[29] Article 74 of the Constitution. The signature of the minister is added to indicate government responsibility. Constitutional lawyers maintain that the absence of the signature would not affect the validity of the law because it is made before the signature is added.

promulgation of law in the technical sense. Once voted legislation is sent to the tenno by the chairman of one or other of the
Houses by way of the cabinet to be published by the tenno in
the name of the people.[30] Laws must be published within thirty
days of the date of their being sent to the tenno (article 66 of
the law on Parliament). The form of publication is not provided
by law, but, according to usage that has been followed for a long
time, publication is effected by insertion in the official gazette
(*kampo*).[31] A law comes into force twenty days after its publication, unless some other date has been set for it.[32]

Under the Meiji Constitution all laws were preceded by the
following formula, which gave the sanction of the tenno: "We
sanction the law on . . . , which has been voted by the Imperial
Diet and We order its publication." Sanctioning by the tenno
was suppressed by the present Constitution, and the formula of
publication now reads: "We hereby publish the law on . . . ."
The formula is followed by the signature of the tenno and his
seal, as well as by the date and signature of the prime minister.
The official gazette does not print the tenno's signature but prints
the characters "*gyomei*," which mean His Imperial Highness's
name. This perpetuates an old tradition according to which it was
considered improper to say or write the name of the tenno. In
Japanese psychology there is still a commandment similar to that
which was made to Israel in Exodus 20: 7—"Thou shalt not take
the name of the Lord thy God in vain." The date of the law is
that of publication; all laws made during a year are numbered
according to the order of their publication.[33]

[30] Article 65 of the law on Parliament; article 7 of the Constitution.

[31] Ordinance No. 6 of 1907 called *koshikirei* (ordinance on the publication of
laws and regulations) laid down that the publication of law was effected by insertion of the law in the official gazette. It was abrogated with the promulgation of the
present Constitution, and no new law has been enacted to fill the gap. The former
practice is still observed and a judgment of 28 December, 1957, of the Supreme Court
explicitly affirmed its legality.

[32] Article 1 of the statute called *horei*.

[33] As far as the time when laws come into force is concerned there is a certain
amount of academic controversy because there is no legislation on the point. A judgment of the full court of the Supreme Court of 15 October, 1958, set the time as the
moment at which the nation could read the official gazette in which the law in
question was published, i.e., the day when the issue of the official gazette containing
the law arrived at the official distributor of the journal in Tokyo. This solution is
unreasonable because the placing of the official gazette at the disposition of the
Tokyo reader in no way means that it can be read in other places. It would be more
reasonable to recognize, as French law does, that laws do not acquire obligatory
force at the same point in time in all parts of the country.

The present Constitution devotes a whole chapter to state finances, and in that chapter article 83 provides that the power to administer state finances must be exercised in conformity with decisions of Parliament. The most important matter in Parliament's competence in this field is the voting of the budget. The cabinet is bound to prepare the budget for each fiscal year[34] and to present it to Parliament for consideration and approval (article 86 of the Constitution). The budget must be presented first to the House of Representatives (article 60 of the Constitution). It is presented to the budget committee and then discussed at a public sitting (article 56 of the law on Parliament). Every amendment to the budget must be supported by at least fifty members in the House of Representatives and twenty in the House of Councillors (article 57B of the law on Parliament). The budget is in principle adopted when it has been voted by both Houses, but the Constitution provides for two cases when the will of the House of Representatives alone is deemed to be that of Parliament.

The first such case arises when the House of Councillors has taken a decision different from that of the lower House and the two Houses cannot reach agreement after the joint committee of the two Houses has met. In this case the decision of the House of Representatives becomes the decision of Parliament (article 60 of the Constitution). In such a case a meeting of the joint committee is obligatory. Neither House can refuse. The second case arises when the House of Councillors does not vote on the budget within thirty days after its receipt and it has been adopted by the other House (article 60 of the Constitution). In neither of these cases is a decision of the House of Representatives necessary to make the budget law. There is, therefore, a difference between this and the case where the will of the lower House alone becomes law (article 59 of the Constitution). When the budget has not been voted on before the beginning of the following fiscal year, the cabinet can present a provisional budget which can be executed within a limited period of time. The provisional budget falls when the annual budget is voted (article 30 of the law on finance).

[34] The fiscal year is from 1 April to 31 March.

The budget (*yosan*) amounts in Japanese law to a special kind of state law. It is to be distinguished from *horitsu*. It is never called a financial law in Japan because this term evokes ideas of laws other than the budget and the term bill is not used in relation to the budget even before it is voted on. The Constitution does not require the publication of the budget, but as it directly affects the life of the people it is in fact published in the official gazette.

Beyond the preliminary formal control of state finances assured by the voting of the budget, Parliament watches over the implementation of the budget by controlling the accounts. Article 90 of the Constitution provides that "final accounts of the expenditures and revenues of the state shall be audited annually by a board of audit[35] and submitted by the cabinet to Parliament, together with the statement of audit for the fiscal year immediately following the period covered." On the basis of this text each House approves or rejects the budget. Rejection does not affect the validity of the payments made in execution of the budget.

PARLIAMENT IN PRACTICE

Parliament is an institution designed to harmonize the various interests of all members of the nation. It must therefore satisfy to the greatest extent possible not only the needs of the majority but also those of the minority. Yet, sometimes the interests of even the majority are not protected. If Parliament does not properly reflect the different interests within the state, the interest of a very small number of men can, behind the façade of a parliamentary majority, prevail over the general interest. Where a popular political conscience is not well developed, this can easily happen, and Japan is such a case. Although Japanese parliamen-

[35] The board of audit (*kaikei kensain*) is a constitutional institution (article 90 of the Constitution) whose independence from the government is guaranteed by law (article 1 of the law relating to the board of audit).

tarianism is more than eighty years old, it has functioned until recent times almost completely independently of the interests of the greater part of the nation. The policies of the ruling class have acted on the mentality of the people and accustomed them to blind obedience and political indifference. There is still an attitude current in Japan unfavorable to the good functioning of Parliament.

Japanese political parties are not closely related to the life of the people. In fact it is not too much of an exaggeration to say that these parties exist only for the elections. They do all they can to attract votes during the electoral campaign and prevail on electors to vote for them by using a respectful manner of address, such as is usually reserved only for the most important people. Once in Parliament they make no effort to represent their electors' interests and consider that they have a "blank check" to do as they like.

There are at present five major parties—the Liberal Democratic, the Socialist, the Communist, Komei, and the Social Democratic. The Liberal Democratic Party is the biggest, is conservative,[36] and is strongly supported by big business and country people. It has 280 seats in the House of Representatives and 126[37] in the House of Councillors. The Socialist Party is second largest, with 118 seats in the House of Representatives and 62 in the House of Councillors. Next comes the Communist Party, with 40 seats in the House of Representatives and 20 in the House of Councillors. The fourth largest is the Komei Party, a group with support among the followers of a Buddhist sect which adheres fervently to the teaching of Nichiren, a great patriotic priest of the middle ages. The Komei Party has been active in the world of politics since 1962 and has 30 seats in the House of Representatives and

[36] The conservative parties were continually forming and breaking coalitions from the end of the war, but from 1955 they have formed a single party. With one minor exception it has always been the conservative party (in spite of its name it has a reactionary tendency) which has been given political responsibility.
[37] Ten further members, the nine independents and the representative of a minor party, usually also vote with the Liberal Democrats.

24 in the House of Councillors. Finally, there are the Social Democrats, a right-wing socialist party that separated from the Socialist Party in 1951.[38] It has 20 seats in the House of Representatives and 10 in the House of Councillors. Thus the conservative party is assured of a very strong majority in both Houses. It is often said that Japan has a two-party system of the English kind, but in reality the present system belongs rather to the type that Maurice Duverger calls the regime of the dominant party.[39]

The numbers of party members in 1974 were 970,000 for the Liberal Democratic Party, 400,000 for the Socialist Party, 300,000 for the Communist Party, 160,000 for the Komei, and 50,000 for the Social Democrats. The opposition parties have little importance in parliamentary life because the government party takes almost no account of the opinion of its rivals. There is a kind of tyranny of the majority. Recognizing that what they say has little effect, the opposition parties are often tempted to resort to physical action to prevent unreasonable procedures in the debates imposed by the government party. Any such action serves as a pretext for the government party to then appeal for police intervention. Their constant and inevitable defeat gives the opposition parties an inferiority complex which makes them more sportsmen than intellectuals. The pattern is as usual favored by the psychological attitude of the people. Accustomed to blind submission to political power over a long period, the people have a strong inclination to put up with whatever is done by the political power without thinking very much about it. Even now the great part of the populace believes for no clear reason that the persons who take on political responsibility are, by their nature, those most qualified and fitted for the job. The attitude

---

[38]   From 1 June until 4 October, 1948, the Socialist Party was in power in coalition with the Democratic Party, which has now been absorbed into the Liberal Democratic Party. This was the only chance that the Socialists had to form a government.

[39]   Maurice Duverger, *Institutions politiques et droit constitutionel*, 6th ed. (Paris: Presses Universitaires de France, 1962), p. 397. Japan is not an underdeveloped country, but what Duverger says about political parties in underdeveloped countries applies with equal force to the political parties in Japan. Japan is a politically underdeveloped country.

generally held when public business is being discussed is that it is best to leave politics to those "important" people.[40]

---

[40] Two surveys undertaken by the Institute of Mathematical Statistics in 1953 and 1958 shed light on the general attitude of the Japanese to politics. In these surveys the following question was asked: "It is said that if we have good politicians the best way to assure the prosperity of the country is to leave all political matters in the control of these leaders rather than to discuss them among ourselves. Do you accept this proposition?" In the first survey 43:38, and in the second 35:44, answered in the affirmative. The proportion of affirmative answers in relation to negative answers was reversed in the two inquiries, but the results show, nevertheless, that a tendency to subjection to authority and a belief, or faith, in the ability of political leaders is still marked in Japan.

CHAPTER VI

THE EXECUTIVE

The term *gyosei ken* (administrative power) is understood in Japan in a very broad sense. No distinction is made between such terms as executive, executive power, political power, and administrative power. The function of the executive is by definition very imprecise. Miyasawa explains it more specifically as the mass of state functions that relate to the execution of laws, foreign affairs, appointing and supervising public officials, maintaining public order, and taking measures necessary to assure security and progress in the nation as a whole. Within the notion of the executive there are two clearly recognizable categories of organs, the organ that takes decisions on principle and the one that adapts the decisions of principle to particular cases. The organ that exercises political power is the *naikaku* (cabinet); those that exercise administrative power are the subordinate organs of the Naikaku.[1]

THE CABINET

Under the Meiji Constitution, all governmental powers were concentrated in the hands of the tenno, but under the new Constitution all executive power was transferred to the cabinet. The tenno no longer participates in the exercise of this power, and many public lawyers consider that acts of state of the tenno do not properly come within the notion of executive power at all.

---

[1] *Naikaku* means literally interior of the palace. The Naikaku is often called *seifu* (government), derived from *gyoseifu*, which means political body.

The cabinet is composed of the prime minister, who is its head,[2] and the other ministers (article 66 of the Constitution). In Japanese the prime minister is called *naikaku sori-daijin* (*sori* means general direction, and *daijin* important person). The other members of cabinet are called *kokumu-daijin*, that is to say *daijin* with responsibility for state business. The notion of *kokumu-daijin* is ambiguous, as it is used to describe all the members of the cabinet including the *sori-daijin*, those other than prime minister, and also those who direct no department. The *kokumu-daijin* are usually departmental heads or heads of some other administrative organ; those with no such post are called *muninsho-daijin* (minister without portfolio).

All cabinet members must be non-military personnel (article 66 of the Constitution).[3] However, since the Constitution forbids the forming of any armed force, no military group could exist under the present regime anyway, and from this point of view the text is superfluous, at least while article 9 prohibiting the forming of armed forces remains unamended.[4]

The prime minister is chosen by Parliament from among parliamentarians (article 67 of the Constitution). He is then appointed by the tenno who must accept the nomination made by Parliament. The nomination of the prime minister by Parliament must be given priority over all other business (article 6 of the Constitution). In those cases where the House of Representatives has nominated person A as prime minister and the other House person B, a conciliation committee tries to work out agreement between the two Houses on one name. If no agreement is reached, the nomination of the House of Representatives is deemed to be that of Parliament. The same result follows if the House of Councillors does not make a nomination within ten days after the vote of the other House (article 67 of the Constitution). In reality it is the will of the House of Representatives which decides

[2]   The prime minister presides over and effectively controls the Naikaku. Under the old regime he was simply *primus inter pares*, but today his position is particularly strong.

[3]   This provision was included because of a fear of falling under the type of military domination which led Japan into World War II.

[4]   A theory supported by a large number of influential constitutional lawyers requires that this provision be understood to mean that no person who was previously a military officer can be a minister.

on the head of government, and consequently it is the head of the party with the greatest number of seats in the House of Representatives who will normally become *naikaku sori-daijin*.

The prime minister can resign at any time, but if he does, the collective resignation of the cabinet follows; the resignation or dismissal of the *naikaku sori-daijin* individually is not possible. The same result also follows if the post of prime minister becomes vacant for some reason (article 70 of the Constitution).[5] The prime minister can be removed against his will only by a vote of no confidence (article 69 of the Constitution). Where a vote of no confidence has been passed the prime minister may choose between his own dismissal and the dissolution of the House of Representatives (article 69 of the Constitution).

All ministers are nominated by the prime minister and the tenno attests the nomination (articles 7 and 68 of the Constitution). Any minister can resign with the authorization of the prime minister and the ratification of the tenno. Further, the prime minister may dismiss the members of the cabinet against their will (article 68 of the Constitution), a very strong power that enables him to maintain unity in the cabinet. Removal must be attested by the tenno, but since the attestation is only a formal act the nomination or removal of a minister is not invalid if there is no attestation.

The prime minister must have a seat in one or the other of the two Houses during the period of his premiership. It is not sufficient to have one only at the time of his appointment. If he loses his status of parliamentarian, he must resign. The status of parliamentarian is thus basic to being prime minister, except in the case of dissolution.[6] This rule seeks to guarantee a parliamentary system of government. For this same reason the Constitution demands that a majority of the members of cabinet be parliamentarians (article 68 of the Constitution). It follows that

---

[5] Foreseeing the possibility of the prime minister's being disqualified, article 9 of the law on the Naikaku permits him to nominate one of his ministers in advance to stand in his place. This minister is officially called deputy prime minister. No such nomination is, however, usually made.

[6] In this case there is no deputy who can replace him. He therefore stays in office until the opening of the new legislative session at the beginning of which his government must resign collectively (article 70 of the Constitution).

the status of parliamentarian is not always a condition for being a minister, but a half plus one of the members of cabinet must have a seat in one or the other of the Houses. That is, a half plus one of the members who effectively form the cabinet, not of the legal number of those who could be in the cabinet. If one minister loses his status as a parliamentarian he does not immediately cease to be a member of the cabinet, for, so long as the majority of the members of the cabinet are still parliamentarians, he can continue to exercise his role. If the majority is lost, the prime minister substitutes non-parliamentary members by parliamentary members as necessary. Usually members of the cabinet are both ministers and members of Parliament. It is very rare for non-parliamentarians to have a place in the government.

The Constitution provides that the executive power belongs to the cabinet (article 65) and that the cabinet is collectively responsible to Parliament for the exercise of its power (article 66). The powers of the cabinet[7] are the following:

1. to administer the law and conduct state business;
2. to control foreign affairs;
3. to conclude treaties;
4. to administer the civil service;
5. to prepare and present the budget;
6. to issue decrees;
7. to perform acts of grace; and
8. to perform general administrative acts.

Item 6 of article 73 deserves mention in this connection. It provides that cabinet may issue decrees (*seirei*) for the purpose of executing the provisions of the Constitution and the laws. It is ambiguous in that it suggests that the cabinet can issue *seirei* to apply the Constitution directly. According to Miyasawa this interpretation is incorrect. If it were correct the cabinet could issue *seirei* in matters which are not regulated by law, which would be contrary to article 41 of the Constitution establishing Parliament as the sole legislative organ of the state. *Seirei* must therefore be understood as a type of administrative regulation made by the cabinet in its capacity as a collective organ. Strictly speaking, it is incorrect to translate *seirei* as decree, a term which

---

[7] Article 73 of the Constitution.

relates not only to regulations but also to individual acts. *Seirei* may not include penal sanctions without explicit delegation by law (article 73 of the Constitution), and may neither create rules which impose new obligations nor limit existing rights without a delegation of law (article 11 of the law on the cabinet).

The strict limitation placed on the regulatory power of the government derives from the legal nature of Parliament. It is necessary to avoid a repetition of past mistakes made when a government endowed with vast law-making powers was abstracted from the control of Parliament and fundamental human rights were extensively violated. The Naikaku exercises its powers according to the decisions of the ministers (*kakugi*). The tenno never sits in the cabinet and is not even allowed to attend. The cabinet is called to session by the prime minister whenever he considers it necessary and whenever a minister calls on him to convoke the assembly to consider a designated matter (article 4 of the law on the cabinet).[8]

Cabinet functions entirely on the basis of customary rules; its procedure is not regulated by any written rules. Complete secrecy must be maintained by all present concerning matters discussed in cabinet, and all decisions taken by cabinet are unanimous. Majority rule is not applicable here, though the rule was different under the Meiji Constitution. To avoid instability in cabinet caused by the kind of disagreement among members criticized in the preceding era, the principle of unanimity was adopted. If a minister persists in a dissident opinion, the prime minister can dismiss him and thus maintain the unity of the cabinet.

The prime minister is head of the cabinet (article 66 of the Constitution), and in this capacity he nominates and dismisses members of the cabinet and directs and controls all branches of the administration. All bills, the budget, and other Matters are presented through him, in the name of cabinet, to Parliament. He also heads an administrative service, the *sorifu* (Prime minister's Office). He signs laws and *seirei* as competent minister, or signs them along with the competent minister as prime minister. He also settles disputes relating to power and jurisdiction that arise among his ministers.

[8] Law of 16 January, 1947.

Ministers other than the prime minister have much more limited powers. Each minister has in principle the portfolio of one department. When he is head of an administrative service, he is called the competent minister (*shunin no daijin* or *gyosei-daijin*, administrative minister) (article 3 of the law on the cabinet). A minister signs laws and *seirei* as competent minister; he participates in governmental duties in the cabinet; and can, as has been mentioned, require the prime minister to call a meeting of cabinet if the need should arise.

The draftsmen of the Meiji Constitution seem to have wished, as far as the relations between the government and the Diet were concerned, to follow the example of the German system of the nineteenth century, which accentuated the independence of the government vis-à-vis Parliament. This system left the plenitude of powers in the monarch intact to the greatest extent possible, by withdrawing them from the democratic control of Parliament. Although the Meiji Constitution did not mention this principle, governments in the first years of its application followed a political practice called *chozenshugi* (indifference)—the government was an arbiter in the struggles between the political parties. This principle was expressed in a famous speech by Prime Minister Kuroda on the day after the promulgation of the Constitution, at a reunion of the prefects. "It goes without saying," he said, "that the citizens have nothing to say either for or against the Constitution. However, as there exists political diversity and as each person has his own opinion, it is quite natural that those who have similar opinions will unite to form political parties. This being so, the government must always place itself with indifference above the political parties in order to be as impartial and just in terms of the law as it can toward everyone. All the prefects are invited to adopt this attitude and to govern their subjects impartially. Let each fulfill this guiding role faultlessly and do his best for the prosperity of the state." This principle of *chozenshugi* was not, however, suitable to the good functioning of politics based on parliamentarianism. The influence of political parties on political life could not be overlooked, and so the practice of the English-type parliamentary regime came to be used more and more. An effort was made to justify it in the name of fundamental constitutional principles (*kensei no jodo*), but it was of course stifled by the militaristic governments at the end of the former regime.

The new Constitution formally adopted a parliamentary regime of the English type, which was and still is considered in Japan as the ideal. It very carefully regulates the relations between Parliament and the government, and the existence of the government is conditioned on the confidence it enjoys in Parliament. When a motion of censure is passed by the House of Representatives, the collective removal of the cabinet must follow (article 69). However, the parliamentary majority does not always faithfully represent the nation, in which in the final analysis sovereignty rests. If the government, therefore, thinks that national opinion favors it, it will go directly to the people. The Constitution permits the government to dissolve the House of Representatives in a case of a vote of no confidence within ten days (article 69). Whether the right of dissolution can be exercised only in the case of a vote of no confidence has been much discussed, but the present practice and the strongest body of theory admits that the right of dissolution is not limited to the case described in article 69. According to Miyasawa, since the aim of dissolution is to provide for direct recourse to the people when there is an unresolved difference of opinion between Parliament and the government, it is of critical importance in the parliamentary system. The right of dissolution is the way the government can balance the power relationship between itself and Parliament. Without this power the government would be obliged to obey the will of Parliament in every case.

ADMINISTRATIVE ORGANIZATION

The state is, with few exceptions, concerned with the administration of business concerning the whole country, and autonomous local bodies attend to those matters that effect only a particular area of Japan. Japan no longer has a state organ like the prefects in France to represent the state at the local level.

Auxiliary to the cabinet are two organs of importance. One is the cabinet secretariat (*naikaku kambo*), which ensures the smooth functioning of cabinet and prepares the cabinet agenda. The other is the Cabinet Legislation Bureau (*naikaku hosei kyoku*), which is directly subordinate to the cabinet.

The Cabinet Legislation Bureau is responsible for all the legislative business of government. It prepares drafts of laws, *seirei*, and treaties for discussion in cabinet. Bills are usually drawn up by the competent minister in collaboration with the *hosei kyoku*, but the latter often draws up bills and *seirei* on its own initiative. The Bureau[9] also gives advice on legal problems that arise in cabinet and on those that concern the ministers. Its members are all lawyers and draftsmen. They are punctilious of spirit and often go beyond reasonable limits in their quest for an exactitude in legal language that does not exist in the language of everyday life. For example, they find a difference between *chitainaku* (without delay) and *tadachini* (immediately).[10]

With the exception of the Board of Audit and the Public Service Council (*Jinjiin*) all state administrative services are submitted to the authority of cabinet and all are regulated by the law on state administrative organization of 10 July, 1948.

The *Jinjiin* is an institution that aims at guaranteeing impartiality of selection and security of tenure to state employees and particularly at eliminating the influence of political parties in this field. It was created by the law on public officers of 21 October, 1947. Unlike the Board of Audit the *Jinjiin* is not a constitutional body, and the question arises whether its independence from the cabinet is compatible with article 65 of the Constitution. The *Jinjiin* is composed of three administrators

[9] It is an institution which in function corresponds more or less exactly to the administrative sections of the French Conseil d'Etat.

[10] A former president of the Bureau explains in his work entitled *Good Legislative Terminology* that in the case of *chitainaku* a slight delay for legitimate reasons can be tolerated, while in the case of *tadachini* no delay at all is permitted. Legal technicians are only concerned with the precision of legal terminology and are not concerned with the clarification or simplification of the Japanese language in general. The result is that legal terms are often quite foreign to the citizens' daily life; for example, marriage is called *kon-in*, a learned word in law, while people in the street call it *kekkon*. It is obviously a very delicate matter to meet the needs both of ready comprehensibility and of inevitably technical legal material, as can be imagined, for example, by following the procedure involved in the preparation of the French Civil Code between 1789 and 1804. Cf. Jean Ray, *Essai sur la structure logique du code civil français* (Paris: F. Alcan, 1926), p. 26f.

(*jinjikan*), one of whom is the president (*sosai*). All three are appointed by cabinet with the approval of Parliament. In order to guarantee the political impartiality of its members, the law forbids the appointing as *jinjikan* of anyone who has been an executive member of or counsellor to a political party during the five years preceding his appointment. The law also prohibits the appointment at any one time of persons who belong to the same party or of persons who have graduated from the same faculty.

The Council has great power in the field of administration of state services, and since it is independent of Parliament and of the government this organism is considered by both as something of an embarrassment. On several occasions attempts have been made to do away with it but there has never been any public support for such action. Although there are doubts as to its constitutional character because of its independent position, it does fulfill the function of guaranteeing the status of public servants.

Within the central administration there are five important categories of organs: *fu*, of which there is only one, the *sorifu* (Prime Minister's Office), *sho* (ministry), *iinkai* (administrative committee), and *cho* (agency).

There is no legal difference between the *fu* and the *sho*. Both are organs which share important state administrative business. The total number of *fu* and *sho* is now thirteen: Prime Minister's Office, Ministry of Legal Affairs, Ministry of Foreign Affairs, Ministry of Finance, Ministry of Education, Ministry of Health and Welfare, Ministry of Agriculture and Forestry, Ministry of International Trade and Industry, Ministry of Transport, Ministry of Posts and Telecommunications, Ministry of Construction, Ministry of Labor, and Ministry of Home Affairs. Each ministry has its own internal government.[11]

Only persons known as *seimujikan*,[12] recruited from among the members of Parliament and with offices in each ministry, have their fate linked to that of the cabinet. There is generally one *seimujikan* in each ministry.[13] He assists the minister in policy

---

[11] Cabinet, directorate, etc.
[12] Second-in-charge with policy responsibilities: deputy minister.
[13] There can be two *seimujikan* in the same ministry. At the present time the Ministries of Finance, Agriculture and Forestry, and of International Trade and Industry are permitted by law to have two *seimujikan*.

matters, and if the latter is unable to perform his functions, he replaces him. In each department, besides the *seimujikan*, there is another deputy called *jimujikan* (deputy charged with administrative affairs), who also helps the minister but whose functions continue after the termination of the mandate of the cabinet.

The administrative committees and the *cho* are central services which, though independent of the ministries, are nevertheless to a certain extent subject to ministerial supervision. The committees (*iinkai*) were set up to attend to business that by its nature demanded greater independence vis-à-vis a government composed of members of political parties. The impartiality of deliberation of these committees is assured by the participation of specialists or representatives of the public interest. These administrative committees are not to be confused with consultative committees, which are also called *iinkai* and whose purpose is to study a defined topic or to answer requests for information from the government. The administrative committees are modeled on the American system of administrative commissions or boards. They constitute a true administrative authority endowed with administrative power and sometimes also with regulatory or decision-making power. At the present time there are nine: four attached to the Prime Minister's Office, two to the Ministry of Legal Affairs, one to the Ministry of Transport, and two to the Ministry of Labor. In principle they can exercise their powers without direction from a minister, though in some cases the law requires the president of an *iinkai* to be a minister.

The *cho* were set up to handle business beyond the capacity of the internal services of any one ministry. Their structure is not very different from that of a ministry, but they are something of a provisional institution that, constitutionally, is placed between a simple ministerial service and an independent ministry. A *cho* is set up when, under the pressure of new social conditions, a ministerial service becomes so important that it can no longer be handled within the framework of the ministry to which it properly belongs. The law frequently provides that the president of a *cho* must be a minister. At present there are twenty-three *cho:* nine within the prime minister's jurisdiction, one under the Ministry of Legal Affairs, one under the Ministry of Finance, one under the Ministry of Education, three under the Ministry of Agriculture and Forestry, three under the Ministry of International Trade and Industry, three under the Ministry of Transport, one under the Ministry of Home Affairs, and one under the Ministry of Health and Welfare.

Those who fulfill any state function in Japan are called *kokka komuin* (he who is responsible for state business). The notion of *komuin* includes everybody who has any responsibility of a governmental nature, whether at a national or local level. It is a very broad concept and has two divisions—*kokka komuin* and *chiho komuin* (*komuin* of local government areas)—each of which is regulated by statute. The law relating to the *kokka komuin* is of 21 October, 1947, and it in its turn divides *kokka komuin* into two classes, a general and a special class. The *komuin* who belong to the special class are listed in article 2 and include the prime minister, ministers, high public officials, and judges. The *komuin* of this category are in general terms outside the provisions of the law of 21 October, 1947.

The *komuin* classed in the general category are what would commonly be referred to as civil servants. Civil servants were called *kanri* under the Meiji Constitution (officers of the government).[14] The relationship between the emperor and the *kanri* was like a bond of personal subordination which required the *kanri* to render unlimited service to the emperor. This bond was related to that of vassalage and extended even into the private life of the state official. By way of counterbalance the *kanri* constituted a privileged class as far as the populace was concerned. In a word, the *kanri* were the emperor's servants, not those of the people. The new Constitution rejected this concept and provided in article 15 that the *komuin* are the servants of the whole nation and not of any one part of it. The law relating to *kokka komuin* serves to make the relationships between state functionaries and the state more rational, and those between the functionaries and the populace more democratic (article 1). But the general mental attitude of the Japanese people still favors the survival of the concept of the former era.[15]

[14]   Government in this case meant the emperor.
[15]   Public officials still have a special outlook and consider, though they do not say so, that they belong to a privileged class.

State servants are subject to various restrictions that do not concern the ordinary citizen. For instance, though the right to associate is, with some few exceptions, not suppressed, the State Services Association is to be distinguished from a union of workers, and the law relating to the latter does not apply to the former. The right to collective bargaining is admitted, but the right to enter into collective agreements and the right to strike are entirely abrogated. Since article 28 of the Constitution guarantees workers the right of collective action, these restrictions are a priori suspect. Certain classes of political activity defined in great detail by the regulations of the *Jinjiin* of 19 September, 1949, are forbidden for public servants (article 102 of the law relating to *komuin*). Violation of these prohibitions is punished by imprisonment with hard labor for up to three years or by a fine of not more than 100,000 yen (article 110 of the law relating to *komuin*). This restriction on the freedom of political opinion of state functionaries may seem unconstitutional but was upheld by the Supreme Court in 1958 and again by a majority (10:4) on 6 November, 1974.

LOCAL ADMINISTRATION

Even under the Meiji Constitution local administration was in the hands of territorial authorities, but the decentralization was imperfect. The prefects were appointed by the government. Mayors were elected by the inhabitants, but their election was submitted to the confirmation of the prefect, and when this confirmation was refused a new election had to take place. If the result of the new election was not acceptable, the minister of the interior could himself choose a provisional substitute or send a state official to take over the duties of mayor. The prefects represented the interests of the state more than the interests of the inhabitants. They were placed under the general control of the minister of the interior and received orders from other ministers for those matters that came within their competence. The prefects controlled the police and could, if need be, resort to the use of the army. The result was that the will of government prevailed throughout the country.

By way of contrast with the Meiji Constitution, which made no mention of local administration, the new Constitution declares in article 92 that the organization and administration of local governments will be determined by a law based on the principle of local autonomy. This formula means that all the public business of each area must be administered in accordance with the will of the inhabitants. Inspired by this principle a law was promulgated on 17 April, 1947, with the title of "Law on Local Autonomy." It divides local governments into two types, those of a general and those of a special nature. The latter are exceptional cases, and only the former will be dealt with here.

Local governments of the general class are subdivided into two groups: *todofuken* (corresponding roughly to the *departements* of French law), and *shichoson* (approximately analogous to the *communes* of French law).

The term *todofuken* is made up of four elements, each of which relates to an administrative division. Japan is divided into forty-three *ken*, two *fu*, one *to* and one *do*. Between *ken* and *fu* there is a distinction of title only,[16] and both terms indicate almost the same thing as *departement* in French. *To* and *do* are regulated by special rules. The system of *to* is conceived of as a special kind of urban agglomeration. It is not legally restricted to Tokyo but for the moment there is no other *to* than Tokyo-to.[17] The system of *do* is reserved to Hokkaido. This island was developed relatively late and had a special legal status granted to it in the Meiji Constitution. It is, moreover, of an extent far greater than that of *tofuken*, being six times larger than the biggest *ken*. All these facts suffice, it seems, to give to Hokkaido a special character among the local governments of a general nature.

[16] This purely nominal distinction has existed from the beginning. The political and economic importance of the three cities Tokyo, Kyoto, and Osaka is the reason why the three regions around these cities are distinct in terminology from the others.
[17] The word *to* is the Chinese form of the Japanese word *miyako*, which means the place where the Imperial Palace is. Thus the word could literally be translated by metropolis, i.e., mother city. However, in current usage *miyako* is used to mean large town. The system of *to* was created in 1943 by a special law known as the law on Tokyo-to. This law was abrogated by the law of 17 April, 1947, on local autonomy which contains a few special rules relating to *to*. Before this reform, Tokyo-fu included the city of Tokyo, but this is no longer the case. The 23 *ku*, corresponding to the 20 arrondissements of Paris, which made it up are part of Tokyo-to. Each *ku* is assimilated to a town. Tokyo-to includes besides the *ku* a large number of cities, towns, and villages.

The term *shichoson* also combines distinct elements. *Shi* corresponds to city, *cho* (or *machi*) to town, and *son* (or *mura*) to village. Legally there is no distinction between them,[18] and all constitute administrative constituencies of a secondary nature. This does not mean, however, that the *shichoson* are hierarchically subordinated to the *todofuken*, though they are contained geographically within the framework of the latter. It can happen that there are conflicts of jurisdiction over the sharing of business, because in any one area the competence of two of the groups is cumulative. Where a conflict arises, the law provides that the two bodies should collaborate to establish a division of the work to be done (article 2 of the law on local autonomy). However, the guidelines are not clearly spelled out.

All public business of a local body must be directed according to the will of the people. The inhabitants do not generally participate directly in the administration; rather, they delegate it to elected representatives. Every inhabitant of twenty or more years of age has the right to elect the members and the head of the local assembly. The assembly of a *todofuken* or *shichoson* is the organ that expresses the general will of the inhabitants. The matters that a local assembly can decide are numerous and are set out, although not limitatively, in article 96. Rules made by the local assembly are called *jorei*. *Jorei* cannot derogate from state laws or decrees, and if a *jorei* of a *shichoson* derogates from a *jorei* of a *todofuken* regulating communal affairs, the *jorei* of the *shichoson* is null. Penal sanctions of imprisonment for a period not exceeding two years with or without hard labor or a fine of up to 100,000 yen may be provided by *jorei*.

The head of the *todofuken* is called *chiji* (prefect), and the head of the *shichoson*, *shichoson cho* (mayor).[19] Both are elected by universal suffrage for a period of four years. No person may be both a prefect or mayor and a member of Parliament. The prefect, or

[18] There is no Japanese term of a general nature like the French *commune* which covers these three elements. The total number of *shichoson* was 3,457 in 1962. In 1920 it was 12,188. From this it can be seen that numerous *shichoson* have been created from others. This number is smaller than that of the French communes: 38,000. The division of the *shichoson* is 557 *shi*, 1,980 *cho*, and 920 *son*. Usually a commune with more than 5,000 inhabitants is a *cho*.

[19] This is a comprehensive term. If it is a question of a *shi*, the head is called *shi cho*, and so on for the others.

the mayor, is the executive organ of a local body, and he is also an organ of the state. In his capacity as an organ of state he is under the authority of the competent minister and can issue regulations (*kisoku*). The maximum sanction against a person contravening *kisoku* is a fine of 2,000 yen.

The inhabitants of a local body area can participate directly in the administration of their local affairs by the system of direct demand, of which four types are provided in chapter 5 of the law on local autonomy:

1. *A request relating to the promulgation or to the abrogation of jorei.* The inhabitants of a local body area who have the right to elect members to the local body can demand of the head of the body that he request the local assembly to promulgate or abrogate a *jorei* if the demand is signed by at least one-fiftieth of the total number of inhabitants of the area who have political rights (article 74). No demand under this head can be made in relation to the imposition or receipt of local taxes, or for such things as the rate payable for public services. These limitations were brought in by an amendment to the law when it was feared that there might be abuse of power because ill-considered consent could very easily be given by the inhabitants on these matters. The prefect or mayor who has received a demand in due form must convoke the local assembly within twenty days. The assembly has, however, complete freedom whether or not to act on the demand of the people.

2. *A request for inspection of services.* There are a number of inspectors in each local body area whose job is to see that the public servants carry out their duties faithfully. If the results of the performance of an inspectorate's duties are not satisfactory, the inhabitants can, on the same basis as for the demands to the prefect or mayor, require the inspectors to go into the matter more fully. This system was substituted for the very strict tutelary-type control that the state exercised over local governments under the former regime. The idea is that local autonomy should be protected through the initiative of the inhabitants themselves.

3. *A request for the dissolution of the local assembly.* Under the Meiji Constitution the central power had the right to dissolve the local assemblies. This was a very effective means of control, but in-

compatible with local autonomy. The present law gives this right to the prefect or mayor when the assembly has adopted a vote of no confidence in him (article 178), and to the inhabitants. A third of the total number of inhabitants who have the right to vote can, in prescribed conditions by notice to the committee controlling elections in their area, demand the dissolution of the local assembly. The control body must submit the demand to a vote. If the request is adopted by an absolute majority of voters, the assembly is dissolved (article 76). This method too could lend itself to abuse, so the law forbids recourse to it within one year from the day the members of the assembly take office (article 79).

4. *Request for the dismissal of public servants.* The Constitution provides in article 15 that the people have the inalienable right to choose their public officials and to dismiss them. The law on local autonomy elaborates this principle. The inhabitants of a local body area can by following a set procedure demand the dismissal of the members of the assembly, the head of the local authority, and other important officers (articles 13 and 80 to 88). The request must be directed to the committee controlling elections and, if it fulfills the required conditions, be submitted to the electors. If an absolute majority of the voters accepts it, the person who was the subject of the demand is dismissed, as of that date. As with the right of dissolution, this demand can only be made after one year from the day the official takes up his job.

Besides the direct demand system the law permits inhabitants to go to referendum in certain cases. For instance, statutes of which the application is limited to a given area must be submitted to the vote of the inhabitants of that area. A law of this sort voted by Parliament would be valid only if it obtained an absolute majority of the votes cast by interested persons.[20]

Under article 243 of the law on local autonomy citizens can, if they think that the acts performed by public servants in respect of the local body accounts are illegal or unjustifiable, require those acts to be restricted, forbidden, or annulled, or they can even claim damages for any loss caused by such acts. The inhabitants cannot seek redress in the courts until they have requested

[20]   Article 95 of the Constitution, and article 67 of the law on local autonomy.

the head of the local body to take the necessary measures, and if the measures taken by him have not proved satisfactory. Like the *recours du contribuable* admitted by the case law of the French Conseil d'Etat, this method is considered by Japanese public lawyers as having the character of a popular action.[21]

Do citizens use these methods of direct government to guarantee local autonomy? Inevitably the Japanese mentality is still dominated by archaic modes of thought. The Japanese do not like to get involved in public affairs, and the populace appears not to know that they are masters of their own fate. They feel more at ease when they can leave the controlling of state affairs to the "important people," and so the time has not yet arrived when Japan can fully enjoy the benefits of local autonomy. It is to be hoped that Japan as run by the "important people" does not run on the rocks before that time arrives.

THE POLICE

The freedom of the people is directly linked to the organization of the police. Under the Meiji Constitution the police were organized in a highly centralized manner. The police network went right out to the most distant areas of the country and constituted a hierarchical system of a very well ordered nature, at the top of which was the minister of the interior. The police controlled all fields of human life and were feared by everyone for their strictness and their cruelty. It would not be unfair to say that the police were unduly involved in the life of the Japanese people at a political, economic, and cultural level. Many progressive intellectuals bitterly recall the unpleasant visits of policemen who came to look at the books that they had in their possession. Through ignorance the police would, for instance, confiscate works of Malthus thinking that they were those of Marx. It is rather absurd to think that the oppression of freedom of thought was

[21] In Japan this appeal is allowed only to ratepayers of local bodies, but jurists regard it as a sort of *actio popularis*. The procedure is laid down in articles 42 and 43 of the law of 16 May, 1962. Article 5 defines popular action (*minshu-sosho*) as "that which is brought for the purpose of having acts performed by a state organ or a public body contrary to law rectified." Cf. the taxpayer's suit of the U.S.A.

based on knowledge that was quite contrary to good sense. The Japanese of early times lived in a police state.

The capitulation following World War II required Japan to abolish every aspect of the old police system that was oppressive of democratic ideas, and to this end a law was promulgated immediately after the defeat to democratize and decentralize the police system. This law of 17 December, 1947, had a radical form of decentralization as its basic principle. Under it every commune with more than five thousand inhabitants had its own police force that was under the control of the Public Order Committee of the commune and that was a financial charge on the commune. The Public Order Committee was composed of three members appointed by the mayor with the approval of the local assembly. In communes where the population was less than five thousand the state police in the area had responsibility for police duties. A Public Order Committee at the prefectural level, nominated by the prefect, controlled the various sections of the state police. Finally, there was the State Public Order Commission, which was responsible for the central organization of the state police. Nominated by the prime minister, with the approval of Parliament, this body supervised the administration of the state police but did not control it.

Under the immediate postwar system there was no supreme authority with power to direct the whole of the Japanese police force, but the system did not function very well in the Japanese social setting. From the beginning the defects of the system stood out more clearly than its merits. Because they were accustomed to a centralized police system and due to impatience, the Japanese were not prepared to wait until the system became acceptable at a social level. In 1951 and 1952 the law of 17 December, 1947, was modified and as a result 1,024 communes out of 1,065 abandoned the system of autonomous police. The field of activity of the state police was extended greatly, but the conservatives were not satisfied with this relatively minor measure. In 1954 the government, backed by the conservatives, presented a bill to Parliament that aimed at complete reform of the police system. The progressive parties, supported by the communes who wished to maintain the autonomous system and by intellectuals who feared the reactionary tendencies of the government parties, vigorously opposed the bill. After a violent struggle in Parliament, which included some physical violence, the length of the session was prolonged in the absence of the opposition parties and the bill was passed by the votes of the government parties alone. In spite of a strong body of opinion demanding annulment of this decision, the law dated 8 June, 1954, came into force on 1 July of the same year.

The new police system is characterized by a return to centralism. Two organs guarantee its activities: the central administration and the police administration for the *todofuken* (*todofuken keisatsu*).

The central administration of the police has two elements— the Public Order Commission and the Police Agency (*keisatsu cho*). The commission is the central control organ for the police. It has six members. The president must be a minister. The Police Agency is a part of the commission's organization and is the organ concerned with the improvement of police organization. It is a true public-service system divided into seven branches at the head of which is the president of the agency.

The police administration for the *todofuken* also has two elements: the Public Order Commission for the *todofuken* and the Police Corps of the *todofuken*. The commission is the control body, and the Police Corps the policing force. As the top personnel of the Police Corps are state servants whom the commission can control only by way of appointment or dismissal, and because the Police Corps is largely under the direction of the central administration, the influence of the commission is very slight. There is a strong inclination toward centralism. In the *to* the operation of the Police Corps is guaranteed by the metropolitan police office (*keishi cho*).[22] In the *dofuken* a police center (*keisatsu hombu*) has these responsibilities. In the larger towns is a municipal police office. Each of the *todofuken* is divided into districts and in each district there is a police commissioner. The system is quite complicated, but to avoid abuse of power of the kind in which Japanese policemen readily indulge and to protect fundamental human rights against arbitrariness a certain incon-

[22] This system was adopted from French law in the Meiji era.

venience has to be accepted. The present system may not be sufficient to achieve this goal, however, for although the government does not directly control the police in normal times, the prime minister can assume control of the police in certain emergency situations (articles 71–74 of the law on the police), and in those cases all police forces are under the control of the prime minister. For those who are only just beginning to realize the importance of liberty, a centralized police system represents a great danger.[23]

LEGAL CONTROL OF ADMINISTRATIVE ACTION

Under the Meiji Constitution a person who claimed that his rights had been infringed by an act of the administration could seek a decision on the matter from one of two bodies, depending on whether the action was of a purely administrative nature or whether it was justiciable. As far as the purely administrative matters were concerned it was possible, under the law on *Sogan* (complaints against administrative actions) of 10 October, 1890, and some other laws, to claim directly against the authority which had taken the decision or to the authority superior to it. As far as justiciable matters were concerned there was a special administrative tribunal which sat at first and final instance. A plaintiff had to take his complaint before the administrative authority before he could bring his action to the tribunal, but the system of control was most unsatisfactory because the matters that were referable to this body were strictly limited by law, and in practice administrative authorities were able to abuse citizens' rights with impunity. Very few plaintiffs won cases be-

[23] I cannot but endorse the opinion of Bertrand de Jouvenel: ". . . power differs a great deal from authority. The essential of authority is that it is exercised only over those who accept it willingly." It is erroneous "to contrast authority with liberty. Authority is the ability to get consent. Following authority is a free act. The limit of authority is marked by the point where voluntary assent stops. In every state there is a margin of obedience which is obtained by the use or threat of use of force; this area restricts liberty and exposes a lack of authority. It is very small among free peoples where authority is very great." *De la souveraineté* (Paris: Librairie de Médicis, 1955), pp. 48–49. As de Jouvenel also says, a government is often termed authoritarian when it resorts to violence, both actual and threatened, to achieve obedience. "But this corruption of the word is quite recent." Ibid., p. 45.

fore the tribunal, and this helped favor the attitude held by the Japanese bureaucracy of being in a privileged position.

The role played by the Japanese administrative tribunal contrasts greatly with the role played by the French Conseil d'Etat, which has acted vigorously to protect the rights of individuals against the arbitrary exercise of public powers over the last 150 years. The French administration knows very well that it can expect no sympathy from its tribunal.[24]

Although the new Constitution provides simply that no administrative organ can exercise jurisdiction in final instance, in the new system all jurisdiction in administrative matters belongs to the ordinary courts. According to article 3 of the law on the courts, all legal disputes are to be judged by the ordinary courts except those special cases mentioned in the Constitution. This principle alone, however, does not exclude the possibility of complaints against administrative actions, and the same article provides that administrative organs may deal with administrative matters at first instance. The law on *Sogan* of 1890 was therefore not abrogated, and since administrative matters are by their nature different from those arising under civil law, special rules were drawn up to provide for those cases not covered by the Code of Civil Procedure. These rules were promulgated in 1948, but because they were prepared in a hurry, practice disclosed many defects. The law on *Sogan* was revised again in 1962, and the result is two statutes—the law on administrative procedure of 16 May and the law on administrative actions of 15 September.[25] The law on *Sogan* of 1890 was incomplete and the whole system of administrative actions was regulated by special laws and was very disorganized. There was even controversy about the nature of a complaint against administrative action. Some thought that its purpose was to make the administration reflect on its action. Others thought that its principal object was to protect the rights of individuals. According to one opinion *reformatio in peius* was possible, and an administrative authority against which an action was brought could take a

[24] Jean Rivero, *Précis de droit administratif*, (Paris: Librairie Dalloz, 1960), para. 134.
[25] Both came into force on 1 October, 1962.

decision that was less favorable to the plaintiff than its earlier one. According to another view this was not possible. The laws of 1962 aimed at putting everything in order, and it is declared in article 1 of the law on administrative actions that "the present law has as its aim both the protection of the rights of the people and the guaranteeing of the proper functioning of the public administration." Further, by articles 40 and 47 an administrative authority seised of a claim cannot take a more unfavorable view or decision on the plaintiff's claim than its earlier one.

There are two levels of complaints against administrative action admitted under the law of 15 September. An applicant can claim either directly from the authority which took the decision or from the body superior to it. The first type of action is called *igimoshitate* (an action by way of objection) and the second *shinsaseikyu* (a request for a review). The first is usually admitted only where there is no superior body. *Shinsaseikyu* is, therefore, the usual method. Ordinary appeal against the decision at first instance (*saishinsaseikyu*) is admitted only in limited cases.

Persons who do not have a knowledge of how the administrative machinery works will not usually know whether appeal is possible or how to make an appeal, so for their protection the law has a system of information (*kyoji*) that requires that interested parties be informed of what they have to do to appeal. Article 57 declares, "When an administrative authority gives a written decision against which an appeal may be entered, the document that contains the decision must inform the persons to whom the decision is directed that there is a right to appeal, of the authority to whom they must address themselves, and of the period within which the right can be exercised." This information must also be given to other interested parties when they request it.

The pre-1962 law stated that administrative actions were subject to the rules in the Code of Civil Procedure, and though it contained some rules that derogated from the code, the Code of Civil Procedure remained the fundamental law. Administrative actions were therefore considered a type of civil matter. The 1962 law seems to proceed on the basis that it is itself the basic text and that the Code of Civil Procedure only serves to complement it. Jurisdiction in administrative actions remains in the ordinary courts, however, even under the system of 1962.

Under the former law jurists distinguished four types of administrative action, but it was not clear whether the law admitted all of them. The new law specifically enumerates those four types in article 2, and though the enumeration is not considered exhaustive the types mentioned are:

1. *Action by way of objection (kokokusosho)*. Actions of this type are defined by law as those brought against the exercise of power by an administrative authority. They in turn are categorized in three ways—

(a) *Action for nullification.* This corresponds to the action for *excès de pouvoir* in French law. It may take the form of an action for nullification of an administrative act or of an action for nullification of a decision on complaint.

(b) *Action for a declaration.* This action is brought in order to have the court declare the existence or non-existence or the validity or invalidity of an act or decision taken by an administrative authority. This action can be brought only when the interests of the plaintiff cannot be protected by a claim relating to the present legal situation, because bringing the action would presuppose the existence, the non-existence, validity, or the invalidity of an act or decision taken by an administrative authority.

(c) *Claim for a declaration of the illegality of a failure to act.* This action is brought in order to have a court declare the illegality of an administrative authority's failure to make a decision within a reasonable period when the authority was bound to decide on the matter as far as it related to the person making the claim. For example, a person who is unable to obtain the authorization necessary to exercise a profession can by this means require the administrative authority to pronounce on the matter. Since the principle of the separation of powers requires that the judicial power should not interfere in the exercise of the administrative power, the law limits itself to providing for a declaration by the court that the inaction of the administrative authority is illegal. The administration is not bound to decide according to the wish of the plaintiff, but it cannot refuse to give a decision one way or the other. Certain public lawyers claim that the court can oblige the administrative authority to do a particular act in a particular case, but prevailing opinion is to the contrary.

2. *Claims between parties.* This action brings two parties who are subject to public law into court. An example of this is the case where a civil servant makes a pay claim against the state.

3. *Popular claims.* This is the claim an elector, or sometimes a person who has no direct interest, makes in order to have an illegal act of a state organ or a public body corrected.

4. *Claims between state organs.* These are actions between state organs or public bodies concerning questions of jurisdiction or the exercise of powers. In principle the problem has to be resolved within the administration, and so the law strictly limits the number of cases in which this type of action is possible.

Article 2 of the old law required that a plaintiff first seek settlement of his claim before the administrative body concerned before going to court. This was called the rule of prior administrative complaint and was made, Japanese public lawyers say, to guarantee the proper functioning of the administration—the administration should be able to rectify its own mistakes because this takes less time and costs less than a court action and because the administration already has knowledge of the matter. The rule did not work well and has been abrogated. Now a plaintiff can in most cases choose between the two modes of proceeding. Certain public lawyers think that the rule of prior administrative appeal ought to have been retained since, according to them, the ill-functioning of the system was due to the defects of the law on *Sogan*, and now that there is a better law the problems experienced previously will not arise.

The courts concerned with administrative cases are always the ordinary courts, and jurisdiction at first instance is in the district courts. Under the Code of Civil Procedure the competent tribunal is the tribunal of the domicile of the defendant and the law on administrative procedure follows this principle. Where the defendant is an administrative authority, jurisdiction is in the court of the place of this authority. If the action concerns a piece of land, the tribunal of the place where the land is situated is also competent.

A plaintiff who wishes to claim must act within three months of notice of the decision that he wishes to contest, and the right is lost at the end of a year from the date of the decision if proceedings have not been commenced. Except in the case of popular actions or actions between administrative organs, a plaintiff must have a legally protected interest in the subject matter before he can enter into litigation. No claim can be made on the basis of an illegality unless that illegality affects the plaintiff's own legal interests.

Article 25 of the administrative procedure law provides that making a claim does not affect the validity of the decision attacked, nor does it prevent the decision's being executed or the continuation of any procedure that is being followed. A stay of execution is thus in principle excluded. The court can, however, order a stay of execution at the request of the plaintiff when it thinks that this is necessary to prevent the occasioning of irreparable damage. A stay of execution is not admitted when it would be against the public interest to do so. Furthermore, the prime minister can oppose any request for a stay, and if such opposition is lodged the court cannot order a stay of execution and must annul any stay of proceedings already ordered. Although the law provides several measures to prevent the abuse of this procedure by the prime minister, there is reason to fear that this is an unjustified encroachment of the executive into the field of the judiciary. It would have been reassuring if the legislator had shown greater trust in the courts.

As is to be expected, a judge must admit a request for the annulment of a decision taken by an administrative authority when he thinks that a decision was illegal. However, article 31 of the law on administrative procedure provides that if a court thinks that the nullification of an illegal decision would be against the public interest, it can dismiss the request provided that the prejudice that the plaintiff will have to suffer and all other relevant matters are taken into account. In this case the judge will in his judgment limit himself to stating that the decision attacked is illegal.

According to the principles of civil procedure, the principle of *res judicata* affects only the parties in cause (article 201 of the Code of Civil Procedure). The law on procedure in administrative matters, on the other hand, states explicitly that a judgment of annulment also affects third parties (article 32). This provision is new and makes the effects of a judgment of annulment analogous to the effects *ergo omnes* of a judgment of nullification in a claim for *excès de pouvoir* at French law.

In general, the court can annul the acts of the administration or order it to fulfill an obligation, but it cannot oblige it to accomplish a designated administrative act in place of an annulled act. The Supreme Court, however, can order a prefect to perform a certain act when the competent minister requires it under the law on local autonomy (article 146). The same principle applies when a prefect requires a district court to order a mayor to perform a certain act. This does not mean that the court is substituted for the administration. The court intervenes only to guarantee the impartiality of decisions taken by the competent minister or prefect, and this procedure is in fact little used.

Unlike French law, Japanese law does not forbid execution against the administration. However, in the case of action by way of objection, the judgment does not require any particular act to be performed and therefore the problem of forced execution does not arise. Where the dispute is between individuals the ordinary rules apply.

CHAPTER VII

THE JUDICIARY

The judiciary was the state institution most radically reformed after the fall of the old regime, and the influence of United States law is very noticeable.

BASIC PRINCIPLES

The principle of judicial supremacy was adopted on the American model, and consequently the judiciary is placed above Parliament because of its control over the constitutionality of laws. The extent to which the principle of judicial supremacy is contradictory to the other basic constitutional idea, that Parliament is the supreme state organ (article 41), is an open question. Should laws voted by a body which directly represents the people be subjected to the control of another body composed of a small number of persons who are not directly responsible to the nation? It is inevitable in such a system that the courts will get involved in political questions. However, when used prudently it can play a very important role in the life of a nation. As Duverger points out, "The control of the constitutionality of laws is again taking on the democratic meaning that it had in the 18th and 19th centuries in states that had newly set up a democracy in which it was particularly necessary to avoid the abuse of power."[1]

The Japanese Constitution provides in article 81 that "the Supreme Court is the court of last resort with power to give a decision on the constitutionality of laws, orders, regulations or

---

[1] Duverger, *Institutions politiques*, p. 225.

official acts." Yet there is also jurisdiction in the lower courts,[2] since according to the Constitution all courts must declare null state acts that contravene the Constitution. Article 98 says that laws, regulations, rescripts, and other governmental acts contrary to the provisions of the Constitution are null and of no effect.

There are two ways to contest the constitutionality of laws. It is possible to conceive of control either by way of action or by way of exception. "In the first system a special action is brought in respect of the law either by an individual or by a public authority. If the law is acknowledged as being contrary to the Constitution, it is annulled in a general way as regards everyone and not just the parties to the case. . . . Control by way of exception, on the other hand, presupposes a case proceeding before an ordinary court in the course of which the ordinary law is going to be applied. One of the parties to the case then can raise the question of non-constitutionality by arguing that the relevant legislation cannot apply because it is contrary to the Constitution. If the court admits this plea, it will set aside the law but only in respect of that particular case. The piece of legislation will not be struck down and could possibly be applied in the future in other cases."[3] There is no precise provision in the Constitution to say which of the two systems the Japanese Constitution adopts. Some think that article 81 invested the Supreme Court with the powers of a constitutional court as well as with those of an ordinary court. If this is so, the Constitution has adopted the first system, but judicial practice and prevailing theory does not accept this answer.

The Supreme Court has refused, since a judgment of 8 October, 1952, to accept any demands for the annulling of laws outside

---

[2]   The judgment of the Supreme Court of 1 February, 1950, states: "Every judge is required and empowered by the Constitution to decide on the constitutionality of laws when he has to apply them to an actual dispute. This is true not only of judges of the Supreme Court but also is a duty of the judges of the subordinate courts. Article 81 of the Constitution states that the Supreme Court is competent in the last resort to decide on the constitutionality of laws; this in no way prevents the lower courts from exercising this power."

[3]   Duverger, *Institutions politiques*, pp. 223–224.

concrete cases,[4] and the predominant body of theory is in agreement with the Supreme Court on this matter. The result is that anyone who wishes to have a law annulled is often obliged to present his claim during a case of a more or less artificial nature. Since according to the main body of legal opinion the non-constitutionality of a law cannot by itself be the object of a claim, the consideration by the court of the constitutional issue will not appear in the judgment section of the decision, but only in the reasoning. If the Supreme Court thinks that a certain law dealt with in a case is unconstitutional, it will refuse to apply that law but it will not annul it.[5] The law in question continues therefore to have validity until it is abrogated by Parliament.

A certain group of public lawyers and proceduralists are, however, of a different opinion. According to them, control by way of exception renders article 81 of the Constitution almost meaningless. They believe that article 81 imbues the judgment declaring the non-constitutionality of a law with a special quality that other decisions do not have. It follows from this line of argument that a piece of legislation once declared unconstitutional by the Supreme Court becomes null and void. All state organs as well as all citizens must thenceforth consider the law as having no legal effect. Laws declared unconstitutional are presumed null *in toto* or in part from the date of their promulgation to the

---

[4] "The function given us by the present law," the Supreme Court said, "is the exercise of the judicial power and for this power to be brought into play there must be an actual dispute before us. We have no power to give an abstract judgment or exercise authority over future cases which can result from the interpretation of the Constitution and laws and regulations, if they do not arise in a concrete case." This judgment was in answer to a claim by the head of the Socialist Party who wished to attack the constitutionality of the reserve forces, which he regarded as contrary to article 9 of the Constitution. Concerning the details of this problem, cf. the interesting article by Tadakazu Fukase, "Théorie et réalités de la formule constitutionnelle japonaise de renonciation à la guerre," in *Revue du droit public et de la science politique en France et à l'etranger* (1963), p. 1109–1141f. On the same point cf. the judgment of the Supreme Court of 15 April, 1953.

[5] The same of course is true for subordinate courts. If the decision of a lower court had effect *ergo omnes* as far as constitutionality was concerned, the result would be that the opinion of the lower court alone would be able to establish definitively the non-constitutionality of the law. Indeed, if no one of the parties appeals against a decision of the lower court, the Supreme Court has no chance to review the decision, and so on the *ergo omnes* theory no one could then claim that the law in question was constitutional even if the Supreme Court disagreed with the lower court because that law would have already fallen by the judgment of the lower court.

extent that the decision of the Supreme Court has considered the law. As far as the retroactive effect of any nullity is concerned opinions are divided.

The Supreme Court must sit in plenary session to examine a problem concerning the constitutionality of a law. To declare a law unconstitutional at least eight of the fifteen judges must be in agreement, though this absolute majority is not required when a law is found to be constitutional. When the Supreme Court gives a decision declaring a law unconstitutional, it must by law send a copy of the decision to cabinet and to Parliament.[6] This rule would tend to indicate that the Supreme Court itself accepts the theory of the absolute effect of the decision on the non-constitutionality of laws, but there is no case law on the point. The Supreme Court is very conservative: in its first twenty-five years of operation it has annulled only one legal provision for reasons of non-constitutionality.[7] The total number of decisions of the Supreme Court handed down between 1948 and 1956 that involved some constitutional point was 41,991—an average of more than 5,000 a year!

"It has always been difficult for a Frenchman to consider that courts and tribunals exercise a power comparable to that exercised by Parliament or government. The French judiciary does not have the same glamor that the English bench has. It has not and does not seek to have the powers and responsibilities of the judges of the United States either."[8] The French Constitution of 1958, therefore, speaks not of judicial power but of judicial authority. The Japanese judiciary does not enjoy a position as exalted as that of the judiciary in England nor do the Japanese judges have the standing, at least for the time being, of their colleagues in the United States. Nevertheless, it can be said that the Japanese courts exercise a true judicial power that exists alongside the legislative and executive powers. Under the Meiji Constitution this was not the case. Although the independence of the judiciary was very carefully guarded by the constant efforts

---

[6]   Article 14 of the Rules of the Supreme Court of 1 November, 1947.

[7]   This was article 200 of the Penal Code which provided a heavier penalty for homicide in respect of an ascendant. The judgment was of 4 April, 1973.

[8]   René David, *Le droit français* (Paris: Librairie Générale de Droit et de Jurisprudence, 1960), Vol. I, p. 25.

of the judiciary itself, the judges handed down justice in the name of the tenno and they were like the members of the ministère public, under the authority of the minister of justice. A noted judge who was director of the Legal Training and Research Institute admitted that the feeling of fidelity that the judges had toward the tenno in rendering justice in his name exercised an undue influence on their independence. Another former judge states in referring to the past: "Since the chancellery portfolio was usually in the hands of a person who had worked his way up through the parquet, judges who wanted to advance—which was a natural aspiration for those who were also servants of the tenno—were very much concerned with the reaction of the ministère public to their decisions." In these circumstances the judges sought only to apply the laws strictly, and protection of the rights of individuals was often neglected. The courts were virtually part of the executive.

The present Constitution made radical changes in the system. Article 76 provides that the whole judicial power is vested in the Supreme Court and the lower courts. The Supreme Court is a constitutional organ, under no authority other than that of the Constitution. It is placed at the top of the judiciary, and all other courts, with the exception of the court of impeachment of judges provided for in article 64 of the Constitution, are subjected to its authority. The courts no longer come under the jurisdiction of the minister of justice even insofar as judicial administration is concerned. It could even be said that there can be no ministry of justice under the Constitution, for all matters concerning justice are outside the competence of the government. The Ministry of Legal Affairs, though it is responsible for some business which belonged to the Ministry of Justice under the former regime, is no longer responsible for the administration of the courts.[9]

The head of the judiciary is the chief judge of the Supreme

[9] The *Homu-sho*, translated here as Ministry of Legal Affairs, replaces the former *Shiho-sho* (Ministry of Justice), and deals with the ministère public, penitentiaries, the pardon and welfare of prisoners, cases involving the state, nationality, civil status, civil status documentation, registration, control of entry to and exit from Japan, registration of aliens, preparation of bills, the retention of records, and like matters. It has no control over the courts, this is the big difference between the *Homu-sho* and the *Shiho-sho*.

Court. He is nominated by the cabinet and appointed by the tenno. Article 6 of the Constitution provides for the appointment of the chief judge of the Supreme Court along with that of the prime minister, which indicates that these two persons are placed on the same rank by the Constitution as far as the hierarchy of state offices is concerned. The independence of the judiciary is further guaranteed by the Constitution's having given the Supreme Court a rule-making power. The Supreme Court can issue regulations concerning practice and procedure, lawyers, the internal organization of courts, and judicial administration (article 77). The regulations can be made for the matters that are enumerated in article 77 without any delegation by statute, but if there is a statute on the same matter, then the regulation is null to the extent that it contradicts the statute. It is therefore up to Parliament to respect the rule-making power of the Supreme Court. Professor Kaneko, while admitting the superiority of a statute, also recognizes the superiority of regulations when the matter dealt with is the practice and procedure or the administration of the Supreme Court itself. This opinion is based on the fact that the Supreme Court is a constitutional organ whose existence and functioning do not depend on statute except where express reservations are made in the Constitution.

When the Constitution is silent on this matter judicial administration is considered as coming within the competence of the Supreme Court. The appointment of judges is effected if not formally, at least in practice, by the Supreme Court. Further, disciplinary measures against judges cannot be taken by the executive (article 78 of the Constitution); the judiciary itself takes care of this. Court personnel other than judges are appointed and dismissed by the courts, and the budget of the courts, which under the old regime was that of the Ministry of Justice, now constitutes an independent item on the state budget.

THE COURTS

Since 1947, Japan has had a unitary court system. The whole judicial system for civil, criminal, and administrative matters is within a single hierarchy of courts. The jurisdictional unity of this system is perfect, because the creation of courts independent of the hierarchy that has the Supreme Court at its head is, with one exception, forbidden by the Constitution (article 76), and administrative agencies can deal only with administrative claims (article 3 of the law on courts).

Within the judicial order two classes of courts can be distinguished, the Supreme Court and the subordinate courts established by the law on courts of 16 April, 1947.[10]

The present Japanese law makes no terminological distinction between courts of first and second instance, such as between a tribunal and a court, nor is there any distinction in the appellation of various ranks of judge or judgments of various courts.[11] All courts are called *saibansho*—the place where justice is administered.[12] Further, there is no special title for criminal courts and no equivalent for terms like assizes or police courts.[13]

The Supreme Court (*saiko saibansho*) is by definition unique. It sits in Tokyo[14] and is made up of fifteen members—a chief judge and fourteen judges. The Supreme Court decides on matters of law as the French Court of Cassation does and is in principle a jurisdiction that decides on points of law only. It is bound to accept the facts of the case as stated in the decision against which appeal is being made (article 403 of the Code of Civil Procedure).[15] Unlike French jurists, however, Japanese jurists consider that their Supreme Court is a third level of jurisdiction; all agree that Japan has a three-tier court system.[16]

[10]   In accordance with article 76 of the Constitution.

[11]   Such as magistrate and judge, or decision and judgment.

[12]   Before the court reform of 1947 the Supreme Court (*Daishinin*) and the court of appeal (*Kosoin*) had a separate title, *in*, distinguishing them from the other courts (*saibansho*), such as the district courts (*chiho saibansho*) and ward courts (*ku saibansho*).

[13]   Nor is there any categorization of criminal acts (e.g., crime, offense, misdemeanor) though this type of distinction was made in the Penal Code prepared by Boissonade.

[14]   Article 6 of the law on courts.

[15]   According to Kaneko the distinction between a judge of the law and a judge of the facts is not absolute in Japanese law; since the Supreme Court has in its capacity as the sovereign organ the plenitude of powers it has jurisdiction in all cases. In practice it avoids concerning itself with matters of fact but it is not prevented from doing so.

[16]   Perhaps this is because the Supreme Court is not concerned solely with matters of law.

The Japanese Supreme Court has jurisdiction to control the constitutionality of laws and regulations, besides the role of unifying the interpretation of laws and regulations, which it has in common with the French Court of Cassation.

The Supreme Court sits either as a full court (*daihotei*) or in divisions (*shohotei*). The full court is composed of the fifteen judges sitting together, and a quorum is nine judges. The chief judge of the Supreme Court presides over every session of the full court. If he is unable to be present, another judge takes his place according to a ranking system drawn up each year by the judges themselves. One judge is appointed as rapporteur for each case. He is called *shunin saiban-kan*, the judge with principle responsibility for the case, and it is he who, with the assistance of the judges' assistants,[17] examines the dossier, determines what the issues are, does the necessary research and prepares the draft of the judgment. Decision is taken by a majority of the judges present, but to declare a law or a regulation unconstitutional a majority of at least eight is required.

A division[18] of the Supreme Court is made up of five judges, and three is the quorum for judgment. The distribution of work among divisions of the court is decided on by the judges in conference. The president of each division is appointed by co-optation, and he presides at every session of the division to which he belongs. A rapporteur is provided for each case. All cases other than those that clearly come within the competence of the full court are examined first of all by a division. When the division thinks that the case it is hearing is one in which it is necessary to decide on the constitutionality of a law or a regulation, when the opinion of the division on the interpretation of the Constitution or of a law or a regulation is different from that

[17]   There are judges' assistants (*saibansho chosakan*) in the Supreme Court and in each of the superior courts. These assistants, under the judges' guidance, do all research necessary for the hearing and deciding of cases (article 57 of the law on the courts). They are recruited from among persons (including judges) who have an extensive knowledge of law.

[18]   There are three divisions in the Supreme Court: the first, second, and third. Once judges have been appointed to one of these divisions, no change is usually made during the judicial year. Everything concerning the composition of a division is provided for by the Regulations of the Supreme Court, No. 6, of 1 November, 1947.

which has previously been given by the Supreme Court,[19] when the judges are divided equally in their decision, or when the division considers that the case should be decided by the full court, the president of the division notifies the chief judge and the case is heard by the full court.[20]

Decisions of the Supreme Court must show in the minutes of the judgment the opinion of each judge in the case (article 11 of the law on courts). This practice was introduced on the model of Anglo-American law, but is not followed in the judgments of the lower courts. In spite of vigorous opposition the system functions quite well and helps to democratize the administration of justice. Thanks to it the nation can have some idea of the tendencies and abilities of each of the judges in the Supreme Court and sufficient knowledge of the personal work of each judge to be able to participate in the national revision of the list of judges of the Supreme Court.

When matters arise concerning judicial administration, the court meets as a judicial assembly (saiban-kan kaigi).[21] All judges attend and the meeting is chaired by the chief judge. It is this body that makes the court rules.

By comparison with the French Court of Cassation the number of judges of the Supreme Court is small. This court does, however, deal with a large number of cases. According to statistics for 1967 the number of civil cases heard by the court in that year was 1,723. Since its establishment there have been worries about its slowness. The former Supreme Court (Daishinin) had more than fifty judges and it did not hear cases dealing with constitutional or administrative matters. The number of cases pending rose to

---

[19] This rule was made to guarantee uniform interpretation of the laws and to provide against a difference of opinion between divisions on the same point. The law provides that a change of mind in the Supreme Court can only come about after a hearing in the full court. Cf. article 41 of French law of 23 July, 1947, which required the president of the Court of Cassation to seize the plenary civil assembly of the matter when the answer to a particular problem is likely to create a conflict of opinion in the case law. Article 14 of the law of 3 July, 1967, is almost analogous with this article.

[20] Article 9 of Regulations of the Supreme Court of 1 November, 1947.

[21] A full assembly of the judges exists in all jurisdictions except the summary courts. Each judges' conference is concerned only with judicial administration. In the case of the Supreme Court the system works well because there are only fifteen judges, but in the other courts where the number of judges is large the body is ill-suited to dealing with the judicial business as it should.

more than 7,000 in 1952 but by 1967 had reduced to 1,374. Because of this backlog several plans for reform have been drawn up by different bodies, including a plan submitted by the Supreme Court itself. The most official of the plans was that prepared by the Council for Legislation, a permanent body within the Ministry of Legal Affairs with the task of assisting in law-drafting for the government. Its reform project was drafted by two of its specialized sections—the judicial organization and civil-procedure sections—working together. The project required a dividing of the judges of the Supreme Court into two classes, judges of the full court and the judges of divisions. The number of judges in the first class would be nine, and those in the second thirty. The appointment of judges to the full court and the appointment of the presidents of the divisions would be made differently from those of judges to the divisions. The sharing of business between the two sections of the court would be almost the same as at present. In 1957 a government bill was drawn up on the basis of this project and introduced into Parliament, but it was not adopted. The structure of the Supreme Court, therefore, remains unchanged.

The second level of jurisdiction is formed by the superior courts (*koto saibansho*). These courts correspond to the former courts of appeal (*kosoin*). There are eight of them, and they sit in Tokyo, Osaka, Nagoya, Hiroshima, Fukuoka, Sendai, Sapporo, and Takamatsu. Since the regional jurisdiction of each superior court is very great, the Supreme Court can create within each of these territorial divisions one or several court agencies (*shibu*) which deal with some of the cases that the principal court has to decide. There are six such agencies at the moment: one in each of the areas of the superior courts of Nagoya, Fukuoka, Sendai, and Sapporo, and two in that of the Hiroshima court.

Each superior court has a president (*chokan*) and a certain number of other judges. The total number of judges in the superior courts is determined by law but the allocation of judges is left to the Supreme Court, which provides each court with the number of judges it thinks necessary. In each of the superior courts there are chambers (*bu*). The Supreme Court also decides, in accordance with the advice of each superior court, how many chambers are to be created within each tribunal. A chamber is made up of three or five judges,[22] as fixed by law; the control of the business of each chamber is in the hands of one of its members called *sokatsu-hanji* (judge director). All a chamber's business must, however, be carried on in accordance with the decisions taken by all the members of the chamber.

A superior court is in the main an appeal court and hears all types of appeals[23] from judgments given at first instance. The superior courts are not, however, simply a second instance jurisdiction. Decisions given by the summary courts are heard on appeal in the district courts, and a further appeal is then brought to the superior courts instead of to the Supreme Court. Cassation jurisdiction is thus dualist in Japan. In order to avoid diverse interpretations of laws and regulations, the law requires a superior tribunal hearing a final appeal in a case where there is a conflict of precedents to send the case on for hearing in the Supreme Court. The superior courts also decide some cases at first instance.[24]

The district court (*chiho saibansho*)[25] is the court of first instance, for both civil and criminal matters. There is a district court in each prefecture, Tokyo included, and four in Hokkaido. The total number of district courts is fifty. This figure is not as great, for instance, as that of the French *tribunaux de grande instance*, but in practice the difference is more apparent than real because there are, besides the main branch, several court agencies (*shibu*).

[22] For example, all matters concerning offenses against state security. When the court is required to pronounce on a disciplinary matter involving a judge, it must also have five judges.
[23] In Japan court decisions are of three kinds: judgments (*hanketsu*), resolutions (*kettei*), and orders (*meirei*). Judgments and resolutions are made by the court, while orders are the act of a judge alone. When the court as a collegiate body is being considered, the distinction is clear. When, however, a court sits as a judge alone it is often difficult to distinguish between the two categories. *Kettei* is a translation of the German word *Beschluss*, which means "decision." A resolution (*kettei*) is a decision taken according to a series of formalities that are simpler than those required for a judgment. It can be taken without hearing any oral argument and does not have to be given in open court. Important decisions in a case must therefore be taken by way of judgment. Appeal against a judgment is called *koso* and that against a resolution or an order is called *kokoku*.
[24] E.g., offenses against state security: articles 77–79 of the Penal Code, and article 16 of the law on courts.
[25] This court existed under the same name before the reform of 1947.

The agencies are of two sorts: A type and B type. A-type agencies deal with cases other than appeals and administrative actions. B-type agencies deal only with matters that come within the competence of a judge sitting alone. There are 81 agencies of type A and 159 of type B.

A district court is composed of a number of judges and assistant judges, as determined by the Supreme Court. One of the judges is nominated head (*shocho*)[26] of the district court by the Supreme Court. The assistant judges do not have full judicial powers: they cannot judge a case sitting alone, and they cannot preside in a bench of judges. Also, a bench of judges may not include more than one assistant judge. Each district court is divided into chambers,[27] and to each chamber is allocated a certain number of judges and assistant judges.

The district courts have jurisdiction at first instance in both civil and criminal cases. The only cases excluded from their jurisdiction are those heard at first instance by the superior courts or by the summary courts. The district courts function also as appeal courts and hear civil appeals from summary courts. In criminal matters all appeals have, following a reform of the Code of Criminal Procedure in 1948, to be brought before the superior courts.

In the district courts the principle of collegiality is not always followed. A court is usually composed of a judge sitting alone, though a bench of judges is required for more important cases, such as offenses punishable by death or by imprisonment for a term exceeding one year, and for appeals from the summary courts. In addition, the court can itself decide to sit as a bench to hear cases normally heard by a judge alone. Where the court sits as a bench it is composed of three judges.

The family courts (*katei saibansho*) constitute a special category of lower court. They deal principally with domestic matters and cases of juvenile delinquency. This jurisdiction was not provided

[26] The word *shocho* has not been translated as president because president has already been used to translate *chokan*, which is used solely with reference to the Supreme Court and the superior courts.

[27] The number of chambers is large in the courts of big cities. For example, the superior court of Tokyo has 30 chambers, and that of Osaka 16; the district court of Tokyo has 55 chambers, and that of Osaka 29.

for in the law on courts of 1947 and is of a somewhat exceptional nature. It was instituted in 1948 by a reform which combined the Domestic Affairs Office (a branch of the district courts) and the Juvenile Affairs Office (which was within the Ministry of Legal Affairs). This tribunal is specialized in the sense that it has no jurisdiction in ordinary disputes. Its jurisdiction is, with a few exceptions, a non-contentious one.

The family courts occupy a special place in the judicial hierarchy because they rank at the same level as the district courts but do not constitute a jurisdiction above the summary courts. The offices and territorial jurisdiction of the family courts are the same as those of the district courts. There are therefore 50 family courts. As far as agencies are concerned there are 81 of type A and 161 of type B. The agencies deal solely with domestic matters. Apart from the agencies there are 74 separate offices (*shutchosho*) in which domestic matters are dealt with by judges sent on a temporary basis from a family court itself or its agency.

The family court is composed of a number of judges and assistant judges as determined by the Supreme Court. The head of each family court is appointed by the Supreme Court. Chambers can be created in any court as the need arises, but at the present time only the family court of Tokyo is divided into chambers. Family courts rarely sit as a bench.

A family court has the following jurisdiction:

1. to hear and settle family matters of the kind enumerated in the law on procedure in domestic affairs of 6 December, 1947;[28]

2. to deal with cases concerning the protection of delinquent minors as determined by the law on children of 15 July, 1948;

3. to give judgment at first instance for offenses listed in article 37 of the law on children. These offences are not those of children, but those committed by adults, such as parents who have a duty to control children and who do not prevent the commission of offenses by their children. The law provides that the family court deal with these matters in the interests of the child;

4. to deal with other matters as are prescribed by law, such

[28] Article 9. This article has 49 headings.

as civil status problems (e.g., articles 107, 110, 113, 114 of the law on civil status of 22 December, 1947).

The summary court (*kan-i saibansho*) is the lowest court in the hierarchy, but from the jurisdictional point of view it ranks with the district courts and the family courts. The relationship between the district court and the summary court is analogous to that existing between a French *tribunal de grande instance* and a *tribunal d'instance*, save that the district court is usually the jurisdiction to hear appeals from the decisions of the summary court. The summary courts with their quick and simple procedure were created in order to make justice more accessible to the people. There are 570 summary courts composed of one or more judges who constitute a special category of magistrate. They are usually lawyers but may be laymen because it is said that the judge of a summary tribunal has not so much need of a special knowledge of law as of a rich experience of human life. The judge need know only enough law to allow him to fulfill his duties.

In the summary courts cases are always heard by a judge alone, and there are no chambers. However, in order to get some lay common sense into the administration of justice at this level, the law permits ordinary citizens to take part in proceedings as judicial commissioners (*shihoin*). Judicial commissioners are chosen for each case from a list drawn up each year by the district court. They assist and give advice but they do not form part of the summary court. They are neither jurors nor assessors and reference to their advice is at the discretion of the court.

In civil cases a summary court has jurisdiction in matters of which the value does not exceed 300,000 yen. In criminal cases they handle minor offenses, but exceptionally they may hear cases for which the maximum punishment is imprisonment with hard labor on the condition that they do not impose a sentence of imprisonment of more than three years (article 33 of the law on the courts). The summary courts also have some special jurisdiction in matters relating to proof (article 344 of the Code of Civil Procedure), and in pre-litigation conciliation procedures (article 356 of the Code of Civil Procedure). They have no jurisdiction in administrative matters.

COURT OFFICIALS

There is a great array of personnel employed either directly by the courts or by public institutions set up within the framework of the judiciary, and these persons constitute a special class of civil servant. Their appointment and dismissal is controlled by the courts and they are not under the authority of the *Jinjiin* (the Public Service Council). The most important court officers are the registrars and the sheriffs.

The registrars are called *shoki-kan* or more precisely, as there are *shoki-kan* in other branches of the administration, *saibansho shoki-kan*. *Shoki* means writer, and under the former regime a registrar was called just *shoki*. The addition of the term *kan* (state official) gives him more dignity. In each court there is a separate administrative body composed of *shoki-kan*. Its duty is to attend to the documentation required to facilitate the court proceedings, to draw up and store the transcripts of court hearings, to give permission to refer to dossiers, to distribute copies and extracts from judicial acts, and so on. The registrar carries out his duties under the direction of the court to which he is attached, but his powers as registrar are personal to him and even a judge cannot perform the tasks assigned to a registrar.

The registrars are appointed by the Supreme Court. Their qualifications are not determined by law but in practice they are recruited either from among assistant registrars, assistants in the family courts, civil administrators of the courts who have passed an exam for this purpose, or from among those who have completed studies at the Training and Research Institute for Court Clerks.

In the Supreme Court there are registrars-in-chief for the full court and the divisions. In the superior courts and the district courts there is a registrar-in-chief for civil cases and another for criminal cases. There are also registrars in each summary court and in each chamber of each court. Assistant registrars are the assistants of the titular registrars, and are chosen from among persons who have completed their studies at the Training and Research Institute for Court Clerks.

Sheriffs are called *shikko-kan*[29] (*shikko* means execution, and *kan* officer) and should be distinguished from the *tei-ri*, a different class of court officer who is more like a court orderly. The sheriffs are public officers whose duty it is to see that judgments and notarized documents are executed and to serve procedural documents. They are recruited from among persons who have the qualifications specified in the Supreme Court regulation of 8 November, 1966, and who have passed a written and oral examination. They then follow a course prescribed by the Supreme Court. They are appointed by and attached to the district courts.

Sheriffs can perform their tasks only within the jurisdiction of the district court to which they are attached. They receive no salary from the state, and their income is what the parties in question pay them for their services. The tariff of payments is strictly regulated by law, and when the annual income of a sheriff does not reach a certain amount,[30] he can claim a state subsidy to make up the deficit.

Besides registrars and sheriffs there are many other officers who facilitate the proper functioning of the courts. They can be classed in two groups: those persons employed in the judicial administration and judicial assistants.

The first group includes the secretary-general of the Supreme Court, the directors of judicial administration of the superior courts, district courts, and family courts, the civil administrators of each of the courts, and the secretaries to the presidents of the Supreme Court and the superior courts.

The second group includes a variety of court assistants. They are not always judges, but they collaborate in the administration of justice because of their specialized knowledge. They do research on problems that arise during cases when judges make a request for their assistance. The assistants in the family courts play a particularly important role in this respect. They are not always legal specialists, for in domestic and juvenile matters a straight legal solution is not always sufficient to resolve properly

[29] Regulated by a law of 1 July, 1966.
[30] This is a system borrowed from French law. The minimum annual revenue for a sheriff is set at ¥1,136,000.

all the problems that arise, and the court must therefore resort to sociological, psychological, medical, physiological, and other data.

The directors who educate lawyers in various fields must also be mentioned. The institutions to which they belong are within the structure of the Supreme Court and are the Legal Training and Research Institute, the Training and Research Institute for Court Clerks, and the Institute for Family Court Assistants. The directors are like professors. They are appointed by the Supreme Court and may be recruited from among judges, members of the ministère public, or lawyers.

THE MINISTÈRE PUBLIC

The ministère public is a state organ with the function of prosecuting criminal offenders, watching over the serving of sentences, and representing the public interest in civil matters. The ministry is part of the executive, but it is convenient to consider it here because it is by function very closely linked to the courts.

Under the Meiji Constitution the ministère public system was very similar to that of France. Each court had a parquet that was under the authority of the minister of justice and the members of the ministère public were a part of the judicial corps. It was therefore possible to describe both them and judges as "*magistrats*," but since the reform of 1947 the courts have become independent of the executive and the ministère public is no longer part of the same body of persons as the judges.

The ministère public is regulated by a law of the same date as that on the courts, 16 April, 1947. The body of authorities that make up the ministère public is called *kensatsu-cho*,[31] translated here as "parquet." The members of this body are called *kensatsu-kan*, agents of the ministère public. There are several ranks of *kensatsu-cho*, making up a hierarchy of which each rank corresponds to the different ranks of the court hierarchy. Thus, the

[31] *Kensatsu* means the function of searching out and detailing, and *cho* means agency.

supreme parquet (*saiko kensatsu-cho*) corresponds to the Supreme Court, the superior parquet (*koto kensatsu-cho*) to the superior court, the district parquet (*chiho kensatsu-cho*) to the district courts, and the local parquet (*ku kensatsu-cho*) to the summary court. The control of the parquet is in descending order in the hands of the procurator-general (*kenji-socho*), the head procurator (*kenji-cho*) and the directing procurator (*kenji-sei*). In a local parquet the member in charge has no special title. In the supreme parquet there is a deputy procurator-general called *jicho-kenji*. Every member of the ministère public has the general title *kenji* with or without a qualifier indicating rank.

The functions of the ministère public are always performed by a single *kenji*. There is no grouping of *kenji*, and *kenji* do not enjoy a functional independence like judges. It is said that the ministère public is one and indivisible. All subordinate members perform their duties under the orders of their superior. At the top of the hierarchy is the minister of legal affairs and the procurator-general must obey the minister's orders. With a government of political parties there is the chance that undesirable influence can be exercised over the ministère public through the Ministry of Legal Affairs, and so the law forbids the minister to intervene directly in any hearing or other activity undertaken by the *kensatsu-kan*. He can only give directives of a general nature and can participate in a particular case only through the intermediary of the procurator-general (article 14 of the law on the ministère public). It would not be desirable, however, to grant the ministère public an independence similar to that of judges. If that happened the ministère public could easily abuse its position, as it is not responsible to the people. By placing the procurator-general as a sort of buffer between the minister of legal affairs and the active *kensatsu-kan*, the law has tried to reduce to the minimum the possibility that undue political pressure may be placed on the ministère public.

The right to prosecute a criminal action is monopolized by the ministère public, but it does not always act as the citizens would wish. In order to meet this difficulty Japanese law has set up a supervisory council (*kensatsu shinsa-kai*) to watch over the functioning of the ministère public in the prosecution of offenders.

The council is not a jury of indictment that decides for itself whether to prosecute a person or not, but is simply a control body that makes certain that the ministère public does not improperly abstain from prosecuting.

The law relating to the supervisory council of the ministère public of 12 July, 1948, provides for more than two hundred councils throughout Japan and for at least one council in every district court area. A council is made up of eleven members elected by ballot from among the electors in the area for a term of six months. The council examines decisions taken by the ministère public to judge whether the decision to indict or stay proceedings was reasonable. It is seised of a matter by members of the public, by the victim of a criminal act, or *proprio motu*. Where the council wishes to act *proprio motu*, a decision of the majority of the members is required.

The examination carried out by the council is done independently and freely. If the council thinks prosecution is required, its decision must be taken by a majority of at least eight. The decision does not compel the ministère public to prosecute, and it has no effect on the charge. It simply causes the prosecutor who receives notification of the council's decision to consider or reconsider his action.

THE JURY

The jury is in many countries considered to be an apt way of reflecting the justice of laymen on procedures and judgments which would become more legal than human if they were left to judges alone. The system has been used in England for a long time, both in civil and in criminal cases, and in recent times by other countries. In Japan neither the civil nor the criminal jury now exists, though Japan did try the system. In 1926 a law on the jury was promulgated and it came into force on 1 January, 1928. It provided for a criminal jury; in each criminal case twelve jurymen were to be drawn by lot from among ordinary citizens and were to participate in hearings at first instance. Their duty was limited to giving a decision on the facts by answering yes or no to the question asked them by the president of the court concerning the guilt or innocence of the defendant. The court was not bound to decide according to the jury verdict. If a conviction was not brought in by the verdict of one jury a court could submit the case to another jury. The reason for this was that it would have been contrary to the Constitution had the court been obliged to follow a verdict different from what its own would have been, because the Constitution by article 24 provided that a Japanese citizen could not be deprived of his right to be judged under the law by a judge.

The jury system was at first very well received as a means of making the administration of justice more democratic. However, use in practice did not measure up to expectations. A significant number of defendants refused jury trial in the case of the statutory jury for crimes punished by death or life imprisonment, and very few offenders in less serious cases exercised their right to have a jury. Japanese people seemed to have no confidence in the legal sense of laymen. Another factor was that it was not possible to appeal a sentence handed down by a jury. In 1943 the law on the jury was suspended to simplify the administration of justice in time of war, and this suspension has continued. There are supporters of a revival of the jury, but discussion is limited to legal circles.

CHAPTER VIII

THE PROFESSION

LEGAL EDUCATION

The education of lawyers in Japan is almost the same as in countries of the Romano-Germanic family of law, and this is as would be expected since the Japanese legal system is modeled on the French and German ones. The education of lawyers is basically a university and academic one. During the Meiji era the faculties of law of the imperial universities were nurseries for bureaucrats who were trained to work in with the political power. These jurists took great care to apply the rules of law literally but were not much concerned with protecting individual rights. They lived in a world apart from that of ordinary people; they were citizens of a kingdom of pure law, such as that conceived of by Kelsen, and the exegetical method dominated their thinking; the formula, *Gesetz ist Gesetz* (law is law), which was imposed on German lawyers as a categorical imperative before the war, was not alien to the Japanese lawyers of Meiji times. The positivist conception of law cultivated in lawyers an attitude of unthinking submission to the dictates of the governmental power and facilitated greatly the work of the dictatorship.

Since the war, a more humane and critical outlook has been developing in the teaching in the faculties of law, but the present reactionary tendency in Japan sometimes threatens to override the new outlook in all areas of Japanese culture. It is clear that the struggle between the two tendencies, the new and the old, will go on for some time.

Basic legal education is given by university law faculties

(*hogaku-bu*).[1] Students begin university at about eighteen years of age, and the period of course work is four years. University training is divided into two parts. The first part is dedicated almost entirely to humanities and the second to specialized studies. Students of the first part therefore do not usually take specialist courses. At the University of Tokyo students who want to do law do not enter the law faculty immediately but belong for the first two years to the College of General Education. At the end of their general studies they become law students. The result is that the length of the period of law studies, whether relating to general legal culture or of a more specialized nature, is in fact only two years. This period of time is obviously too short for specialization, but in spite of efforts to lengthen the period for the law studies the best that has been done to date in the Tokyo faculty is to reach agreement with the College of General Education that a certain number of courses relevant to the law degree be taught in the last semester of the first part.

The Tokyo law faculty is divided into three departments: the private law department, the public law department, and the political science department.[2] The subjects taught in the first department can only be taken by those students who want to become lawyers. In 1971 the number of students in each department was 842 in the first, 489 in the second, and 246 in the third. Formerly most students chose to study in the second department because the subjects studied there are very varied in nature: public law, some private law, and a little political science and economics.

After completion of their undergraduate studies, students can extend their knowledge in the *daigakuin*. Training in the *daigakuin* is divided into two cycles. At the end of two years of study in the

---

[1] All institutions of tertiary education in Japan are called universities and faculties whether they are national or private. Faculties can grant their students degrees of which the value is legally identical, though they may not be recognized as of equal value in practice. The total number of universities (*daigaku*) is considerable; there are 389 and a further 486 universities of short term. The number of universities which have law faculties is much lower. There are 51, plus 2 law faculties of short term. (Figures are for 1971.) The number of graduates coming out of these faculties was 13,165 in 1959, not counting the graduates of the faculties of universities of short term.

[2] Economic sciences are studied in another faculty.

first cycle, a student can present a thesis. If this thesis is accepted by the jury, its author receives the title of *shushi* (master). *Shushi* can go on to the second cycle and at the end of three years present a doctoral thesis. If he succeeds he receives the title of *hakushi* (doctor).

Few students who want to become lawyers go to the *daigakuin*.[3] Law faculties usually content themselves with giving students a purely theoretical training. The idea is to arm students with a minimum technical knowledge of law and a general legal culture. Practical matters do receive some attention, but it is impossible in two years to teach students enough law to enable them to practice as lawyers. Of course, not all students who join a law faculty want to become lawyers. Law faculties, particularly those with a good reputation, attract a great number of students, but it is not because the Japanese hold a view like the French that a knowledge of law is an aspect of general cultural knowledge that should be acquired by everyone.[4] A law degree, provided it is from a faculty with a good reputation, opens the door to socially elevated positions in big companies or within the government. In fact, the top personnel of the big companies and of the administration are almost exclusively persons who have law degrees. Since most law students only seek a degree that will assure them of a good position and are not much concerned with an appropriate knowledge of law, it would be difficult to require them to do any extensive professional training.

Because a university education is not sufficient to prepare professional lawyers for their jobs, other specialized organizations provide the necessary training. The most important of these is the Legal Training and Research Institute (*Shiho kenshujo*), which was founded on 3 May, 1947, the day that the Constitution came into force. The Institute began to operate on 1 December, 1947, and between 1949 and 1960 it trained 2,893 lawyers. From the beginning of the new regime there has been a certain tendency toward unity within the Japanese legal world (*hoso ichigenron*)—persons who deal professionally with the law are educated by the same

[3] The *daigakuin* is reserved almost exclusively for those seeking university chairs.
[4] "At least an elementary knowledge of law is considered desirable in France. The French consider such knowledge almost as a normal attribute of general culture." David, *Le droit français*, Vol. I, p. 46.

body, so that they can easily change from one legal occupation to the other, which also makes it possible to recruit judges from among attorneys of good standing, as is done in England.

For the moment, however, few of the top attorneys would want to leave their profession to become judges, because judges' salaries are too low and the honor of being a judge is not great. Perhaps for this same reason the proportion of those who study at the Institute who wish to become attorneys is increasing all the time. In the last few years more than half of those at the Institute have wanted to become attorneys—140 out of 256 in 1958, 150 out of 282 in 1959, and 160 out of 391 in 1960.[5] Because of this there is vigorous opposition to the present system, particularly from the point of view of state finances. Should the state pay to educate persons who have no intention to serve it now or in the future? The Finance Ministry, in particular, does not favor the education of attorneys in the Institute. It is nevertheless to be hoped that things will change, with an improvement in the social standing of judges, as the present system has great value since it contributes to understanding between lawyers of various categories. Each learns how the other thinks and behaves. By giving them a vision of their common mission and by emphasizing the necessity for collaboration, the system creates a certain amount of professional solidarity between these different categories.

Prospective students of the Legal Training and Research Institute must take a state law examination (*shiho shiken*), which consists of two parts. The first exam aims at finding out whether a candidate has sufficient knowledge of general cultural matters, such as are taught in the universities. Those who have a university degree in any subject are therefore not required to take this exam. The second exam is in two parts, written and oral. The written part has compulsory tests on constitutional law, civil law, commercial law, penal law, penal procedure, and civil procedure, and some optional topics which in turn are divided into two groups. In the first group is the procedural law of the branch that the candidate has not chosen as an obligatory subject, administra-

---

[5] In 1964, of the 365 new jurists, 57 became judges, 45 entered the ministère public, and 261 became attorneys. In 1965, out of 441, 72 became judges, 52 members of the ministère public, and 315 attorneys. In 1974, out of 506 graduates (29 women), 85 became judges, 47 entered the ministère public, and 366 became attorneys.

tive law, bankruptcy law, labor law, international law, conflict of laws, and penal policy. The second group of optional topics includes political science, general theories of political economics, economics, accountancy, psychology, economic policy, and social politics. The candidate must choose one topic in each of these two groups. He has then to write seven essays. It is to be noted, however, that since the number of candidates sitting for these exams increases yearly,[6] it has become necessary to introduce a sort of elimination process. Since 1956 each candidate has had to answer ten simple questions in each of the subjects. These questions are asked in a way that requires an answer of yes or no, and they have to be answered at the same time as the essays are written. The examination committee need not examine the essays of a candidate who does not obtain a certain number of marks in the preliminary questions. Those who pass the written exam then take oral exams in the same subjects as those in which they did the written exam. The examination takes place at least once a year at a date and place announced in the official journal.

A committee for the control of the exams for the *Magistrature*, composed of the deputy head of the Ministry of Legal Affairs with responsibility for administrative matters (*jimuji-kan*), the secretary general of the Supreme Court, and an attorney nominated by the Bar Federation of Japan, has been set up by the Ministry of Legal Affairs to organize the exams. The members of the examination panel are nominated for each exam by the Ministry of Legal Affairs, and are in practice chosen from among university professors.

The Supreme Court calls the candidates admitted to the Institute auditors (*shiho shushusei*) or, more precisely, legal apprentices. In practice all candidates who pass, except those who are thought to be incapable of completing the course because of illness or those who have been legally excluded because, for instance of a criminal background, are admitted. The auditors receive instruction and complete the work necessary to become a judge, member of the ministère public, or attorney.[7] They are

[6] More than 8,000 in 1960 and 20,000 in 1970 as against 2,500 in 1949.
[7] The Institute not only arranges for the teaching and the practical work for the auditors, but also for in-depth teaching for assistant judges.

under the general supervision of the Supreme Court, but the director of the Institute is the person who controls their instruction and the practical work.

The length of studies and the practical work comprise two years. In the first four months the auditors gain a knowledge of judicial practice in the Institute itself. Then they are sent for eight months to the courts, for four months to a parquet, and for four months to a bar. Each auditor does the practical work determined for him by the director. Although the Institute is in Tokyo auditors are also sent to other towns. After finishing their practical work, they return to the Institute to receive a further four months of teaching to improve their standard. At the end of this period of studies they take an exam which is held before a panel made up of the chief judge of the Supreme Court and members recruited from among the *saiban-kan*, *kensatsu-kan*, attorneys, course directors, and other qualified persons. This panel grants or refuses admission to the auditors on the basis of the results of their practical work and the marks obtained by each participant at this last exam.

The teaching the Institute gives the auditors is of a purely professional nature, though there is some time spent on general cultural matters too. For the general cultural studies the Institute employs university professors, but the purely professional teaching is carried out by course directors who are recruited from among *saiban-kan*, *kensatsu-kan*, and attorneys. The directing of the practical work is entrusted by the director to the district courts, to the district parquets, and to the bar councils. The study of comparative law is also included in the teaching of the Institute, and during their two years at the Institute auditors study German, Anglo-American, or French law.

The auditors are not public officers, but they have a status very similar to that of public officers and they receive a government allowance[8] for the period of their studies.

ATTORNEYS

The Japanese attorney, *bengoshi* (he who takes on the defense

---

[8]   In 1974, ¥72,000 a month.

of others), does not correspond exactly in function to a barrister for he may represent parties in the way a solicitor does. Though he may perform both functions, parties to court proceedings need not retain his services. For want of a better term *bengoshi* will be translated as attorney.

In Europe the barrister's profession has a very long tradition, and during that long history barristers have played a brilliant role in explaining matters to judges and in working with judges to achieve justice. Their eloquence has also contributed a great deal to the embellishing of language and giving it more precision. Barristers are a very proud professional group, and from the Japanese point of view they enjoy a social standing and respect worthy of them.

In Japan the profession of attorney did not exist before the Meiji era. An attorney's duty is to uphold justice and to defend the rights of individuals against injustice, and it is therefore quite natural that the profession was not known in feudal Japan since individuals were not then considered as the proper subjects of rights. In the Edo period persons called *kujishi* (*kuji* means procedure, *shi* a person who specializes in a particular matter) took charge of consultations and gave assistance to litigants, but this profession was not legalized; thus, in the occupation of *kujishi* there was not a germ of the profession of attorney. It was only in 1872 that Japan began to take account of the importance of the legal professions. Four years later a law called *daigennin kisoku* (regulations concerning spokesmen) was promulgated to regulate the attorney's profession. The object of the law was to suppress the activities of professionals who appeared in court and who were of very low standing. These professionals were called *sambyaku daigen* (three-hundred-cent spokesmen) because they stirred up trouble in order to make profit even for such small amounts as three hundred cents, and the epithet is still used to describe attorneys unworthy of their profession. Since that time many efforts have been made to improve the standing of the profession, but much is still left to be desired.

The authority and respect that European barristers enjoy is, it seems, beyond the reach of their Japanese counterparts. In John I: 2, verse 1, the following phrase occurs: "Should anyone sin he has an advocate before the Father in Jesus Christ the just." Somewhat surprised at this assimilation of Christ to an attorney, I looked up this phrase in the Japanese edition of the New Testament. The word attorney is not used there. The Japanese translation of the Bible uses the word *tasukenushi* (savior).[9] The English translator of the Bible quite naturally thought the word advocate was suitable as a description of Jesus Christ who was a model man because the English advocate enjoyed a standing which made him worthy of this comparison. If the standing of the advocate was not so respected by everyone, no one would think of qualifying Christ in this way. On the other hand, in Japan, where the notion of attorney is not so respected, such an analogy is inconceivable.

The attorney's profession is regulated now by a law on attorneys of 10 June, 1949. Under the present system those who want to become attorneys must go to the Legal Training and Research Institute and take the course there along with those who want to be judges or members of the ministère public. Those students of the Institute who pass the final exam successfully can become attorneys (article 4).[10] Before he can practice, the attorney must also be on the roll of attorneys of the Japanese Bar Federation. An application for entry on the role is addressed to the bar before which the candidate wishes to practice. When it receives an application, the Bar Council examines the professional qualifications of the candidate, and may refuse to send the name on to the Bar Federation if the candidate does not fulfill the conditions or if it considers him unfit to be an attorney. The candidate can appeal against this decision of the Bar Council to the Federation. The Federation can in its turn refuse to admit the candidate, even in cases where the attorney's application has received the approval of a Bar Council. A candidate can appeal to the superior court of Tokyo against his rejection by the Federation or against the decision given on appeal from the Bar Council.

An attorney must have his office within the area of the bar to

---

[9] The meaning of the Greek word used in the original is "he who is called to help," which corresponds exactly to the meaning of the Latin word *advocatus*.

[10] There are other ways of becoming an attorney but they are exceptional. Cf. article 5 of the law on attorneys.

which he belongs, and he must obey the rules of that bar and of the Federation. He is also bound to professional secrecy (article 134 of the Criminal Code), can neither request nor receive money from any party who opposes him in court, nor may he participate in a case in which he has any personal interest. He may not, for example, accept a brief in a case in which he has previously advised the opposing party. The profession of attorney is incompatible with certain public offices, and an attorney cannot be a professor in the law faculty of a national university. Where an attorney becomes a member of Parliament or a minister, he must suspend his activities as attorney while he holds office.

The discipline of attorneys is within the competence of the bar to which they belong or of the Bar Federation. Disciplinary measures are taken by these bodies following a decision of their disciplinary council, which is made up of attorneys, judges, *kensatsu-kan*, and other suitably qualified persons. The decision of a disciplinary council can be challenged by appeal to the Bar Federation; the decision of the Bar Federation on such an appeal may in turn be appealed against to the superior court of Tokyo.

Fees are freely arrived at between clients and attorneys. The Bar Federation has internally set up a tariff for fees, but this tariff is not mandatory. Certain lawyers seek a mandatory list of tariffs so that expenses can easily be worked out, but attorneys generally do not wish their scale of fees to be legislated. For the time being attorneys' fees do not form part of court costs and therefore cannot be recovered from the defendant.

The bar (*bengoshi-kai*) is an autonomous organ that directs, controls, and groups attorneys. Every attorney is obliged to belong to a bar, of which there is one in the district of each district court except Tokyo, where there are three. The present law preserves the earlier system. Within each bar there are three councils—the admission council, the control council, and the disciplinary council. The control council watches over the activities of members to see that professional etiquette is observed. The Bar Federation of Japan directs, controls, and brings together all attorneys, and its members are both the attorneys individually and each of the bar councils. The Federation has almost perfect autonomy in that it is not subject to any state control. Only the Supreme Court has power over the bar councils, and this power is of a regulatory nature allowing the Supreme Court, if need be, to require the Federation to make reports to it and to do any research necessary before the Supreme Court promulgates regulations relating to attorneys.

No one other than an attorney can give legal advice for a fee, under pain of imprisonment with hard labor for a term not exceeding two years or of a fine of up to 50,000 yen, and no one but an attorney may use the title of attorney, or run an office or advertise the giving of legal advice.

Unlike, say, French barristers, who show a strong professional pride before the courts, Japanese attorneys show no sentiment of independence worthy of their task before judges. The Japanese attorney lives in an environment where everyone thinks the government is good and where private initiative is disdained. Because of this he is obsessed by an inferiority complex when in court. Some attorneys address the judges with great deference, as if they were begging them to give judgment in their favor, and out of court they display an ill-founded mistrust of the judiciary.

One of the causes for this attitude is the training of attorneys in the Meiji era. At the time of the *Jiyu Minken* movement, Japanese attorneys showed a lively spirit of resistance against the arbitrariness of state power, but in the absolutist political regime which repressed that movement their spirit was gradually weakened, and the new tendency was accentuated by the method of recruiting lawyers. From 1893 to 1923 law graduates from an imperial university could become attorneys without taking any exams, while those of piivate universities had to pass a competitive exam. The members of the panel that conducted the examination were mostly professors from the imperial universities and for this reason private universities sought the assistance of the professors of the imperial universities for their law courses. The influence of the imperial universities thus dominated the private universities and, since the imperial universities were training grounds for bureaucrats, the spirit of independence or resistance was hard to maintain.

Since the end of World War II a great change of temperament has taken place. From an inquiry carried out in 1960 it appears that there is a very clear distinction to be drawn between the generation of attorneys over fifty and those under fifty. It is interesting to note that the generation who are now in their forties showed in their answers to every question that they were middle-of-the-line men; the older generation was conservative, and the younger more progressive. In the group of under-30's, two attorneys supported the Liberal Democratic Party, and three the Socialist Party; in the age group 30 to 40 the ratio was 8 to 18; in the age group 40 to 50 the ratio was 8 to 5 and in the age group 50 to 60 the ratio was 29 to 12; in the age group 60 to 70 it was 32 to 2; and in the age group over 70 more than 10 to 1. For the group below 30 and the group over 70, the number of persons questioned was too small to draw a proper conclusion, but nevertheless the figures do tend to show that the outlook of Japanese attorneys is changing.

MEMBERS OF THE MINISTÈRE PUBLIC

Generally speaking, *kensatsu-kan* still have the authoritarian mental attitude that was developed under the earlier regime. A representative of the ministère public is too busy trying to discover offenders to be really very much concerned with the rights of the persons he interrogates. The judicial police of the Edo period never hesitated to use torture to get admissions from suspects. Even after Boissonade's call for its suppression, torture was used by the judicial police. They considered it their duty to find guilty parties at any cost. As a consequence it often happened that they got confessions from persons who were not guilty. This defect has not really been rectified by the present *kensatsu-kan*. For fear of causing the police to lose face the *kensatsu-kan* frequently accept the results of a police inquiry without proper consideration. The principle of *in dubio pro reo* does not direct the activities of the *kensatsu-kan,* and there is a strong tendency within the ministère public to consider *kensatsu-kan* who have a habit of deciding against the prosecution of suspects as being cowards.

There are two classes of *kensatsu-kan*. To be a *kensatsu-kan* of the first class—the procurator-general, the deputy head of the supreme parquet, the procurators-in-chief, and the *kenji* of the first class—a candidate must have practiced one of several listed professions for at least eight years. He should, for example, have been a *kensatsu-kan* of the second class, attorney, assistant judge, or judge of a summary court. The basic law relating to the ministère public is that of 16 April, 1947, *Kensatsucho ho* (the law on the parquet). The *kensatsu-kan* of the second class—*kenji* of the second class and the *fukukenji* (*kenji* of lower rank)—are appointed generally from among auditors who have been admitted to the final exam of the Legal Training and Research Institute. The procurator-general, the deputy head of the supreme parquet, and the procurators-in-chief are appointed and dismissed by the Naikaku under the attestation of the tenno. The other *kensatsu-kan* are appointed and dismissed by the minister of legal affairs.

All *kensatsu-kan* are subject to a general review of their professional activities every three years. Further, an unscheduled survey can be made either at the request of the minister of legal affairs or *proprio motu* by the review body, the screening committee for *kensatsu-kan*. This committee is under the control of the prime minister and is made up of eleven members elected from among members of Parliament, *kensatsu-kan*, judges, attorneys, and members of the Japan Academy. If it finds a *kensatsu-kan* guilty of moral turpitude or physically incapable, the minister of legal affairs must, if the officer is the procurator-general, a deputy head of the Supreme Parquet, or a procurator-in-chief, ask for that officer's resignation. If the person involved is a *kenji* or a *fukukenji*, the minister dismisses him directly.

The *kensatsu-kan* enjoy certain guarantees of office. They cannot be dismissed, suspended, or have their salary reduced without their consent. Unlike judges, however, they cannot refuse a new posting, and since they are classed within the general category of public officials, they can be dismissed by disciplinary measures taken against them according to the ordinary procedures set out in the law on the public service. The age limit for the procurator-general is fixed at sixty-five; for the other *kensatsu-kan* the limit is sixty-three.

THE PROFESSION 151

JUDGES

All state officials responsible for handing down justice are called *saiban-kan*.[11] They fall into two broad groups: the chief judge and judges of the Supreme Court, and the judges of the other courts. Judges in the strict sense are called *hanji* (*han*, to judge; *ji*, thing). With the exception of the president all the *saiban-kan* have *hanji* as part of their title. The word used without qualification refers to the judges of the superior courts and the judges of the district and family courts. The judges of the Supreme Court are always called *saiko saibansho hanji* and those of the summary court *kan-i saibansho hanji*. Assistant judges are called *hanji ho*.[12] When a *hanji* is appointed to a specific court he bears a title designating his duties. For example, a *hanji* of the superior court of Osaka is called *Osaka koto saibansho hanji*. Judges who are presidents of the district courts and family courts do not constitute a special class of *hanji*. They are simply *hanji* invested with the power of president.[13] The presidents of the Supreme Court or superior courts on the other hand are not called *hanji*. They are simply chief judge or president of a superior court. In Japanese the president is called *chokan*, and *hanji* with the duties of president are called *cho* or *shocho*.

The number of *saiban-kan* is determined by law. For the Supreme Court the number is set out in the law on courts as being a chief judge and fourteen Supreme Court *hanji* (article 5). In January, 1963, there were eight presidents of superior courts, 1,210 judges, 527 assistant judges, and 715 summary court judges. The

[11] *Saiban* means every activity concerned with the practice of justice, and *kan* means state official. The word judge comes from the Latin *iudex*. The Roman *iudex* was originally a private individual. This etymological sense is still retained in the word judge, as a judge need not be a public officer. The Japanese word *saiban-kan*, on the other hand, is always applied to a state official concerned with the administration of justice. There is another term, *hanji*, which in itself does not have the meaning of public official. Unfortunately the present use of this term is limited to judges who are public functionaries.

[12] *Ho* means subordinate.

[13] This term has not, however, been translated as president because the Japanese terminology distinguishes the title of head of the district court or family court from that of the head of the Supreme Court and the superior courts. Only in the latter case is the word president used.

total number of *saiban-kan* therefore was 2,475, a much lower figure than in France, which had 4,500 in 1965.[14] The number of judges in relation to the number of inhabitants is therefore very much lower in Japan than in France (2.15 judges per 100,000 Japanese as against 9.2 judges per 100,000 French). The total number of judges has not increased much in Japan since the Meiji era (1,531 in 1890), although the population has almost tripled in the same period. The need to increase the number of judges is urgent.

The *saiban-kan* of the Supreme Court must be persons of upright character, advanced education, and be at least forty years of age. They must have an adequate knowledge of law, but there is no requirement that they be specialists in law. Because of this the law requires that ten of the fifteen judges be lawyers of at least twenty years standing in one of a prescribed number of legal professions among which are listed lower court judge, member of the ministère public, attorney, and law professor. The chief judge of the Supreme Court is appointed by the tenno according to the nomination of the Naikaku; the judges of the Supreme Court are appointed by the Naikaku, and their appointment is witnessed by the tenno.

All appointments to the Supreme Court are also submitted to a democratic control (*kokumin shinsa*). That is to say, they are submitted to the people for approval. In this way the nation indicates whether or not it extends its confidence to the judges who have been nominated. This control system is reminiscent of the recall system practiced for the nomination of public servants in the U.S. Article 79 of the Constitution provides that the nomination of judges to the Supreme Court, the chief judge included, must be submitted to the nation for approval at the first general election of representatives following the nomination. The control must be repeated every ten years after the first vote, at the first available general election. If the majority of the voters vote for the dismissal of a judge he is dismissed *ipso jure*. Detailed formalities for the national control are set out in the Law on the National Control of Judges of the Supreme Court of 20 November, 1947. The holding of office by the chief judge and judges of

[14] France has less than half the population of Japan.

the Supreme Court is thus qualified by the confidence of the people, which is manifested every ten years.[15] Each voter places a cross on his voting slip opposite the name of any judge whose nomination he does not approve. Those who approve the nomination or those who wish to abstain put the slip on which the names of all the judges are written into the ballot box without making any special mark on it. No one may take his voting slip out of the voting hall. Those abstaining are presumed to have approved the nomination. Some think that this institution is superfluous, because the Japanese are not used to the election of judges and are therefore incapable of discerning the quality of judges. For the time being this may be so, but . . . *chi va piano va sano!*

The presidents of the superior courts and the judges, in the strict sense of the word, are recruited from among lawyers who have practiced their profession of, for example, assistant judge, summary court judge, member of the ministère public, attorney, court assistant, course director at the Legal Training and Research Institute, or law professor for at least ten years. Assistant judges are appointed from among auditors of the Legal Training and Research Institute who have completed their studies and period of practice and who have been admitted to the final examination of the Legal Training and Research Institute. The judges of the summary courts are recruited either from among lawyers who have practiced their profession for at least three years, from among those who have been employed in the judiciary other than as a judge for a sufficiently long time, or those who have sufficient knowledge and experience to be considered by the recruitment board as suitable material for judges of the summary courts. The appointment of lower court judges is entrusted to the Naikaku, which appoints them from a list drawn up by the Supreme Court. The choice of persons to be appointed depends exclusively on the Supreme Court, and the nomination is therefore in principle quite formal. In this way an effort has been made to preserve the independence of the judges from politics and, at the same time, to avoid any arbitrary method of recruitment by the Supreme Court by permitting the Naikaku to exercise a right of veto when necessary.

[15] No judge has yet been dismissed by this means.

A characteristic of this branch of the law is the system of appointment of lower court judges for a set term of ten years. This was a radical innovation brought in after World War II. By this system all judges, except judges of the Supreme Court, are appointed for ten years. They are automatically out of office on the date ten years after their nomination. They can be reappointed indefinitely until the age of retirement, but even if a judge wants to be reappointed he may not be, since reappointment depends on the Supreme Court, in the exercise of its discretion, including his name on the list submitted to the cabinet. Judges are therefore obliged to fall in with the opinion of the Supreme Court in the exercise of their functions. That includes falling in with its political standpoint, for there is no way of exercising control over the choice of the Supreme Court. Some, therefore, think that the independence of the lower court judges is more apparent than real.

Judges enjoy complete independence from all influences external to the judiciary. The Constitution declares that all *saibankan* perform their duties in complete independence and according to the dictates of their conscience. They are only subject to the Constitution and the law (article 76 of the Constitution). They cannot therefore be pressured into resigning, accepting a different post, suspension, or accepting reduction of salary, except in those cases where they have, in accordance with the proper procedure, been declared incapable of performing their duties for physical or mental reasons. To better guarantee the independence of judges, the Constitution forbids the government to take disciplinary measures against them (article 78). Disciplining the judges is within the competence of the judiciary itself.

For judges of the district courts, the family courts, and the summary courts, jurisdiction in disciplinary matters is vested in the superior court of the area in which the lower court is situated. For all other judges disciplinary jurisdiction is in the Supreme Court. Unlike other public officers, judges can never suffer disciplinary measures, such as dismissal, suspension, or reduction of salary. Censure and disciplinary fines, of which the value may not exceed 10,000 yen, are the only measures that may be taken.

Judges cannot be dismissed except by a procedure of public accusation (article 78 of the Constitution), and for this type of trial a special court is set up within the framework of Parliament with fourteen judges, half elected by each House. It is called the Court of Impeachment and is governed by the rules set out in articles 125 to 129 of the law on Parliament and by a special law on the prosecution of judges of 20 November, 1947. The court performs its duties independently of Parliament and can act even when Parliament is not in session. Its judges sit for the period set out in their parliamentary mandate. The process of accusation is instituted by the Prosecution of Judges Committee, composed of twenty members, ten of whom are elected by each House from among its members. The causes for prosecution are (a) serious violation of professional obligation or inexcusable negligence in the exercise of judicial functions, and (b) conduct which seriously affects the dignity and standing of the judiciary, whether occurring in the performance of judicial functions or not (article 2 of the law on prosecution of judges). Dismissal can be ordered only on the vote of two-thirds of the judges voting at the hearing.[16]

Judges' salaries are guaranteed by the Constitution (article 79). The salary must be reasonable and cannot be lowered during the term of duty of the judge. When the new judicial system was set up, the lowest salary for judges of the middle rank was equal to the highest salary for a public officer, but as a result of successive increases in salary, which have been given to officers in the executive, the position has changed. The inadequacy of the judges' salary in relationship to the revenue of attorneys obviously constitutes one of the main reasons why attorneys of good reputation do not wish to become judges, although the new system provides for their appointment to the bench. Quite independently of this, however, it would be desirable to raise judges' salaries as much

[16] It has happened on several occasions that the prosecuting body begins gathering information on cases that are still pending before the courts. A judge presiding in a case who did not allow the accused persons to intercede for their companions at a public hearing was called upon to appear during the procedure before the prosecution committee. Such activities of the committee have been vigorously criticized as being a threat by Parliament to the independence of the judges. There is the feeling that judicial independence is properly guaranteed vis-à-vis the government, but very much less between Parliament and the Supreme Court!

as possible so that they can perform their duties in an impartial manner.

The age limit for judges varies depending on the category to which they belong. It is seventy years for *saiban-kan* in the Supreme Court and summary courts and sixty-five years for *saiban-kan* of other courts.

JAPANESE AND THE LAW

CHAPTER IX

JAPANESE AND THE LAW

In most European countries the word law applies both to objective and subjective law, and the term always implies some idea of the protection of the legitimate interests of individuals. In Japan, on the contrary, the corresponding word *ho*,[1] or *horitsu*, means only the body of legal rules. Japanese have no clear idea of subjective law and as a consequence objective law interrelates very poorly with subjective law. It should not be forgotten that the legal term *kenri*[2] (subjective right) was invented only in the last days of the Edo period when a knowledge of Western law was first acquired. Even after the reception of the modern legal system, state law hardly ever functioned for the protection of individual rights.

With the exception of lawyers and persons with some knowledge of law, Japanese generally conceive of law as an instrument of constraint that the state uses when it wishes to impose its will. Law is thus synonymous with pain or penalty. To an honorable Japanese the law is something that is undesirable, even detestable, something to keep as far away from as possible. To never use the law, or be involved with the law, is the normal hope of honorable people. To take someone to court to guarantee the protection of

---

[1] The Chinese character corresponding to *ho* had originally three elements: water; an imaginary animal which knows how to distinguish the just from the unjust; and the action of going away or disappearing. The element "animal" is eliminated in the present form. Water here signifies impartiality because of the evenness of its surface. Thus the word *ho* means a desire to have justice rule and injustice disappear. In Japan the justice represented by *ho* was usually that of the ruling class.

[2]   In the complex grouping of characters which expresses this notion in Chinese the first character has the meaning of balance or impartiality but at the same time has an original meaning of fraud. The second means interest. At the present time almost everyone disregards the sense of impartiality that the word implies. For the average Japanese this word conjures up something related to egoism.

one's own interests, or to be mentioned in court, even in a civil matter, is a shameful thing;[3] and the idea of shame, as will be seen, is the keystone to the system of Japanese civilization. In a word, Japanese do not like law. There is no wish at all to be involved with justice in the European sense of the word.[4] Japanese are even surprised to see justice personified as in the goddess Themis, or Dike, because the word law, synonymous for them with justice, evokes a prison. Femininity, which is a symbol of tenderness, has no association at all in the Japanese mind with justice.

After reading René David's chapter on the Chinese legal system in his *Traité elementairé de droit civil comparé* it might be thought that this attitude of the Japanese derives from Confucian influence. However, though Confucian influence is undeniable, Chinese ideas constitute only one of the many factors which have gone into the formation of the Japanese conception of law. Indeed the essential factors appear to be, along with Chinese and Buddhist ideas, geographical and historical conditions and the basic character of the Japanese themselves.

The problem of the national character of the Japanese is a very difficult one and outside the general field of legal knowledge. It will, however, be dealt with here for the purpose of shedding some light on the topic in hand.

CHARACTERISTICS OF JAPANESE MENTAL ATTITUDES

It is very difficult to state with scientific precision what the characteristic traits of the mental life of a people are. Indeed it may be questioned whether there is a character type to which

---

[3] To enforce *kenri* is something that weighs on the conscience of a good citizen even if he considers his rights beyond dispute.

[4] Cf. Takeyoshi Kawashima, "Dispute Resolution in Contemporary Japan," in *Law in Japan*, p. 41f.

at least the greater part of a nation conforms.[5] In spite of the efforts made by anthropologists, ethnologists, characterologists, and psychologists to throw light on the matter the results so far have not been very convincing. But this does not prevent the perception in each people of something that can be called, in general terms, a national temperament, or a national character —Gustave Le Bon called it "the soul of the races," and André Sigfrid "the soul of the nations."[6]

While leaving to specialists the difficult task of establishing the methodical basis on which to determine national character and trying to avoid falling into the traps of amateurism, an effort will be made to delineate the Japanese national character.[7] The researches of Paul Griéger published in 1961 under the title of *La caractérologie ethnique*[8] will be used as a guide.[9] Griéger affirms that "there exists in the behavior of groups of men, in the orientation and style of their actions, even in the tools that they use (instruments, houses, language), a body of *characteristic traits* which are *relatively static*. The form and the content of these traits translate the reality of specific phenomena common to the members of a group and differentiates them from those of another group."[10] Griéger calls the discipline which studies the psychological characteristics of groups of men "ethnic characterology."

[5] René Le Senne thinks such a type can be found. Cf. *Traité de caractérologie*, 7th ed. (Paris: Presses Universitaires de France, 1963), p. 572–573. Along the same lines, cf. Paul Griéger, *La caractérologie ethnique* (Paris: Presses Universitaires de France, 1961), p. 22–24. Alex Inkels and Daniel J. Levinson on the other hand cast doubt on the scientific possibility of establishing the existence of a character type for a given nation. They categorically deny the existence of any such type, and state that "national character" is a hypothesis which has not yet been proved. Cf. "The Study of Modal Personality and Socio-Cultural Systems," in *Handbook of Social Psychology*, ed., Gardner Lindzey (Cambridge: Adisson-Wesley, 1954), Vol. II.

[6] The studies by these authors did not get much past the level of amateurism, but they nevertheless helped promote more methodical and systematic studies of the subject.

[7] "It is the study of the characterological makeup of a nation or its typical representative which will teach us about it and permit us to better foresee, if not the very acts taken in certain circumstances, at least the general patterns of that nation's conduct." Le Senne, *Traité*, p. 575.

[8] Paul Griéger, *La caractérologie ethnique: Approche et comprehension des peuples*, preface by Morot-Sir (Paris: Presses Universitaires de France, 1961). This work is volume 16 in the collection *Caractères* established by Le Senne and edited by Morot-Sir.

[9] There are very helpful bibliographies on the subject in the cited works of Griéger, Inkels, and Levinson. Cf. also, Heuse, *La psychologie ethnique* (1953).

[10] Griéger, *La caractérologie ethnique*, p. 16. Italics by Griéger himself.

By "ethnic" is meant a body of common cultural and historical elements by which nations, great or small, are psychologically recognizable.[11]

In order to distinguish one group of people from another according to character Griéger suggests the following four types as criteria: introverted, fluctuant, perpetual, and extroverted.[12] These types are called by him ethno-types, and are built up on the basis of two fundamental psychological factors: structuration and reactivity. If a people manifests a stable character, that is to say, a well-structured character, to a degree above average, that people belongs to a character ethno-type of a greater structuration. If the degree of a factor passes the average, the structuration factor is given by a capital S, and when the degree is lower than average, it is symbolized by a small s. In the same way, if a people, as a matter of habit, reacts very violently to stimulants and if the degree of reactivity is greater than average, that people ranges in an ethno-type category of a greater reactivity. By a procedure identical to that for the structuration factor, the reactivity factor if greater than average is expressed by an R, and if smaller than average by an r. By a combination of these two properties, as they exist in varying degrees, it is possible to obtain the following four ethno-types, the letter m being average:[13]

Constituent properties	Ethno-types
$R>m, S>m$: RS	Introverted
$R>m, s<m$: Rs	Fluctuant
$r<m, S>m$: rS	Perpetual
$r<m, s<m$: rs	Extroverted

According to Griéger, "each of these types is characteristic of a whole group of people. . . . It corresponds to the notion of synthesis that statisticians call typical value or central value. That is to say the value which is most frequently met in individuals of the ethnic group under consideration."[14] Using this

[11]   Ibid., p. 13.
[12]   Ibid., Chapter 3.
[13]   Ibid., p. 58.
[14]   Ibid. The word "mode" is also used in this connection in the statistical science sense of "the most frequently met value."

method as a guide it can now be determined to which of the four types the Japanese people belong. Without studying the matter in detail Griéger himself suggests that the Japanese ethnotype is introvert of R predominance (introverted R>S),[15] which means that there is a tendency toward a fluctuant type.

In order to bring out in clearer fashion what the characteristic traits of the Japanese people are, they may be compared with another type of an opposite kind, such as the French, which comes closer to an extroverted ethno-type.[16]

An introverted type is characterized by subjectivity. All his behavior is oriented toward subjectivity. He has a tendency to live within himself and tends to dwell on his own innermost thoughts. Because of this he likes dreaming and fantasy and has an aversion to rigorous logic and conceptual thinking. The extroverted type, on the other hand, is distinguished by objectivity. For him the object is more important than the subject, for he is, says Griéger, "basically directed by his objective attitude which turns his thoughts toward things, that is, outward; his kingdom is the exterior." Because of this a liking for practical decisions and an aversion to the obscure, the confused, and the indefinite is the rule.[17] Thus these two types constitute two poles in a series of character types. The others are intermediate types.

An aversion to rigorous logic and conceptual structures must be considered as the most important of the factors characterizing the legal thought of the introverted type, and there is among Japanese a very strong disposition of this kind. Japanese people to a large degree lack a sense of logic. "The principal defect of

[15] Ibid., p. 106.
[16] More precisely the French ethno-type is more complex. Le Senne thinks that the French people "fall into two characterological groups that are mixed, though somewhat unequally, according to the province: the one is called *français actif-primaire*, covering the range Danton to Voltaire, the other *français emotif-secondaire*, which includes Robespierre and Colbert." Le Senne, *Traité*, p. 576. But according to Le Senne's diagnosis the typical representative of the French nation would be *actif-emotif sous-primaire*, which distinguishes him from the extroverted type. Cf. Le Senne, *Traité*, p. 577. It nevertheless seems sufficient to refer to the extreme interest of the French in logical precision to rank them in the broad category of types with extrovert tendencies. Cf. Griéger, *La caractérologie ethnique*, p. 272–273. These two opposite character types were first discussed by the Swiss psychologist, Carl Jung in *Psychologische Typen* (1920). On this point Griéger's study is based on Jung's theory.
[17] Griéger, La *Caractérologie ethnique*, pp. 124, 152.

the Oriental spirit is the absence of any methodical reasoning. The Oriental spirit rebels against any exercise of an analytical kind or any synthesis which would enable a clear view to be obtained of an undertaking or of a study, and which alone gives thought vigor, precision and stability."[18] Edwin O. Reischauer, professor at Harvard University and former U.S. ambassador to Japan, states, "The peoples of the Far East have constantly shown much less interest in logical systems than the North Americans. They are more at home in the expression of emotion with art or in poetry than in the field of reasoned analysis."[19] These two witnesses do not speak specifically about the Japanese mentality, but since they are very knowledgeable about things Japanese there can be no doubt that they are thinking particularly of the Japanese in these passages. Finally, Grosbois, former director of the Franco-Japanese Institute of Kyoto, reaches a similar conclusion and speaks specifically about the Japanese: "Logic and rationality frighten the Japanese. They study Descartes and Kant because they must, but they prefer Bergson and Schopenhauer who are more intuitive, more fluid."[20] Indeed, the Japanese do not like logical solutions to any problem because this appears to them too decisive and too distant from the actual state of things. They prefer seeing things as they are. They have little interest in knowing if A can at the same time be not-A. The clarity and precision of thought which is so dear to the French seem to the Japanese to be incompatible with the integrity of existing things. To clarify and to give logical precision to things is to limit them, and therefore to denaturize them, from a Japanese point of view.

Remarkable evidence of the contrast between the two character types, French and Japanese, can be seen in the difference which exists between the gardening arts of the two countries. In a typical Japanese garden things are never placed symmetrically though that is one of the most characteristic elements of a French garden. A Japanese gardener deliberately avoids everything that appears artificial to him. Trees are planted in a Japanese garden

---

[18]   Bousquet, *Le Japon de nos jours*, Vol. II, p. 286.

[19]   Passages cited by Griéger, *La caractérologie ethnique*, pp. 133, 136.

[20]   Michel-Droit, *J'ai vu vivre le Japon* (Paris: Librairie Arthème Fayard, 1960), p. 120.

as if they were growing there solely by force of nature. The stones are placed in a way that gives viewers the impression that nature itself had placed them where they are.[21] Michel-Droit points out an analogous factor in ikebana (floral art): "The basic principle of ikebana is to reproduce the great impulses of nature. . . . For this long branches are used, always of an uneven number, on which flowers are still in bud form. All symmetry in the arrangement is rigorously proscribed."[22] It is a spirit of finesse in direct contrast with a geometrical spirit. Dominated noticeably by emotivity, the Japanese spirit, as Pascal said in another connection, "hardly sees things; it feels them rather than sees them. One must see a thing at a glance and not through the process of reasoning, at least to a certain degree."[23] Such a mentality, of course, is not readily compatible with law, which in the European sense requires a faultless logic.

Michel Villey has shown that the European conception of law rests on Aristotelian logic. According to him, the European jurist "knows how to abstract the general problem, compare it, and harmonize it with similar or analogous cases and draw out the rule from which the decision flows logically." This Aristotelian method is, he says, "a method that we perhaps believe to be one natural to man because it is our own but in fact it is neither natural nor universally used."[24] This is true. The peoples of the Far East, who had no knowledge of Aristotelian logic until fairly recent times, did not think of law in the same way as Europeans, and so even after the reception of European law the logical conception of law did not take root easily in their mentality.

The Japanese in particular, belonging as they do to a charac-

[21] An inquiry conducted in 1958 by the Institute of Statistical Mathematics arrived at a very interesting result on this point. Two photographs were shown to the subjects of the inquiry, asking them to choose the one they preferred. One was of the garden of the palace at Versailles and the other was that of Japanese gardens. Seventy-eight percent of those questioned chose the latter. Three other photos were then shown to the same people. They were of the Arc de Triomphe in Paris, a mosque in Iran, and the U.N. building in New York. Forty-five percent preferred the Arc de Triomphe, 28 percent the mosque, and 19 percent the U.N. building.
[22] Michel-Droit, *J'ai vu vivre le Japon*, p. 121.
[23] Blaise Pascal, *Pensées, Oeuvres complètes* (Bibliothéque de la Pleiade), p. 1092.
[24] Michel Villey, *Leçons d'histoire de la philosophie du droit* (Paris: Dalloz, 1957), p. 167.

ter-type of emotive predominance, feel an aversion to law. It should not, however, be thought that this conclusion is reached because it is reasoned through as: "constraint, because it is incompatible with liberty, is detestable; law is a means of constraint; therefore law is detestable." Such a syllogism, familiar in particular to the French, is not familiar to the Japanese. The latter only feel, without any argument, that they have an aversion to law. In these cases the Japanese will always use a cliche: "I hate (or I like) such and such a thing *tada nantonaku.*" *Tada nantonaku* is a truly Japanese expression and, for want of a better one it can be rendered as "for no particular reason." This translation is not good because there may be no particular reason for acting in a certain way, though there may be a perfectly good general reason for so acting. The Japanese cliche, on the other hand, implies that *a priori* all reasoning is excluded in the determination of one's conduct. One acts in such and such a way because one feels compelled to by emotive impulse. Even electors vote *tada nantonaku*;[25] the Japanese people are not at all used to the detailed processes of legal reasoning.[26] Indeed, in the field of law, as Radbruch says, every delicate nuance of feeling is ignored or repulsed, "legal thought is based on extreme abstraction. Man is considered without taking account of his individuality and the law constructs the legally important elements from a mass of facts. In the result there is almost nothing left of the rich forms of life with their various colors."[27] The jurist only knows the antithesis between yea and nay. As far as he is concerned he has a right or he has not. Law takes no account of the more or the less.

But the world, full as it is of life and beauty, is a world of

---

[25] At the general election of 21 November, 1963, a frivolous candidate obtained about 10,000 votes against every expectation. A high public official who had been involved with the election explained: "Among the voters there were obviously parents and friends; but there are persons who vote at every election *tada nantonaku!*"

[26] From this it may be assumed that there is a strict relationship between the structure of the language of a people and their way of thinking. Stoetzel affirms that different languages lead those who speak them to think in different ways. Cf. Jean Stoetzel, *La psychologie sociale* (1963), p. 132. Salvador de Madariaga tries to point up this correlation in his book *Portrait of Europe* (London: Hollis and Carter, 1952). Cf. also Griéger, *La caractérologie ethnique*, p. 180.

[27] G. Radbruch "*Il diritto nella visione goethiana del mondo*," in *Rivista internazionale di filosofia del dirrito* (1940), pp. 202–203.

infinite variety, and artists and poets who live in a world of subtle shades find themselves ill at ease and sometimes even lost when they move into the world of sharp antithesis. It is the same with the Japanese people who, according to Reischauer, are artists by nature: "From the top to the bottom of the social scale the Japanese give evidence of a developed artistic sense for things which are by their own tradition and good sense generalized in a thousand tiny details of daily life. The passion of Japanese for natural beauty and the high level of artistry which exists throughout the nation is clear proof of this emotive impulse."[28]

What a contrast with the national character of the French. Professor David gives a very neatly drawn portrait: "French people love legal discussions," he says "just as they like grammatical and linguistic problems, and in France those who are, on legal matters, the most exacting and punctilious are not always the lawyers."[29] "We find discussions about grammar are the most satisfying."[30] And in Molière's *Femmes savantes* (Act II, scene 6), Philaminte reproaches the kitchen maid Martine for her grammatical mistakes:

> She has with an insolence that has no equal
> After thirty lessons insulted our ears
> With the impropriety of a vulgar and savage word
> Which Vaugelas condemns in decisive terms.

Then she solemnly declares the intangible dignity of grammatical rules:

> Grammar controls the kings
> And makes even them, with all their power, obey its laws.

---

[28] Edwin O. Reischauer, *Le Japon*, p. 25, cited by Griéger, *La caractérologie ethnique*, p. 146.

[29] David, *Le droit français*, Vol. II, p. 66. He also says: "The French consider this knowledge [of law] as an almost normal element of the general culture. . . . From this derives the tendency that the French have to see problems from a legal point of view in a way that often surprises foreigners," p. 46. E. R. Curtius also emphasises this legal attitude of the French in his study of French culture, *Die französische Kultur* (Stuttgart: Deutsche Verlags-Anstalt, 1930), Chapter VIII.

[30] A. Siegfried, *L'âme des peuples* (Paris: Hachette, 1950), p. 74.

Such a tirade is inconceivable in Japanese theater. Those who go to the theater in Japan to laugh or cry[31] would be very surprised to be given a grammar lesson there. They would be even more surprised to hear a notary giving a little lecture on the law of marriage contracts.[32] In short, the French experience pleasure in detailed reasoning,[33] while the Japanese find pleasure in the stirring of their emotions.

It is not surprising to see among the Germans, whose character, like the Japanese, has a noticeable tendency toward the introverted ethno-type, many people who have given up their law studies halfway through the course in order to go and seek their vocation in some other field. Radbruch gives several examples of this, among whom Schiller, Schumann, and Heine are three of the most well known.[34] And Anselm von Feuerbach made the following admission: "From my youth" he wrote to Anselm, his son, "I was unable to get to grips with legal science, as it was contrary to my native predisposition. Even today it does not greatly arouse my interest. I was interested in history and, among other things, in philosophy too, but alas what luck. Just at that moment I met your mother. I was therefore obliged to choose an occupation which would bring me in more money than would the teaching of philosophy. I therefore decided to give up what was dear to my heart, philosophy, and get on with the law that I hated."[35] There are many Japanese, too, who have had this sort of experience.[36]

Analogous cases are not likely to be found in France. Honoré de Balzac studied law but he did not give up halfway through, and according to one author he took quite an interest in his legal

[31] Much less to laugh than to cry.

[32] Molière, *L'école des femmes*, Act IV, scene 2.

[33] "It is to the Latins that basically we owe our ability to reason and express ourselves. The French analytical ability is extraordinary. The least among us, the man in the street, possesses a singular capacity to generalize as well as the gift of being able to discern in a problem the principle which is involved and the consequence likely to follow." Siegfried, *L'âme des peuples*, p. 67.

[34] G. Radbruch, *Einführung in die Rechtswissenschaft*, 9th ed., ed., K. Zweigert (Stuttgat: K.F. Koehler Verlag, 1952), p. 250f.

[35] Ibid., p. 256.

[36] This was the author's experience too, but for a reason different from that of Feuerbach. Regrettably he did not have the luck of meeting an attractive woman at the beginning of his career. He was simply obliged to study law in spite of his complete aversion to it.

studies.[37] In 1819 he graduated bachelor of law and worked for some time in a notary's office. He used his legal knowledge in a great number of his books, and there are works dedicated to him which are entitled *Balzac as Legal Historian*,[38] and *Balzac, Romantic Lawyer*.[39] By way of further example, it is known that Stendhal read several pages of the Civil Code each day to improve his style, and this evidently also served him as some kind of exercise in reasoning. He, therefore, was not put off by the rigorous logic of legal thought.

These examples show the marked liking that French have for law. The absence of rigorous logic—or rather an indifference to logic—can on the other hand be noted in the Japanese character right from the earliest period.

Japanese people have adopted and still do adopt strange or foreign things very readily, and this is another of the characteristics of the introverted ethno-type who is, according to Griéger, avid for the acquisition of new knowledge.[40] Japan has received ideas from China, India, and Europe and, with little regard for logical coherence, the Japanese have allowed these ideas from different sources to coexist without ever asking whether one system of thought is compatible with the others.[41] Systematic thought is broken down by the Japanese into isolated conceptual elements which in the process lose their logical affinity and are reduced to basic elements, without any relationship between one another, which can then be exchanged with elements from a system which is heterogeneous from a logical

---

[37] A. Peytel, *Balzac, juriste romantique* (Paris: Editions M. Ponsot, 1950), p. 8.

[38] Saint-Germes (Madeleine), "Balzac, consideré comme historien du droit," (thesis, Dijon, 1936).

[39] A. Peytel, *Balzac*.

[40] Griéger, *La caractérologie ethique*, p. 130.

[41] "An important effect of introverted thought can be stated to be lack of clarity. The clarity which characterizes every intellectual operation in pure state is lacking as far as emotional matters are concerned from their very nature, and it is not possible to apply rigorous logic to an emotion or to a sentiment, but only to the outward manifestations accompanying the emotional state. Intellectualizing and emotionalism vary in an inverse ratio the one to the other. Emotionalism has its basis in the innermost recesses of our being and this is why a person whose mental life is controlled by emotions demonstrates little inclination or liking for rigorous logical structures. He is little worried about pure rationality in thought or conciseness in expression." Griéger, ibid., p. 135.

point of view.[42] Ideas are for the Japanese nothing more than tools that can be used for various purposes. If a saw does not do the job, you can use an axe. In the same way, if Confucianism does not give the desired result, resort may be had to Buddhism.[43]

The systems of thought that have been introduced to Japan one after the other have thus undergone no logical confrontation with each other. While one system reigns, the other systems dwell in a kingdom of oblivion, like Sleeping Beauty until a Prince Charming comes to revive them. As Maruyama Masao[44] says, diverse ideas introduced at different times and from different cultural settings, cut off as they are from their original cultural background, can coexist in the Japanese mind without any difficulty. The new idea is not structured with the preexisting ideas, which in turn were not structured with each other.[45]

The historical basis of thought is never questioned in Japan, and strictly speaking there is no history of thought in Japan because, as Denis de Rougemont points out: "The feeling of history is a characteristic of the West which was wanting in the Orient until Western influence was felt."[46] "Many ideas are crowded together

[42]   This does not of course mean a total lack of systematization. As far as the introverted person is concerned, systematization has a special attraction: "While systematization of the perpetuating ethno-type (rS) moves toward identification, that of the introverted type, with a predominance of the image over the concept, moves from abstract formalism toward *globalization* and a harmonization which integrates all the phenomena into a whole. Emotionalism here contributes toward the globalizing, toward the submersion of the various elements in the totality. Intuitive globalization seems to be a characteristic of introverted thought." (Griéger, ibid., p. 138). But since it has tendencies toward the fluctuant, Japanese thought does not show this introverted tendency in a pure form. It shows a strong tendency toward the "syncretism" in the sense of "clear understanding" or "overall picture of the whole," which characterizes the fluctuant. Cf. Griéger, ibid., p. 196.

[43]   A scholar of the Edo period, Motoori Norinaga, in an effort to point up the Shintoist quality of Japanese thought by comparison with Chinese thought, said: "If it is difficult to rule without Confucianism, rule according to Confucianism. If Buddhism is indispensible to government, use Buddhism. Both Confucianism and Buddhism constitute the temporal aspect of Shintoism." It is possible to notice here, too, the characteristic trait of the fluctuant-type pragmatism. Cf. Griéger, ibid., p. 186.

[44]   A historian of Oriental political thought.

[45]   Masao Maruyama, *Nihon no shiso* [Japanese Thought] (Tokyo: Iwanami Shoten, 1961), p. 4f. For a proper study of Japanese thought, Maruyama, *Thought and Behavior in Modern Japanese Politics*, ed., Ivan Morris (New York: Oxford University Press, 1963), is essential reading.

[46]   Denis de Rougemont, *L'aventure occidentale de l'homme* (Paris: Albin Michel, 1957), p. 123.

in the heads of Japanese without classification or grouping. Their heads are like museums in disorder where the article sought cannot readily be found."[47] Having noted that the German word *Vernunft* is used both by Kant and by every housewife, Wendt writes: "The Japanese word to express the *Vernunft* of Kant, *risei*, has no direct relationship with daily life. The conditions in which this notion of *risei* has been formed through the history of Japanese ideas are very different from those in which the notion of *Vernunft* has been cultivated. Can then a Japanese truly understand why and against what Kant has argued by his *Vernunft?* . . . What does the practical reasoning or the pure reasoning of Kant mean for a Japanese? Can his understanding grasp what Kant said to the cultivated men of central Europe, accessible as it is only to well-disciplined thought?"[48] But such a question cannot be asked of Japanese, because the word *Vernunft* is for them, like other words, a simple and useful tool, just like a European car which operates perfectly well on roads of a peculiarly Japanese type.

In this mental climate it is possible to speak of a fashion in ideas.[49] An idea is not followed because it is rationally convincing, but because it is newer and therefore satisfies curiosity so much the better. Just as fashion garments know only a passing glory, so ideas that are favored today will not be so tomorrow, though no one knows that they will not become the fashion again another day. It is the same as far as legal ideas are concerned. Sometimes French ideas, sometimes German ideas, and at other times Anglo-Saxon ideas are the fashion. If favored ideas have been replaced by new ideas it is not because they have become less convincing at a logical level. They are abandoned simply because they are considered to have become outdated. Bousquet saw one such brusque change in Japanese thought and he wrote:

---

[47] Bousquet, *Le Japon de nos jours*, Vol. II, p. 286.

[48] I. Y. Wendt, *Zen, Japan und der Westen* (München: Paul List Verlag, 1961), p. 114f.

[49] This is also a characteristic trait of the fluctuant type. "By his basic character the fluctuant ethno-type has a maximum predisposition toward the imitation of others. It is for him a basic need, subject of course to the condition that the imitation is easy. From this need is born the influence of fashion. Whether it is a matter of opinion, ideas, literary style, or merely of dress, how many people dare not fall under its influence?" Griéger, *La caractérologie ethnique*, p. 178.

"It is surprising to find the commentary on the Declaration of the Rights of Man written by one of the followers of Confucius who have suddenly become proselytes of Rousseau. . . . Always concerned with advancing quickly rather than advancing straight, the Japanese jump without transition from Louis XI to Robespierre, just as they advance from pedestrian tracks to railways. They deny themselves the time to grow, the time to pass through those necessary stages without which there can be no true progress."[50]

This cast of mind has been clearly accentuated by geographical and historical factors. Geographically isolated on islands far from the continent, the Japanese have had little occasion to mix with people of different types and have conserved their congenital characteristics in a relatively pure state.[51] Historically they have lived for a very long time under despotic regimes and, as Griéger points out, the introvert ethno-type is inclined to accept dictatorship willingly. "What attracts people of this type," he says "is a dictatorship which governs rigorously. Their type of hero will always be of the Caesar class. His manner attracts them, his authority impresses them, and his sabre frightens them. Led to rise up against an authority that is too weak, they will obey a strong authority with respect and faithfulness."[52] From this it follows that there is a lack of critical evaluation and no independence of spirit.

Both Confucianism and Buddhism have favored this state of mind. Confucius taught that the hierarchical order of a society is natural and absolute and cannot be changed at will. Everyone must rigorously observe the duties that this order imposes upon him. Willing obedience is the principal human virtue. Buddhism in its turn preaches resignation. Blessed is submission to fate, for it is the source of all true happiness. Do not rebel against the conditions in which you find yourself, but follow your fate to the end. These two doctrines became deeply ingrained in the subconscious of the Japanese people for over more than a thousand years, and against such a background it is very

[50] Bousquet, *Le Japon de nos jours*, Vol. II, p. 282–283.
[51] Griéger notes that geographical isolation favours exaggeration in certain character types. *La caractérologie ethnique*, p. 74.
[52] Griéger, ibid., p. 116.

difficult for a lively consciousness of subjective rights to be created. However, the dignity of the individual is closely linked to such a consciousness, and both are of the essence of modern law.

The unique value of each individual as a creature of God is without doubt one of the great revelations of Christianity for all mankind. Yet since they were beyond the influence of Christian ideas, except for a short period in the sixteenth century, the Japanese had no thought that all men were equal before God. The Japanese word *jinkaku*, which corresponds to the notion of personality, was not known until 1877. Japanese, even today, worry little about their rights, and this is an aspect of Japanese legal life which attracts the attention of Western observers.[53]

In the long and painful historical process by which individual rights have developed in the West it is not possible to overestimate the role that the politico-legal ideas of the right to resist and of social contract have played. These ideas have been among the effective causes of revolutions which have opened the way to social reform in the West. The history of Japan, however, knew no such revolutionary ideas. Even in China there were many changes of dynasties and of governments. In that country the political ideal maintained was that the emperor was authorized to occupy the throne on condition that he was virtuous, and, although Japan received many other Chinese ideas, its thought never accepted this theory. Even today the tradition is very much alive, and most Japanese regard the word revolution as something slightly frightening. In pure theory they can be persuaded of the legitimacy of the right to resist, but in their hearts they feel, *tada nantonaku*, that they must abstain from resisting any superior authority.[54] They are dumbfounded when a man as prudent as Geny concludes: " 'Resistance to oppression judiciously understood, wisely contained within its limits, manipulated

[53] E.g., cf. K. Takayanagi, "The Development of Japanese Law, 1868–1961," p. 39 in particular; T. Kawashima, "Dispute Resolution in Contemporary Japan"; K. Tanabe, "The Process of Litigation: An Experiment with the Adversary System," p. 77 in particular, in *Law in Japan;* and Arthur von Mehren's commentary on p. 191f.
[54] Cf. p. 91, note 40. The trend to subordination to authority is still strong among the Japanese.

with tact, remains . . . the supreme guarantee of justice and right."[55]

THE RULES OF GIRI

The Japanese manner of thinking clearly favors neither the formation nor the functioning of law as a conceptually arranged system of rights and duties. This does not, however, mean that there is no rule of conduct which functions for the maintenance of the social order. Before the modern system of state law was established, a system of social rules of a non-legal nature directed the lives of Japanese, and that system continues to operate today, side by side with the more clearly defined system of state law. Whether this fluid system be called "custom"[56] or "non-law"[57] its rules play a very important part in Japanese social life. The system of a purely legal nature is penetrating gradually deeper into the life of Japan and the system of the past will eventually disappear, but the evolution will be slow and difficult because the ethnic character of the Japanese both facilitates the survival of the former system and compromises the proper functioning of the modern one. In addition, there is the conservatism of government which supports the natural inclination of the people.

The traditional rules that the Japanese obey are called the rules of *giri*.[58] They are rules of conduct, and do not presuppose the existence of any relationship of clearly defined and quantitatively delimitable rights and duties between the subjects whose conduct they regulate. The rules of *giri* are of a singular nature, and it is very difficult to explain them in an entirely satisfactory fashion.[59]

[55] F. Geny, *Science et technique en droit privé positif* (Paris: Sirey, 1924), Vol. II, p. 134.

[56] H. Levy-Bruhl, *Sociologie du droit* (Paris: Presses Universitaires de France, 1961), p. 41.

[57] J. Carbonnier, "L'hypothese du non-droit," *Archives de philosophie du droit*, No. 8, (1963), p. 55f.

[58] Cf. Stoetzel, *Jeunesse sans chrysanthème ni sabre*, p. 191.

[59] See Ruth Benedict, *The Chrysanthemum and the Sword: Patterns of Japanese Culture* (New York: Houghton Mifflin, 1947). Though it contains certain errors and mistakes of detail this is an excellent book, and one of the best guides to the nature of *giri* for people of the Western world.

The word *giri* is difficult to define, even in Japanese, because it evokes many ideas which are difficult to group together into one general notion.[60] Attempts have been made to define it in a coherent manner, but any such undertaking encounters almost insurmountable difficulties. A Japanese sociologist who studied the problem in detail sees a similarity between the notion of *giri* and that of *potlatch*.[61] Such a comparison undoubtedly defines the notion of *giri* to a certain degree, but does so at the risk of excluding from it certain of its essential elements. It is therefore necessary to be satisfied with listing some of the characteristics of *giri* without worrying too much about conceptualization. *Giri* (*gi*, just or right; *ri*, reason or reasonable behavior) means the manner of behavior required of one person to others in consequence of his social status. More specifically:

1. *Giri* is a duty or the state of a person who is bound to behave in a prescribed way toward a certain other person. The content of this duty or obligation varies greatly according to the situation in which the subject of the duty is placed and of the person toward whom the duty is owed. There is the *giri* of a child to his parents, that of the student to his teacher, that of a beneficiary to his benefactor (*onjin*), that of one friend to another, and so on.

2. The person toward whom the duty is owed has no right to demand its fulfillment from the subject of the duty. He must wait for the latter to fulfill it voluntarily. Anyone who does not satisfy his *giri* in the desired manner is seriously dishonored, but the other party must avoid applying pressure to oblige him to fulfill his duty. If the beneficiary of the duty applies pressure for performance of the duty, he in his turn violates *giri*. Usually the beneficiary of the duty is himself bound by another *giri* relationship of which the content is determined by the special link which unites him to the person bound in his regard, and the two sub-

[60] Imprecision of this kind can already be noted in the relationship between the lord and his vassals in the Kamakura period. Cf. Joüon des Longrais, *L'Est et l'Ouest*, p. 147f.

[61] Cf. S. Sakurai, *On to giri* (Tokyo: Asahi-sha, 1961). To reach this conclusion the author uses the studies of Marcel Mauss, *Sociologie et anthropologie*, 3rd ed. (Paris: Presses Universitaires de France, 1966) and of G. Davy, *La foi jurée* (Paris: F. Alcan, 1922) The definition and explanation of *potlatch* is found in Davy's book, p. 24f.

jects of the rules are thus placed in a condition of reciprocal obligation. This relationship does not, however, constitute a synallagmatic contract sanctioned by the exception *non adimpleti contractus*, as that would presuppose that the two parties had entered into the arrangement of their own free will.[62]

3. The relations of *giri* are perpetual. They are not extinguished, even when a duty deriving from *giri* has been performed by the "debtor." *Giri* relationships are maintained outside time limitations and are continually giving rise to duties. Even between a merchant and his customer the relationship tends to be permanent. If the *giri* relationship has been established between them, the customer who buys from another merchant is considered as failing in his *giri*. In return for continuing custom a merchant gives his customer advantages of both a material and general kind.

4. *Giri* relationships are founded on feelings of affection. They have an emotive quality.[63] The relationship must not be conceived of as being in consideration of an interest or profit that is anticipated, though in practice there are many cases where feelings of *giri* are mixed with selfish desires. Japanese people are, however, bound to behave, at least in appearance, as if they act for reasons of affection coupled with feelings of duty.[64] This feeling of affection is called *ninjo* (natural human affection). The two feelings of *giri* and *ninjo* are so closely related that they are often referred to by the compound *giri-ninjo*. No one wants to be regarded by others as a person who acts only in his own interests, and it is said of a person who does act in that way that "he does not know his *ninjo*," and he is considered abnormal from the social point of view. For this reason few people in Japan would consider entering into a marriage contract or take time to think

---

[62] Benedict considers that the rules of *giri* are strictly rules aiming at guaranteeing something in return: "Repayment of *giri* is thought of as repayment of an exact equivalent." *Chrysanthemum*, pp. 140, 142. Of course, a person who has received the performance of an act of *giri* feels obliged to reciprocate, and this obligation is called *okaeshi* (return). But nevertheless it seems to me that the value of *okaeshi* is not always the equivalent, in objective terms, of the act of *giri* which preceded it.

[63] Remember in this context that the character trait of the Japanese is a predominantly emotional one.

[64] Maruyama says: "Private affairs accordingly involved something shady and were regarded as akin, or even equivalent, to evil. This applied particularly to profit-making and to love." *Thought and Behavior*, p. 7.

about matrimonial property regimes. Everyone believes that conjugal relations must be exclusively ruled according to *ninjo* and that they are by their nature incompatible with monetary preoccupations. A fiancé who would think of regulating the future matrimonial property relationship before marriage would be considered by his future spouse as *mizukusai*, a person who "smells of water," a person whose affection is likely to be submerged by material preoccupation. The force of this attitude is shown by the small number[65] of marriage contracts that have been concluded since the promulgation of the Civil Code, and also by the number of articles in the Japanese Civil Code dealing with matrimonial property regimes, the number of which is very limited by comparison with the French Civil Code.[66]

5. *Giri* relationships are imbued with principles of a hierarchical order characteristic of feudalism. *Giri* duties are derived from the social status of the subject of the duty, and in the feudal hierarchy of Japan until the Restoration of 1868[67] the station in society of each person was strictly determined. To remain faithful in his *bungen*[68] was the chief virtue required of a Japanese in feudal society. It follows that the content of the *giri* of a socially inferior person toward his superior is not the same, even where there is a relationship of reciprocal duties, as that of the *giri* of the superior to the inferior. For example, in the relationships between merchants and their customers, which are governed by the principles of a hierarchy, the customers are always considered

[65] Article 756 of the Civil Code provides that a contract entered into to modify the statutory matrimonial regime does not bind third parties unless it is registered before the marriage declaration. Since the coming into force of the Civil Code on 16 July, 1898, the number of contracts registered in any year has never exceeded 20. The total number of contracts registered from 1898 to 1953 was 337. In the years following World War II there were hardly any contracts registered. Four were registered in 1950, and one in 1953. In the light of this experience the Civil Code Reform Commission proposes the abrogation of the articles of the code relating to marriage contracts.
[66] Eight articles as against one hundred and fifty-nine.
[67] Japanese generally call this social and political change *ishin* (reform) or *fukko* (restoration), and not revolution.
[68] Cf. p. 33. "Inequality is organized. It has a number of ranks. The relation ships of subordination and superiority are complex and the notion which truly characterizes the structure is that of a hierarchy. Already existing in the earliest period, developed with feudalism to a point where, in the Edo era, there were 360 divisions, the hierarchy has left many traces in modern Japan." Stoetzel, *Jeunesse sans chrysanthème ni sabre*, p. 53.

superior to the merchants for the sole reason that they are clients. In the case of a sale, therefore, there is not just a simple legal relationship existing between the seller and the buyer. Of course, the merchant has the duty to deliver the thing sold to his client, but he may not fulfill this duty in just any manner. He must conform to his *giri*. He must show his client the deference appropriate to indicate his own inferiority. A large shop in Tokyo instructs its employees: "We have from time immemorial called our clients Sir and Madam *Zenshu* [former master] to express our feelings of respect toward them. The manner of behaving in front of our clients cannot be democratic." The departmental head of a company has not fully acquitted his *giri* toward his subordinates if he has only given them directions, however perfect, for their professional activity. A good head knows his *giri-ninjo* and always has a concern for the personal and domestic affairs of his inferiors.[69] In return, those inferiors must be ready to help their head of department in his private affairs. For example, when he is involved in a house-shifting operation they must assist him gratuitously.

6.   The rules of *giri* are not imposed by means of a system of public constraint but are sanctioned simply by a feeling of honor. Those who fail in their *giri* are seriously dishonored in the eyes of those around them. They lose face; they will say, "I cannot look the world in the face." Everyone in Japan is very sensitive about his honor; there is an effort to save face at any cost. It is this feeling of shame which prevents a person from acting immorally, or doing any act contrary to *giri*. Restraint is exercised because it is known that if a certain act is committed, a feeling of shame will follow.

Ruth Benedict distinguishes two types of civilization: one

[69]   In the inquiries of 1953 and 1958 a striking result was obtained. Those questioned had to express a preference for one of two different types of bosses described to them—*Type A:* a man who always follows the rules and never orders his subordinates to do anything unreasonable, but who never takes any interest in their personal affairs which have nothing to do with the work situation; *Type B:* a man who sometimes requires his subordinates to do jobs outside the regulations, but who does take an interest in the non-work affairs of his subordinates. In the first inquiry 85 percent preferred type B; and in the second 77 percent.

founded on the idea of shame and the other on the idea of sin.[70] In the second the non-observance of a moral rule is considered a sin. The feeling of sin weighs heavily on the conscience of the individual. Each person in this type of civilization tries to avoid doing evil, simply because he does not wish to have to suffer pangs of conscience. What others think does not matter. In a civilization based on shame, however, people refrain from doing wrong to avoid being criticized by others. Consequently, if there is no one to see the commission of a wrongful act, a person in the latter civilization will readily do it because he will not be likely to suffer dishonor for it. Therefore, in those places where the idea of shame dominates, people are continually concerned about the attitude of others even in regard to the most trivial events of private life. It is because of this psychological sanction that the rules of *giri* are observed scrupulously.

INFLUENCE OF THE RULES OF GIRI

Generally speaking, where the rules of *giri* dominate, the rules of a purely legal nature have difficulty penetrating; the emotional excludes the legal. The nature of the rules of *giri* does not favor the invasion of their domain by the notion of subjective rights, because if this happened social relationships would be regulated in a clear-cut manner by norms with a defined area of relevance, and duties would lose their emotive aspect; they would be qualitatively and quantitatively delimited, and execution would no longer depend on the mental attitude of the person under the obligation. People would take notice of the equality of all subjects before the law, and that would destroy the hierarchical order. It is therefore quite natural that those who are concerned with the maintenance of the social order do their best to create conditions which favor the survival of the rules of *giri*. Even

[70] Benedict, *Chrysanthemum*, pp. 222–223, speaks of "shame culture" and "guilt culture": "In anthropological studies of different cultures the distinction between those which rely heavily on shame and those that rely heavily on guilt is an important one. . . . True shame cultures rely on external sanctions for good behavior, not, as true guilt cultures do, on an internalized conviction of sin. Shame is a reaction to other people's criticism."

after the reception of modern legal thought, state law, which was founded on rational principles incompatible with the idea of *giri*,[71] was unable to regulate the social life of the Japanese people, and social conflicts have been and still are regulated for the most part outside the state law system.[72] Even the courts operate less as instruments of judgment than as organs of conciliation.

In rural areas, where a community conscience remains, resistance to modern law is very strong. There the relationship between owners and farmers, for example,[73] has for a long time been regarded as resting on *giri*. The farmers can cultivate the land thanks to the *go-on*, or favor, of the owners and not because they have rights under any contract of lease. They do pay rent for the use of the land, but this is in execution of their duty of *giri*, which is owed toward the owners, and not in execution of a contractual duty. The owners in their turn are not simply parties to a lease. They are superiors vis-à-vis the farmers in the hierarchical order of the peasant community. In these conditions the lessees must perform their part not only by paying the rent but also by fulfilling other duties that their social position imposes upon them vis-à-vis the landlords, their superiors. In return the latter grant them material and moral favors of various kinds. These relationships can be assimilated very readily to those that exist between parents and children, where human affection (*ninjo*) must dominate. To ask for the satisfaction of one's rights in this type of circumstance would be shameful. According to Kawashima, a peasant who filed a plaint in court to have a joint ownership dispute settled was condemned by the inhabitants of his village, and for three generations he and his descendants were refused the right to take a spouse from among the villagers.

Although the Japanese Civil Code regulates the obligations of contractors in almost the same way as the French Civil Code, in practice these contracts are not regulated as in France. The

---

[71] "In short, a wide discrepancy has existed between state law and the judicial system on the one hand, and operative social behavior, on the other." Kawashima, "Dispute Resolution in Contemporary Japan," p. 46.

[72] Cf. studies by Kawashima, ibid., and Tanabe, "The Process of Litigation."

[73] The relationships between workers are considered in the same way. Cf. Chapter 1.

practice is for the contractor to write to the principal requesting him to fulfil his duties. At the level of pure law the principal must fulfil his contractual duties even without any letter, but in the world of *giri* the contractor, who is hierarchically inferior to the principal, hopes that by this letter future conflicts between the principal and himself will be regulated not in a legal manner but through the grace or special favor of the principal. Parties very rarely appear in court for the enforcement of their rights, and though only a specific type of contract has been mentioned the position is the same for almost all other contracts.

In the field of obligations the Japanese legal solutions to problems do not differ greatly from those of the European legal systems, but Western jurists are often surprised to notice that the average number of court cases in this field of law is very much higher in their own countries.[74] When a person suffers loss in Japan he reacts in a special way. Characteristically:[75]

1. Japanese have difficulty in distinguishing the legitimate exercise of rights from extortion. It is regarded as extortionary, if not avaricious, to bring a claim for damages before the courts, even when the claim is against the author of the damage suffered.

2. Japanese seek to avoid altering their personal relationship with the author of any injury suffered. They do not bring an action, because to do so would seriously affect the feelings and honor of the defendant.

3. The Japanese are not greatly sensitive to the damage which they suffer. Having been continuously exposed over the years to natural and human scourges, such as earthquakes,

[74] E.g., Léon Julliot de La Morandière, *Travaux de la semaine internationale de droit de Paris de 1950* (Paris: Pedone, 1954), p. 894. Unfortunately we do not have accurate statistics of the number of cases in the field, but a general idea of the trend can be gained from the following table relating to road accidents which Kawashima published in his article ("Dispute Resolution in Contemporary Japan," p. 63):

	1953	1954	1955	1956	1957	1958	1959
Cases	20	20	22	20	19	18	24
Persons killed or injured in accidents	4,645	5,158	5,169	5,451	5,818	6,044	6,371

Recently, because of the increasing number of motorcar accidents and public nuisances, the number of cases litigated has increased surprisingly.

[75] Cf. the very interesting article by Kato Ichiro, a specialist in the field of civil liability, "The Treatment of Motor Vehicle Accidents," in *Law in Japan*, p. 400.

typhoons, fires, civil wars, and despotic governments, they are accustomed to accepting with submission the results of external forces, which they regard as inevitable. They readily resign themselves to their fate and do not seek to improve their lot by recourse to the law. The most frequent means of resolving a damage case is for the victim of the injury to renounce his right to indemnity. Usually what happens is that the author of the damage comes to offer his apologies and at the same time offers a sum of money. The sum is frequently much less than the extent of the damage suffered by the victim, but the victim is quickly moved by a more or less sympathetic attitude on the part of the author of the injury. It is not the amount of the indemnity but the sincere attitude worthy of *giri-ninjo* on the part of the offender which is the important thing to the victim. Sometimes the victim is so moved by the sincerity of the author of his loss that he does not accept the sum offered to him. Exceptionally, the victim may seek reparation from the author of his loss, but even in this case he does not want to go to court. He resorts rather to the authority of some person such as a notable in the community or a police officer who has influence over the person who has injured him. More rarely the victim even proceeds to court, but this is only done in order to achieve an amicable settlement of the dispute through the good offices of the court. Such extra-judicial procedures are considered more honorable and desirable than the judicial. They save face for both parties.

The cases that are brought to court mostly concern relationships between large enterprises which are competing with each other for purely economic interests, or between moneylenders and their debtors.[76] Nevertheless, even big companies do not seek a legal answer to their problems when the enterprises concerned are those between which there exists a close business link. People in the business world say that a client who has an obligation toward an enterprise should not be called a debtor, because the very use of the word might leave an unfavorable impression with the client. Even in the business world, therefore, relationships are imbued with *giri-ninjo*.

---

[76]   The usurer has no delicate feelings toward his debtor.

THE FUTURE OF GIRI

The manner of thought and behavior of a people is not something static. It is dynamic and constantly changing, even though there always remains in the spirit of a people a central core which permits them to retain their individuality notwithstanding the continuing transformation. It is particularly important to bear this dynamic quality in mind because all that has been said of the mental outlook of the Japanese people is concerned only with the present attitude, the present outlook, which, though formed by a thousand years of development, in no way precludes the possibility of great development in the future.[77] Indeed, the Japanese state of mind is changing at a rapidly increasing rate. The traits described here as those most characteristic of the Japanese mental outlook are much less marked among the younger than among the older members of the community,[78] and young Japanese do not know the full detail of the rules of *giri* even though they may have the same mental outlook as their elders. The older generation often complain that the young do not know how to behave according to *giri-ninjo*, that they are too hard and calculating.

Present indications are that the Japanese attitude to law will continue to become more Westernized but that the Japanese outlook will not necessarily come to be identical with that of the West. Japan has often adopted European ideas which have enriched the Japanese spirit greatly, particularly with respect to rationality and objectivity, but this has never prevented the Japanese spirit from retaining its congenital characteristics. The Japanese spirit will change in the course of time, but it will always be Japanese.

[77] Concerning ethnic stereotypes, see Otto Klineberg, *Psychologie sociale*, trans. R. Avigdor-Coryell (Paris: Presses Universitaires de France, 1959), Vol. II, p. 544f.

[78] Relying on the results of his inquiry in Japan in 1952, Stoetzel thinks, with certain reservations, that the notion of *giri* represents a tradition that is on the decline. "A precise knowledge of the meaning of *giri* becomes less common the younger the person asked; *giri* is a notion which at present seems to be in decline; young adults who have heard it spoken of frequently make the error of giving it a purely material connotation. The youngest persons asked very clearly knew it least well." *Jeunesse sans chrysanthème ni sabre*, pp. 193, 197.

SOURCES OF LAW

CHAPTER X

LEGISLATION

In Japan the starting point for a study of the sources of law[1] is article 3 of the decree of *Dajokan* no. 103 of 8 June, 1875. This article is reminiscent of article 1 of the Swiss Civil Code, which it predates, and though it is not possible to establish exactly what the origin of the text is,[2] at the time when the article was promulgated, almost all Japanese laws had their origin in Western laws. It would therefore be reasonable to assume that this text was of European origin too.[3]

The decree is entitled "Directives for the Administration of Justice," and article 3 provides that in civil matters a judge must, in the absence of written laws, decide according to custom; in the absence of custom he must decide taking into account *jori*.[4]

---

[1]   On the notion of "sources of law" cf. Paul Amselek, *Méthode phénoménologique et théorie du droit* (Paris: Librairie Générale de Droit et Jurisprudence, 1964), p. 164; Léon Julliot de La Morandière, *Traité de droit civil* (Paris: Dalloz, 1957), Vol. I, No. 178, p. 109; Virally, *La pensée juridique* (Paris: Librairie Générale de Droit et Jurisprudence, 1960), p. 148f.

[2]   Cf. N. Sugiyama, "Le pouvoir du juge et la libre recherche scientifique d'après la loi japonaise du 8 juin, 1875," in *Ma mission en France* (Tokyo: Maison Franco-Japonaise, 1936), p. 75f.

[3]   Article 6 (2) of the Spanish Civil Code is very similar to the Japanese text but the former code was promulgated on 25 July, 1889. The Argentinian Civil Code, promulgated in 1869, has a similar article (article 16), although it does not mention custom. There is no proof, however, that this code was known in Japan at that time. Of more importance, therefore, is article 7 of the Austrian Civil Code of 1811.

[4]   *Jo* (straight line) and *ri* (reason); *jori* corresponds therefore to *recta ratio* in the Ciceronian sense. The term *jori* is much used by jurists at present in those cases where French lawyers would invoke general principles of law. The term, however, was not invented at the time of the reception of Western law, but was known in the Edo period too. An original Japanese philosopher, Miura Baien, understands this term to mean reason or the universal law which dominates all the physical and moral world. It is not known, however, whether the legislator in 1875 took the word from this source.

This text, which has not been abrogated, shows that Japanese law admits a hierarchy of sources of law. Legislation constitutes the primary source, then comes custom, and *jori* is a subsidiary source. The article does not mention case law, though in Japan as in Europe case law is very important, nor is the text of 1875 exclusive. Even between law and custom the hierarchical order is not always clearly indicated. Article 1 of the Commercial Code provides that, "In commercial matters commercial custom shall apply in the absence of provisions in this code, and in the absence of custom the provisions of the Civil Code shall apply." Commercial custom therefore takes precedence over the civil law enactments in commercial affairs.

The Japanese word corresponding to "legislation" is *horitsu*. It may be interpreted widely or restrictively. In the broad sense *horitsu* means law in its entirety, whether written or not. Used in this sense there are the expressions *horitsugaku* (science of law), and *horitsu ka* (jurists). In the narrower and more technical sense *horitsu* means the rules of law established by Parliament. Article 59 of the Constitution uses the term in this narrow sense when it speaks of a bill becoming *horitsu* after it is voted by the two Houses. Not all rules of law voted by Parliament are, however, in the form of *horitsu*. The budget, for example, which is considered by most Japanese public lawyers to have the character of a rule of law, is called *yosan*.

Legislation in Japan, as in Romano-Germanic systems, is the most important of the formal sources of law, and a judge is required to apply it to the cases that come before him in preference to all other sources of law. Legislation is not, of course, as the school of exegesis would have it, the sole source of law, and a judge can refer to other sources of law in the case of the absence, obscurity, or inadequacy of the legislation, for his function is not so much to apply the preexisting law faithfully as to give a reasonable solution to the social conflicts that arise, without the parties having to ask whether laws exist to regulate their dispute or not. In the usual run of cases the judge finds legislation to apply, since all the important matters likely to cause legal disputes are now regulated by legislation. In this sense, and in this sense only, legislation is the primary source of law.

STATUTES

The rules promulgated by Parliament have a value superior
to that of all other state rules.

The Constitution established by Parliament has a peculiar
character and is considered a supreme norm and distinct from
other legislation. Article 98 declares: "This Constitution is the
supreme law of the nation." Japanese people regard their Constitution as a sacred and intangible norm which must rule the
whole nation now and in the future. This political outlook is to
be contrasted with that of the French, who, according to Ardant,
are "intensely legal minded." They have a tendency to hold their
political institutions responsible for the failures of both internal
and external politics. If the institution and the regime are
changed, the situation of the country and of every person in it
will be improved: good institutions cannot but produce good
policies.[5] It is for this very reason that there have been about
twenty constitutions in France in the last 150 years. For the
French the Civil Code occupies a place analogous to that of the
Constitution for the Japanese, and in the period in which there
have been twenty or so constitutions the Civil Code has retained
its basic identity. In systematic studies of French law, constitutional law is not used as the starting point;[6] in Japan, constitutional law is always dealt with at the beginning.

Subordinate to the Constitution a great number of laws
regulate all the legal life of the Japanese people. An attempt is
being made to codify them to facilitate access to the law by the
people, but the end is not yet in sight, and the bulk of the law
remains uncodified. There are so far six codes: the Constitution,
the Civil Code, the Commercial Code, the Code of Civil Procedure, the Criminal Code, and the Code of Criminal Procedure.

[5] Philippe Ardant, "Droit constitutionnel et libertés publiques," in *Le droit
français*, ed., René David, Vol. II, p. 339.
[6] In the Dalloz codes the Constitution appears in the Administrative Law Code.
It is unthinkable to a Japanese lawyer that the Constitution should be found among
administrative laws. Without exception the Constitution of Japan is placed first in
all collections of legislation.

1. The Constitution

The present Constitution was promulgated on 3 November, 1946 and came into force on the 3 May, 1947.[7] It was prepared under the strict supervision of the Occupation Forces in conditions that were unfavorable to the preparation of the basic law of a nation. Certain people think that it is nothing more than a Constitution imposed on the country by a foreign force, and because of this it must be abandoned or completely revised. This claim is at first sight legitimate and finds acceptance with those of conservative tendencies. It is natural, too, that such criticism should provoke a lively reaction among sentimental patriots. Profiting from this situation, governments of a reactionary character have tried to foster a movement for revision of the Constitution.

In 1956 the government created within itself a commission called the Committee for Constitutional Research (*Kempo chosa-kai*) which had the revision of the Constitution as its aim.[8] An effort was made to avoid calling this body by a name which would make any allusion to revision of the Constitution for fear that it would be suspected by the nation that it was intended to modify the Constitution. It was explained in Parliament that the committee was only to make a theoretical study of the Constitution to see if there were any provisions in it that were defective. The committee was composed of thirty parliamentarians and twenty persons from other fields. The nomination of the parliamentarians was to have been made in proportion to the number of seats held by the two largest political parties, the Liberal Democrats and the Socialists. However, though the twenty members of the conservative party were soon named, the Socialist Party, which knew the real intention of the government, categorically refused to participate. As far as the Socialist Party, to whose views all those of progressive tendencies subscribed, was concerned, the committee was bound finally to decide, on the

---

[7] The third of May is the national festival which commemorates the promulgation of the Constitution. In recent years the government has shown itself indifferent to this festival, and this is some proof of its loss of respect for the Constitution.

[8] This committee was set up by law no. 140 of 11 June, 1956.

vote of the majority of its members, in favor of revision, and the participation of the minority would only serve to justify the decision and would not lead the discussions in any worthwhile direction.

Takayanagi, former professor of the Faculty of Law of Tokyo University, was named president, and he had the committee decide at the outset that it would not express any opinion of its own but would simply publish the opinions expressed by its members. The committee worked for almost eight years[9] and then presented a final report to cabinet and Parliament. Theoretically the committee succeeded in following its own basic principle. No decision was taken either for or against the revision of the Constitution. However, a strong tendency toward revision is shown to be the majority opinion, and there is no doubt that the report will be fully used by the revisionists to achieve their aims.

Even the defenders of the Constitution in its present form regret that it was prepared and promulgated during the Occupation. There was at the time of the revision[10] no text analogous to article 89 of the French Constitution to forbid the modification of the Constitution during foreign occupation, and there was no way of contesting what happened because the political and social circumstances were unfavorable to a free manifestation of the national will. The opinion of the revisionists, therefore, has some foundation. Even so, no one should in all conscience agree to a hasty revision of the Constitution, because that would encourage the reactionary political movement which has already manifested itself in different forms since the conclusion of the peace treaty. The revisionists would not be satisfied with a simple reform of the law to affirm Japan's political independence. Their real intention is to reestablish the former absolutist regime. They have a vivid recollection of a political system in which the greatness

[9] The committee held its first full session in August, 1957, and its last in July, 1964. Its report is public. At the time this committee was set up, another committee called the Commission for Constitutional Studies (*Kempo kenkyu-kai*) was set up privately. Made up of progressives this second committee is clearly anti-revisionist, and its works are much more objective. The two committees with their divergent tendencies should not be confused.

[10] The present Constitution is in form a simple revision of the preceding one.

of the empire of Japan shone out. This greatness was in fact based on the general poverty of the nation and a cruel oppression of freedom of thought, but given the fact that the national character of the Japanese is predominantly emotive it is easy to find support for revision by an appeal to sentiment. The Japanese is freely disposed to acting blindly under the impulse of an opinion which appeals to his sensibility or to his national vanity. If there is a general tendency favoring the revision of the Constitution, he will be inclined to follow the fashion without questioning whether the reform really coincides with his own wishes. He is an easy prey for demogogues. While recognizing its imperfections, the Japanese must protect the Constitution until the whole nation understands the true nature of democracy.

The mere existence of a constitutional text which declares the principle of democracy is not enough to establish a truly democratic regime, but a Constitution which is materially democratic can, in spite of the defects of its form, protect a nation against the currents of reaction. The present Constitution is not so defective that it ought to be recast immediately. The experience of almost thirty years of application reveals no serious problem other than a lively controversy of an ideological nature concerning a few of its provisions. Its style and construction are far from perfect, but this sort of defect is not the monopoly of the Japanese Constitution and is not, as Takayanagi, president of the Committee for Constitutional Research, himself concluded, a sufficient reason for revision.

Not all the points discussed by the committee will be dealt with here, but two important problems on which public opinion is clearly divided deserve mention. The first relates to the tenno. The revisionists would like to strengthen the legal position of the tenno and one day bring back a purer form of monarchy. Such a return to the past would not be difficult. The feelings of the nation toward the tenno have not changed much in recent times, and the Japanese would be ready to accord to the emperor greater governmental power without reflecting very much on the political significance of such a reform. Those who defend the Constitution do not lack respect for the tenno, but they have not forgotten that the omnipotence of the tenno surrounded by a militaristic clique in the recent past stifled individual liberty and dignity in the nation, and the danger of militarism has not completely disappeared, as can be seen from a consideration of the second problem.

The second problem concerns the famous article 9 of the Constitution.[11] Article 9 proclaims the decision of the Japanese people to renounce recourse to war as a means of regulating international conflict forever. To achieve this aim the Constitution forbids the maintenance by Japan of armed forces of any sort—land, sea, or air. This solemn declaration, which was born of a deep regret for the tragedy of World War II and from the fearful experience of the explosion of the atomic bombs dropped on Hiroshima and Nagasaki, was received enthusiastically throughout the world. To understand the state of mind of the Japanese people at the time one has only to read the words of the members of government that were pronounced on the occasion of the presentation of this article to Parliament. "The most important characteristic of our present Constitution," said Mr. Ashida, president of the Commission for the Revision of the Constitution, "is that it has courageously and forthrightly declared the renunciation of all war. This is the vow of all those who have passed through the experience of this great war which was undertaken at the cost of tens of millions of victims, and this is, moreover, the way toward world peace. In raising the flag which this ideal symbolizes we mean to direct an appeal to the whole world. (Applause) This is the only opportunity given to Japan to live again, and I thank God that he has given us this chance. (Applause) This having been said, the Constitution, even if it is written in a grand style, will remain meaningless unless the nation understands its aim and is imbued with its spirit. Failing this the rebirth of Japan will be impossible. (Applause)"

"The article concerning the renunciation of war," Yoshida Shigeru, the prime minister, said, in his turn, "does not directly deny the right to legitimate defense, but since its second paragraph suppresses all rearmament and every right of belligerence that

[11] There is an in-depth study on this article by Fukase, "Théorie et réalités de la formule constitutionnelle japonaise de renonciation a la guerre," p. 1109f.

the state may have, the result is that the Constitution has renounced all sorts of war, even those undertaken as operations of
legitimate defense, and equally renounces all forms of belligerence. The recent wars were undertaken on the pretext of
legitimate defense. It was the same with the Manchurian conflict,
and it was the same in the case of the Greater East Asia War.
Japan has manifested in its Constitution its will to renounce
belligerence in all its forms. Some claim that war undertaken in
the name of legitimate defense is just, but I consider that such a
viewpoint is dangerous. (Applause) It is obvious that the recent
wars were fought in the name of legitimate defense. Any view
therefore which accepts the legitimacy of such wars, has the
danger of favoring such events." Finally, Shidehara, who is re-
puted to be the promoter of article 9 said, "The best way to
assure peace is to completely and voluntarily suppress all rearmament and to renounce war instead of having an imperfect
and useless military establishment. What is stronger than arms
is the unity of the nation. A disarmed people is more powerful
than an army, if it is united in solidarity. It is absolutely impossible to carry out the genocide of eighty million people. . . .
If each citizen maintains his belief in justice, he has nothing to
fear if he is disarmed. On the other hand an enormous military
force bankrupts a state, and this in turn leads to great anxiety
in daily life. For these reasons we can be more at ease without
soldiers than with them."

This ideal was not destined to remain that of the conservative
politicians for very long. Immediately after the conclusion of the
peace treaty in San Francisco on 8 September, 1951, which put
an end to the Occupation, there was a reaction against the
Constitution by the conservatives. Even those who had most
loudly praised it began to find in it evidence of national humiliation. The glory of yesterday became the humiliation of today.
The ideal of complete disarmament, which they had been obliged
to espouse when it was difficult for them to express themselves
freely, had been transformed into a yoke. They therefore under-
lined the excessive and illusory idealism of this constitutional
clause as if the ideal had been an ideal only under the Occupation. Under the protection of an occupying army it was easy to

be a pacifist, but as an adult one must be a realist and for this realism an armed force, derisory in the eyes of an idealist and which can be of no use against atomic weapons, may well assure the peaceful existence of the nation. Unfortunately, such an armed force, though useless in the case of a nuclear attack, may nevertheless be enough to ruin the national economy!

The question of constitutional revision, then, remains a crucial political question in Japan.

The Constitution contains no title announcing its fundamental principles, but all constitutional lawyers admit that it is based on the principles of democracy, individualism, liberalism, pacifism, the welfare state, and secularism.[12] Article 1 states explicitly that sovereignty resides in the general will of the people. The Preamble, moreover, states that "government is a sacred trust of the people, the authority for which is derived from the people, the powers of which are exercised by the representatives of the people and the benefits of which are enjoyed by the people." These words express the principle of democracy. Individualism was not assured by the Meiji Constitution. Article 13 of the present Constitution, however, declares that every citizen is to be respected as an individual. As far as marriage is concerned article 24 requires that the laws have due regard to individual dignity and the essential equality of the sexes. Although this principle is not yet instilled in the mentality of the people, it is to be hoped that the Japanese spirit will be influenced by it over the years.

The Constitution guarantees the fundamental rights of people in Chapter 3, and provides that these rights shall be maintained by the constant endeavor of the people. This is a declaration of a modern liberalism which has really only been recognized in Japan since the end of World War II. It is not of course beyond criticism, and has, as in the country where the idea was first enunciated, been complemented by a more socialized principle.

The details of the pacifist principle have already been examined in connection with article 9. This principle is the most

---

[12] This can be deduced from the Preamble and some of the articles of the Constitution.

distinctive characteristic of the Constitution and is an indication, perhaps a slightly premature one, of the political regime of the world of tomorrow. Who in this atomic era can believe that any country can survive other than by "putting full confidence in the justice and goodwill of all peace-loving people of the world," as is proclaimed in the Preamble to the Constitution. Every new idea seems an illusion until it is realized and accepted by the greater part of the world. But Rome was not built in a day, and it is to be hoped that this great ideal will not be cast aside, as a useless scrap of paper, in the cause of realism. Human history has shown on several occasions that short-term realism is more unrealistic than an ideal which is a postulate of practical reason.[13]

Nineteenth-century liberalism has contributed greatly to the guaranteeing of individual rights against political absolutism, but it has as a consequence reinforced the social position of those who are economically the strongest. The constitutions that have come into force in the twentieth century sought to improve the social condition of the poor, and the Japanese Constitution in its turn does not accept the limiting of the field of activity of political power to the protection of individual liberty. It aims at assuring the whole nation of a spiritual and material life worthy of human beings. This is the meaning of the *menschenwürdiges Dasein* mentioned in the Weimar Constitution and of the *moyens convenables d'existence* which were promised to the nation by the French Constitution of 1946. The notion of the welfare state is spoken of everywhere today, and the Japanese Constitution conforms, although in an inadequate fashion, to the worldwide tendency. Article 25 affirms that "all people have the right to

---

[13] In his work *Zum ewigen Frieden* the philosopher Kant says: "Above all seek the reign of pure practical reason and its *justice*, and the end [the benefit of perpetual peace] will follow as of course." "Because morality has this peculiarity, even relative to the principles of public law . . ., that the less it is made to depend on the pursuit of the goal, the physical or moral advantage that is sought, the more in general it leads to it. This is because of the general nature of *a priori* thinking [in a nation or in the relationships between different nations] which alone determines what is law for men; and this union of all wills, provided that it appears subsequently in practice, can at the same time, depending on the circumstances, be the cause which produces the desired effect and which assures the realization of the idea of law." Immanuel Kant, *Vers la paix perpétuelle*, trans. Jean Darbellay (Paris: Presses Universitaires de France, 1958), p. 149.

maintain the minimum standards of wholesome and cultured living. In all spheres of life, the state shall use its endeavours for the promotion and extension of social welfare and security and for public health." The Constitution also guarantees social rights of various sorts, such as the right to equal education (article 26) and the right to associate (article 28).

The Meiji Constitution did not explicitly adopt any system of state religion. Shintoism was not proclaimed as the religion of the state, though it enjoyed a political and social position of a privileged nature, and the emperor was regarded as an incarnate divinity of that religion. The extremists exploited the privileged situation of Shintoism to the full to realize their absurd ideal of a military state. To avert this sort of danger the present Constitution guarantees the freedom of religious belief and forbids the state to grant any religious privileges. It is therefore evident that the principle of secularism is adopted by the Japanese state.

Among the laws which complement the Constitution the most important are that of 30 April, 1947, on Parliament, that of 15 April, 1950, relating to the election of public functionaries, and that of 16 January, 1947, which deals with the imperial family, succession to the throne, regency, and the council of the imperial family.

2. The Civil Code

The Civil Code is divided into five books: the general part, real rights, obligations, family law, and succession.

The general part, following the pattern advocated by the German pandectists, contains the rules common to all the other books.[14] It is composed of the following six chapters: Chapter I, natural persons; Chapter II, legal persons; Chapter III, things;

---

[14] The general part that is supposed to dominate all the books of the Civil Code is concerned in reality only with law of property. The French method of codification is in this respect more practical and wiser than the Japanese. It is to be noted that at the time of the 1947 reform two articles of very wide application were added at the beginning of the general part:

Article 1. Private rights must conform to the public good.
The exercise of rights and the fulfillment of duties must be effected according to the requirements of good faith.

Article 1-2. The present code must be interpreted on the basis of respect for the dignity of the individual and the equality of the sexes.

Chapter IV, legal acts; Chapter V, time limits; Chapter VI, prescription. The first chapter concerns the enjoyment of civil rights, capacity, domicile, and absence. Chapter II includes provisions relating to foundations, and the management and dissolution of corporate bodies. The third chapter contains general rules relating to those things which may be the object of private rights, and corresponds more or less to the title "De la distinction des biens" in Book II of the French Civil Code. Chapter IV contains, in theory, the rules applicable to all legal acts, but in reality acts affecting the legal status of individuals are regulated by rules quite different from those in this chapter. The articles in Chapter IV are therefore analogous to articles 1108 to 1118 of the French Civil Code. The rules relating to defect of consent are found in the section dealing with declaration of intention.

A major difference between the French and Japanese codes is that the Japanese has a special part dealing with agency. This is section 3. Section 4 concerns the nullity and voidability of legal acts. Unlike the French civil law, which distinguishes between absolute and relative nullity, Japanese law divides defective acts into two classes: void and voidable. Voidable acts are valid until avoidance, but they are deemed void *ab initio* when they are avoided.[15] Nullity can be claimed by any interested party, but only a restricted group of persons can bring an action for avoidance.[16] Chapter V provides for the mode of computation of various time limits. Where there is no specific statutory provision, court order, or contractual term to the contrary, the provisions of this chapter apply. Chapter VI groups the provisions relating to acquisitive and extinctive prescription.

Book 2 regulates real rights and provides not only for property and the real rights related to it but also for possession and real securities. Chapter I contains some general rules. Article 175, for instance, declares that no real rights can exist except those provided for by legislation. Article 176 says the creation and

---

[15]   In the case of a void act there is no need to perform another act to render it void, but in the case of avoidance some action must be taken, either in court or outside court, evidencing the desire to annul the voidable act.

[16]   Generally speaking the difference from French law is more theoretical than real.

transfer of all real rights is valid by the simple manifestation of the will of the parties. This article had its origin in articles 1138 and 1583 of the French Civil Code. Inscription on the property register of a change relating to a real right is therefore not a condition of the validity of its transfer, but does, as article 177 says, provide for protection of the right against third parties. On this point Japanese law has clearly followed the model of the French Civil Code and not that of the B.G.B. Though people are accustomed to thinking that the Japanese Civil Code is a faithful copy of the B.G.B., article 177 should suffice to prove that such an opinion is ill-founded.[17] Chapter II deals with possession; Chapter III with ownerships. Articles 209 to 238 relate to what the French call *servitudes*. The Japanese code deals with this matter in a section entitled "Restrictions on Title," but it is studied under the rubric of "relationships with adjoining properties" (*sorin kankei*). While the Code Napoleon is hostile to co-ownership, the Japanese code deals with the subject in detail in articles 249 to 264. Article 208, which provides for co-ownership of apartments, has been replaced by a special law of 4 April, 1962.[18]

As divisions of ownership the Civil Code recognizes superficies, emphyteusis, and real servitudes. Superficies is a real right by which a person may use the land of another for planting or building; the right of emphyteusis permits an owner to cultivate land or to raise stock on it for a set fee. The economic effects of these two rights can be produced by a contract of lease, though a lease, of course, would not create a real right. Since a contract of lease is more favorable to an owner of land, it is very rare to find these real rights in practice. Non-owner cultivators are obliged to enter into leases to assure themselves of their rights to cultivate the land. The rules on real servitudes are similar to those in the French code. The right of usufruct, however, is unknown in Japan.

Real securities are regulated in the same book as real rights, but in spite of this the Japanese system is very close to that of

[17] If not in its form at least in its concepts the Japanese code borrows as many of its rules from the German code as from the French.

[18] Lack of space has obliged the Japanese to change their traditional living pattern and get used to living in apartment blocks. Until very recently almost all Japanese houses were single story or at most two story.

the French code, save that the Japanese code provides in this part for the right of retention, which it treats as a sort of real right. Apart from the right of retention, the code provides for pledge, privilege, and hypothec, and all are modeled quite closely on French law.

Book 3 deals with the law of obligations. In Chapter I the general rules applicable to all obligations are set out, and these correspond to those provided in Chapter III of Book 3 of the French Civil Code. Chapter II deals with contract as the most important source of obligation. Having dealt with the rules common to all contracts in articles 521 to 548, thirteen important contracts are covered: gift, sale, exchange, loan, bailment for use, hire of things, hire of services, labor contracts, agency, deposit, association, annuities, and compromise. Gifts *inter vivos* are considered one of the most important contracts,[19] and legacies are dealt with in the provisions relating to wills in the book on succession.[20] The other three chapters deal in turn with *negotiorum gestio*, unjust enrichment, and civil delict, that is, they deal with what Domat called non-contractually created obligations. The last chapter of this book bears the title "Unlawful Acts,"[21] which undoubtedly comes from the *unerlaubte Handlung* of the B.G.B.

The last two books of the code were drawn up, taking particular account of Japanese family traditions. These books contain many rules which were already out of date at the time of the writing of the code. The ordinary family was already a nuclear one, composed of parents and children, except in remote areas where the concept of the large family still existed. Yet the code sought to maintain the extended family system headed by a head of the family (*koshu*) endowed with great power. Households which, in spite of their material independence, were noted on the civil status register as belonging to a given family were under the authority of the head of that family. Members of a family had to obtain the consent of their head of family to their marriage even after their majority. The head could arbitrarily

---

[19]　A different attitude from that of the French code.

[20]　Japanese law does not know the notion of *liberalité*, which includes both gift and legacy.

[21]　The Japanese word corresponding to delict, *hanzai*, is only used in the criminal law field.

determine the place of residence of members of his family, and those who did not obey him could be excluded from the family. Exclusion was equivalent to being disinherited!

The legal position of the head of the family was a privileged one. It was the object of a special succession, which meant principally that the eldest son of the head of the family succeeded. This succession (*katoku sozoku*) was monopolized by a single legitimate heir on whom devolved all the property, and the other members of the family could not participate. Brothers and sisters of the legitimate heir had to await the head's favor for a share in the succession. The system had the advantage of preventing the excessive subdivision of rural land, but the basic principle of this family-based organization had clearly fallen out of use by the time of the code. Just before the promulgation of the new Constitution the complete reform of Books 4 and 5 was decided upon, and a committee instituted for the purpose drew up a new law to conform with the provisions of the Constitution. In particular, it gave effect in the code to the principles of individual dignity and the legal equality of sexes. The books on the family and succession were thus completely rewritten and became law on 22 December, 1947.

Book 4 is entitled *shinzoku*. According to article 725 the *shinzoku* (the family) includes blood relatives to the sixth degree, spouse, and relatives by marriage to the third degree. In this book there are five chapters which deal respectively with marriage, filiation, paternal authority, guardianship, and the alimentary obligation. As in the draft for the revised French code, the matrimonial regime is dealt with in the chapter on marriage. The fact that this subject is dealt with in only eight articles reflects an important difference between the French and Japanese attitude toward law.

Book 5 deals with succession. The revised code has given up the system of *katoku sozoku*. It therefore deals with succession to all property and not just to moveables, and all heirs can participate in the succession. The book contains eight chapters. Chapter I contains four general articles, and Chapter II lists those who can succeed. In Chapter III, entitled "The Effects of Succession," are found the rules relating to the hereditary shares and to the division of property. Subject to certain exceptions the division between co-heirs is usually on the basis of equality. When rural property is to be divided this principle, of course, brings with it the danger of fractionalization of the arable land, as the inevitable result of the suppression of the system of *katoku sozoku*. Several measures have been taken to deal with this problem of division but none has been satisfactory, and reactionaries would for this reason favor a return to the old system. But in practice there is no great problem. Heirs who do not want to live a rural life renounce their rights in favor of those who want the land, in return for an amount of money equal to the value of their share. Accepting and renouncing successions is dealt with in Chapter IV: acceptance can be simple, or subject to inventory.[22] Chapter V deals with the separation of patrimonies. When there is no heir the succession is disposed of in accordance with the provisions of Chapter VI; Chapter VII relates to wills; and Chapter VIII deals with the reserved share.

Since the promulgation of the code, more than seventy years have passed. During this time the code has been supplemented by special statutes and by case law. The most important of the statutes are the law of 22 December, 1947, relating to civil status,[23] that of 24 February, 1899, on registration of immoveable property, the law of 8 April, 1921, on the leasing of building sites, and the law of 8 April, 1921, concerning the leasing of houses.

3. The Commercial Code

Since coming into force, the Commercial Code has been the object of frequent reforms necessitated by the profound economic and social vicissitudes of a country which only a century ago began to modernize itself on the pattern of the economically advanced states. The many amendments attest the great efforts made by the Japanese people to adapt themselves to world

---

[22] Called in Japanese law "limited acceptance."
[23] The code itself originally contained no rules relating to civil status. Cf. French Civil Code.

economic developments. The reforms of 1911, 1938, and 1952
are particularly important.[24]

The original code had five books. Book 4, however, which dealt
with bills of exchange and cheques, was abrogated in 1933 as a
result of signing the international conventions for unification of
the law relating to bills of exchange and cheques concluded in
1931 and 1932 in Geneva. The present code thus has four books.

Book 1, completely redrafted in 1938, is the general part of
the code. It includes the rules relating to merchants, Chapter
II; the commercial register, Chapter III; trade names, Chapter
IV; commercial books, Chapter V; merchants' employees,
Chapter VI; and commercial agents, Chapter VII. Book 2 deals
with commercial associations. It too has undergone redrafting,
in 1911, 1938, 1950, and 1974. The 1911 revision was made
necessary by the great development of business in Japan following the Russo-Japanese War of 1905, and the 1938 revision was
related to the radical transformation of economic conditions in
Japanese society before the outbreak of World War II. Following
a chapter of general provisions, three chapters deal with the three
types of commercial corporations. The first two chapters provide
for the first two types of association (partnerships) in almost
exactly the same terms as the French law. Chapter III was
drastically revised in 1950 on the advice of the Occupation
authorities, and the influence of Anglo-American law in it is
strong. The provisions on partnerships limited by shares which
existed before the 1950 reform were abrogated because they
were little used; private companies are regulated by a special
law of 5 April, 1938.

The third book deals with acts of commerce. In Chapter I
three types of commercial acts are enumerated:[25] absolute commercial acts (article 501), professional commercial acts (article
502), and accessory commercial acts (article 503). Absolute commercial acts are those which are always such whether performed

[24] Most recently the reform of the Commercial Code realized by law no. 20 of
2 April, 1974, aims at strengthening the audit system of commercial companies;
law no. 22 of the same date obliges joint-stock companies whose capital exceeds
¥500,000,000 to submit their accounts for a special inspection by a certified public
accountant.

[25] These denominations are not those of the code itself.

in the exercise of a profession or not. Professional commercial
acts are those which are not so by their nature but which become
commercial when they are performed professionally. Accessory
commercial acts are all legal acts accomplished by merchants in
order to advance their profession, whatever the nature of the
act. The nine other chapters that make up this book deal with
sale, current accounts, undisclosed partnership, brokerage, commission agents, forwarding agents, transport, deposit, and insurance.[26]

Book 4, which was the fifth book at the time of the promulgation of the code, deals with maritime commerce. Its seven
chapters are headed: ships and ship-owners, crew, transport, loss,
salvage, insurance, and maritime lien creditors.

The most marked difference that exists between the French
and Japanese commercial codes is that the Japanese code does
not deal with bankruptcy or commercial courts.[27] The rules on
bankruptcy are in a separate law, the law on bankruptcy of 25
April, 1922, which is applicable not only to merchants but to all
persons.

Like the Civil Code, the Commercial Code is far from including within its pages all the rules that are relevant to commercial
law. There are numerous complementary laws of which those of
especial importance are the law on limited companies, the law
of 15 July, 1932, relating to bills of exchange, the law of 29 July,
1933, relating to cheques, and the law of 13 June, 1957, relating
to the international transport of goods by sea.

4. The Code of Civil Procedure

The code is modeled almost exactly on the German code. No
Japanese code has been less influenced by French law than this
one, and until recent times Japanese procedural lawyers paid
very little attention to the works of the French procedural
lawyers. The code is divided into eight books. The first, the
general part, has four chapters. Chapter I deals with the jurisdic-

[26] The chapter on insurance deals only with terrestrial insurance. Maritime
insurance is, as in the French Commercial Code, dealt with in the last book of the
Code on Maritime Commerce.
[27] Commercial matters are within the jurisdiction of the ordinary courts.

tion of the various courts and the exclusion,[28] challenge, and withdrawal of judges and registrars. If any of the causes of exclusion set out in the law, whether raised by the parties or not, arises in connection with a judge called to hear a case, that judge cannot participate in the case, and anything done by him in the case is of no effect.[29] Chapter II deals with parties to proceedings. Chapter III relates to costs,[30] and Chapter IV contains a number of general rules for the hearing, time limits, notification of judgment, and adjourning of proceedings.

Book 2 is entitled "Procedure at First Instance." Of the four chapters of this book, the first deals with the statement of claim, the second with the hearing and preparation for it, the third with evidence, and the fourth with special rules for summary tribunals.

Book 3 deals with appeals,[31] and Book 4 with retrial. The fifth book relates to the procedure on orders to pay. This procedure is aimed at facilitating the recovery of debts relating to sums of money, perishable goods, or incorporeal moveables. It is analogous to the procedure created in France for the same purpose by the law of 4 July, 1957.

Book 6 contains the rules dealing with execution of judgment. It provides some general rules, then discusses methods of execution under three main heads. The first type concerns execution of obligations which have payment of a sum of money as their object, and separate procedures are provided for the seizure of moveables, the seizure of immoveables, and the seizure of ships. The second type concerns the execution of obligations which do not have a sum of money as their object. This mode of execution is used when the delivery of a certain piece of property, either moveable or immoveable, is required. The third type has to do

[28] Distinct from challenge, exclusion (*Ausschliessung*) takes effect *ipso jure*.
[29] Where the judgment is given with his participation, it can be challenged by appeal before it becomes *res judicata*, and by retrial after it becomes *res judicata*.
[30] Japanese law makes no terminological distinction between fees and expenses. The general word *hiyo*, which can cover fees of any sort, is also used for expenses. When the expression *sosho-hiyo* (court fees) is used, only the fees prescribed by law are referred to. The law of 16 August, 1890, relating to *sosho-hiyo* (frequently amended) regulates fees in great detail.
[31] To be more precise Book 3 deals with *joso* (hierarchical appeals). Where a term is needed to include appeals between courts of the same rank, the most generally used expression is *fufuku-moshitate hoho*.

with two measures preparatory to execution. One is provisional seizure and the other is *kari-shobun* (provisional disposition), which is similar in nature to an interim injunction. It follows the German *einstweilige Verfügung* and is very much like the French system of *référé*.

Book 7 deals with the procedure by which a court may at the request of an interested party give public notice to unknown creditors, calling on them to declare their rights or have their rights defeated. After this public notice the court can give an excluding judgment (*Ausschlussurteil*), the effect of which is to consolidate the legal position of the plaintiff to his advantage. Book 8 deals with arbitration.

The Code of Civil Procedure is a faithful imitation of the German code. However, the Civil Code, which contains the basic rules of private law, retains, in spite of the generally held belief that it too copies the B.G.B., a great number of rules of French origin. For this reason there exists between the two codes a certain lack of coherence which has given rise to many doctrinal controversies. The provisions of French origin obviously presuppose legal sanctions of a French type, and it is therefore a hopeless task to try to harmonize the rules of the two codes. As an example of the type of problem that arises, consider the law on possessory actions. The Civil Code provides, in articles 197–202, rules relating to possessory actions. Subject to certain modifications which were not always fortunate in their result, the draftsmen of the Civil Code retained the French system of possessory actions, but they did not place the rules of procedure for these actions in the Civil Code because that was, according to them, a matter to be covered by the Code of Civil Procedure. However, the Code of Civil Procedure contains no provision relating to possessory actions, because the German law on which it was founded does not provide any special rules for possessory actions. Under the German code there are two methods of requiring the transfer of a thing: the owner of the property can get it back relying either on his possession or on his title. This is his choice, and he can even combine the proprietory action with the possessory action. The German law of 1898 abrogated a provision which had retained in a somewhat modified form the principle of *non-cumul* of actions borrowed from the French law. The system is therefore quite different from the French. The Japanese lawyers, if they wish to be faithful to the French system, must accept the solutions given by articles 23–27 of the French Code of Civil Procedure. If on the other hand they support the German system they must at the same time accept the logical conclusions that follow from the German procedural system. For the moment, the law on the point is neither clear nor coherent.

The Code of Civil Procedure does not provide all the rules of civil procedure. There are many important laws outside it, ignorance of which would render an investigation of Japanese civil procedure imperfect and inaccurate. Apart from the Supreme Court rules of 1 March, 1956, which are not in statutory form, there is the law of 16 May, 1962, on administrative procedure, the law of 21 June, 1898, on procedure in matters of civil status, the law of 21 June, 1898, on procedure in non-contentious matters, the law of 6 December, 1947, on family law procedure, the law of 25 April, 1922, on bankruptcy, and the law of 9 June, 1951, on conciliation in civil cases. This last law seeks to find equitable and practicable rather than legal solutions to civil cases, based on mutual concessions made by the parties. The Japanese do not like the solution of a dispute to be too decisive or contrary to their native sentiment of what is right, and therefore a large number of cases are dealt with by way of conciliation.

5. The Criminal Code

The first Penal Code was drawn up by Boissonade, and it introduced Japan to the principle of *nulla poena sine lege*. It had the great merit of causing the spirit of humanity to penetrate into penal institutions which previously had been utilized only as instruments of threat and intimidation on the part of those in power. However, under the influence of the new thinking in criminal law at the end of the last century,[32] Japanese lawyers

---

[32] In particular, Professor Makino of Tokyo University Law Faculty studied criminal law under the German criminal lawyer F. von Liszt, who at that time represented a new line of thinking in criminal law and who exercised a profound influence on Makino. Makino was one of the most influential promotors of the new school of Japanese penal law.

came to regard this code as imperfect from the theoretical point of view. In 1907 a new code was promulgated on 24 April to come into force on 1 October, 1908. It is this criminal code which is in force today.[33] It departed from the pattern of the former code in a number of important aspects. In the first place, the new code abandoned the French system of classification of offenses.[34] Second, it extended considerably the power of judges to decide on the appropriate penalty to be imposed. The code allowed a reasonably extensive difference between the maximum and minimum penalties available for each crime, so the judge could within the prescribed limits choose a penalty appropriate to the degree of culpability of the accused, and individualization of penalty was thus much better realized. Third, the new code is more systematic than the earlier one. The provisions relating to self-defense, for example, which are applicable to all offenses, were placed in the old code in the part relating to homicide, assault, and wounding. The new code puts these rules in the first book, which contains general rules. Finally, the new code admits, to a large degree, stay of execution of penalties.

The new code has been amended several times since 1908. The most important of the reforms was that of 1947, when the law was reworked to a fairly large extent to bring it into line with the Constitution. In conformity with the constitutional principles, the law of 26 October, 1947, sought to make the code more democratic, more liberal, and more pacifist, and as a consequence of the constitutional postulate that war would be renounced, a large number of provisions relating to war were abrogated. The principle of individual dignity demanded the improvement and the extending of the system of stay of execution, and the laws relating to outrage were modified, too, so that personal honor would be better respected. Third, the principle of equality before the law made necessary the total abrogation

[33]   The entire reform of this code has been discussed since 1956 on the initiative of the Ministry of Legal Affairs. Under the strong influence of Ono Seichiro, professor emeritus of Tokyo University and a leading authority on penal law, a reform draft was completed in collaboration with a certain number of lawyers and laymen and was published in 1974. The draft has been severely criticized by jurists who consider it to be of too authoritarian character. The Ministry of Legal Affairs will draw up a final draft, taking in consideration the various viewpoints.

[34]   I.e., crimes, delicts, contraventions.

of the provisions relating to offenses against the imperial family.

The code is made up of two books. The first book has thirteen chapters in which are set out rules of a general nature which apply to all crimes: application of the code (Chapter I), penalties (Chapter II), calculation of time (Chapter III), stay of execution (Chapter IV), provisional release (Chapter V), prescription and extinction of penalties (Chapter VI), justification and exonerating circumstances (Chapter VII), attempts (Chapter VIII), concurrent crimes (Chapter IX), recidivism (Chapter X), accomplices (Chapter XI), mitigating circumstances (Chapter XII), reduction or increase of penalties (Chapter XIII).

Book 2, called by Japanese lawyers "the part containing the special rules," is called in the code "Crimes." It is divided into forty chapters, each dealing with a particular class of crime.

Of the numerous special laws which complement the Criminal Code, the most important are the law on minor offenses (*Keihanzai ho*) of 1 May, 1948, and the law of 21 July, 1952, which seeks to prevent subversive activities (*hakai-katsudo boshiho*).[35] This law was promulgated, in spite of lively opposition by intellectuals and the progressive political parties, to repress the violence of the Communist Party in an era when such violence was frequent. This law could undoubtedly be used to oppress freedom of expression in Japan, and the opposition succeeded in having the following clause inserted in it: "This law, having as it does a very close relationship with the fundamental rights of the nation, must be applied in the most limited way possible considering the need to assure public order. Any broad interpretation of the law is strictly proscribed." To date the law has been used—not as originally planned—principally to repress the violence of groups of the extreme right.

6. The Criminal Procedure Code

The Criminal Procedure Code (*Chizai ho*) drawn up by Boissonade remained in force until 1890. When the Constitution of 1889 was promulgated the code had to be revised, and a new law of October, 1890, was promulgated as the Code of Criminal Pro-

[35] This law is referred to by the abbreviation *haboho*.

cedure (*Keijisosho ho*). The change of title preceded the change in France by sixty-eight years. The new code, in spite of the change of title, was not very different from its predecessor and did not enjoy favor for long.

In 1922 a new Code of Criminal Procedure was introduced by the law of 5 May. This code retained many ideas of French origin, such as the *action civile, instruction préliminaire,* and *pourvoi dans l'intérêt de la loi.* The Constitution of 1946 did introduce, however, in its chapter on fundamental rights, many rules of Anglo-American origin[36] destined to guarantee the liberty and dignity of suspected criminals; to keep in line with these rules it was necessary to revise the code again. From this revision came the law of 10 July, 1948, a law presented as a revision of the earlier code but in fact a completely new code, which retained none of the former articles. The change of style alone is enough to show the degree of the change. Whereas the old code used literary style, the new code is written in familiar style.[37]

In the new code the influence of Anglo-American law is predominant. A completely accusatorial type of procedure is adopted, and the accused is no longer an object of investigation but the subject of the proceedings. The preliminary investigation procedure, which had a bleak record, was suppressed, and the civil action was omitted because it was little used in practice.

The new code is in seven books. The first book deals with general matters: the jurisdiction of the courts (Chapter I), disqualification and challenge of judges (Chapter II), capacity (Chapter III), defense and legal aid (Chapter IV), preliminary hearing (Chapter V), procedural acts (Chapter VI), time limits (Chapter VII), summons, imprisonment, and preventive detention of accused persons (Chapter VIII), seizure and search

---

[36] Articles 31–40 of the Constitution.
[37] Before the 1868 Restoration a special style, quite distinct from the spoken language, was used for writing. So different was it that its use was limited to the intelligentsia. It was called *bungo-tai,* the literary style. From 1868 to the end of the Second World War the literary style became more and more unfashionable, and a preference grew for writing in familiar style (*kogo-tai,* literally the style of the spoken language). However, in official documents, particularly in legislative texts, the literary style was even then the only mode of expression. Since the end of the Second World War the literary style has not been used in legislative texts either. The 1946 Constitution was the first law to be published in the familiar style.

(Chapter IX), viewing by the court (Chapter X), witnesses (Chapter XI), experts (Chapter XII), interpreters and translations (Chapter XIII), evidence (Chapter XIV), and costs (Chapter XV).

Book 2 is headed "At First Instance." It has three chapters which deal in turn with information, the prosecution, and procedure in court. Book 3 deals with appeals, Book 4 with retrial proceedings, Book 5 with cases stated for opinion by the court, Book 6 with summary proceedings, and Book 7 with the execution of judgment.

The laws complementing this code are numerous. Apart from the rules of the Supreme Court of 1 December, 1948, relating to penal procedure, there is the law of 1 January, 1950, relating to the indemnification of persons wrongly prosecuted, the law of 15 July, 1948, on juvenile delinquents, that of 28 March, 1908, on prisons, and the law of 1 April, 1954, on probation.

The principal codes, of which a summary exposition has been given, constitute only a small part on the legislation of Japan. Of the remaining body of statute law it should be noted that there is no administrative code.[38] Second, the importance of labor laws must be emphasized. Japanese workers did not really acquire legal independence from their employers until after the war, and so the laws that guarantee their legal position are very important. The three basic work laws are called *rodo sampo*. They are (1) the law of 7 April, 1947, on work conditions, promulgated to give effect to article 27 of the Constitution: "Work conditions, such as salary, length of time on the job, rest periods . . . will be determined by law"; (2) the law of 1 June, 1949, on trade unions, which with (3) the law of 27 September, 1946, on the regulation of work disputes, aim at guaranteeing to workers the right to associate and to collective bargaining in accordance with the principle declared in article 28 of the Constitution. Thirdly, though the Japanese social security system is very backward, the laws in the field of social security are very important.

---

[38] Unlike French administrative law, which is essentially a body of case law, Japanese administrative law is made up basically of legislation. It has, however, not been codified.

SUBSIDIARY LEGISLATION

Apart from statutes there are various other sorts of written law, some emanating from Parliament, some from government, some from the judiciary, and some from local bodies. All these forms of law have a validity that is inferior to that of statutes.

Under article 58 of the Constitution each House of Parliament can make rules for its internal procedures and discipline. Though in principle valid only for the House that created them, such rules do, to a certain extent, have force for the whole nation. They are not submitted to the ordinary formalities of publication for legislation, but are brought to the knowledge of the public by insertion in the official gazette. Apart from such rules each House promulgates rules called *kitei*, which also find their authority in article 58.

There are several categories of regulations of governmental origin of which the most important are *seirei*. *Seirei* are signed by the competent minister, countersigned by the prime minister, and published by the emperor; they bind the administration (article 7 of the Constitution). *Seirei* cannot be made in respect of any matter not already regulated by statute or for which no statute has delegated power to legislate by *seirei*.

To facilitate the application of a statute or *seirei* every minister has the power to make rules of a subsidiary nature. Such enactments are called either *sorifu-rei* or *shorei* (ministerial order), depending on whether they are made by the prime minister or one of the other ministers. Under the authority of such rules the head of an administrative committee or service can make a still more subsidiary form of rule called *kisoku*.

Regulations of judicial origin are those of the Supreme Court. Rules made under this head play a very important role as a source of law, as the two sets of regulations complementing the two procedure codes attest. The idea for rules of this kind is borrowed from Anglo-American law and aims at assuring the independence of the judiciary, at the same time entrusting to the courts the job of providing rules which will improve the administration of justice, based on the belief that the Supreme

Court is in the best position to know what the current practice is or should be. The regulations promulgated by the Supreme Court are decided upon by the assembly of judges and published in the official gazette. The Supreme Court can delegate its legislative power to the inferior courts.[39]

The rules made by local authorities are called *jorei*,[40] and are explicitly authorized by article 94 of the Constitution. *Jorei* are inferior not only to statutes but also to *seirei* and to *shorei*.

TREATIES

The Constitution is silent on the subject of whether a signed and ratified treaty (*joyaku*) has the value of law at a national level, and the point is disputed by theorists. Those who deny the internal validity of a treaty maintain that legislation dealing with the subject matter of the treaty must be promulgated, as the treaty as such has no force as a rule of internal law. This opinion does not meet with general approval. The most favored theory admits that a treaty, once approved by Parliament, has in itself the same value as legislation, and this thesis finds some support in article 98 of the Constitution, which declares that "Treaties concluded by Japan and the established rules of international law shall be faithfully observed." The conclusion, however, by no means follows necessarily from this article, as even under the Meiji Constitution treaties were considered to have the force of law without the promulgation of legislation with the same content as the treaty being necessary, and it could be maintained that this constitutional practice is still valid.

A treaty is concluded by the Naikaku (article 73 of the Constitution), but it must be approved by Parliament before or, when necessary, after its conclusion. Thus the agreement of the Naikaku and the approval of Parliament are two conditions necessary for the validity of a treaty. The conclusion of a treaty is perfected by ratification of the Naikaku, and for this reason

[39] It is still a matter of some controversy whether the regulations of the Supreme Court are inferior to legislation or not.

[40] Cf. Chapter 6.

the Naikaku must usually seek the approval of Parliament before it ratifies. In order to have a treaty ratified by Parliament, the House of Representatives must be seised of the matter first (article 61 of the Constitution), and as in the case of debates on the budget, irreconcilable disagreement between the two Houses, or the silence of the House of Councillors for thirty days following its being seised of the matter, can provide the House of Representatives with the chance to manifest alone the will of Parliament.

Certain constitutional lawyers basing themselves on the pacifist and internationalist spirit of the Constitution accept the view that a regularly approved treaty has a validity superior to that of national law. The main body of opinion maintains, however, that a law which derogates from a treaty supersedes it until it is modified to bring it into line with the treaty.

COLLECTIONS OF LEGISLATION[41]

The most complete collection of legislation is the *Horei Zensho* (complete collection of statutes and subsidiary legislation), an official publication that contains all the legislation promulgated from 1867 till today. All the laws appear in chronological order. To find out which laws are still in force reference must be made to a collection called *Genko-hoki-shu* (collection of laws and regulations in force), which is edited by the office of legal research to the cabinet of the Ministry of Legal Affairs. The collection is ordered methodically, divided into 46 volumes, and is regularly brought up to date by loose-leaf supplements.

Treaties can be found in the *Genko joyaku shuran* (collection of treaties in force) and in an official publication edited under the direction of the Treaties Branch of the Ministry of Foreign Affairs. It is regularly brought up to date by loose-leaf additions.

All the official collections of legislation are in immense volumes and are difficult to use. To get over this problem private editors publish several sorts of more manageable collections at moderate

---

[41] All statutes can be found in English in the *E.H.S. Law Bulletin* series, published in Tokyo (1946–) by Eibun Horeisha.

prices. Such collections are usually called *Roppo Zensho* (complete collection of the six codes) but they contain not only the six codes,[42] but also the statutes and most important subsidiary legislation in all fields. The two most popular private collections are the *Iwanami Roppo Zensho* (collection of six codes edited by the Iwanami publishing company) and *Yuhikaku Roppo Zensho* (collection of the six codes edited by the Yuhikaku publishing company). Both collections are published in two editions of different format. The smallest edition is called *Kihon Roppo* by Iwanami (basic collection of the six codes), and *Sho Roppo* (small collection of the six codes) by Yuhikaku, and this is the most popular edition among teachers and law students. The bigger edition, however, contains many more laws. Both editions of the two collections are reprinted annually.

---

[42] Constitution, Civil Code, Commercial Code, Code of Civil Procedure, Criminal Code, Code of Criminal Procedure.

CHAPTER XI

CUSTOM AND JORI

CUSTOM

Custom is understood as those rules of conduct which are generally followed in a society, although they are not established by any public body. They are rules of popular origin formed unconciously by the force of habit. They are produced, one might say, by a sort of law of social inertia. When Portalis said that "people's codes develop with time; strictly speaking they are not made,"[1] he was evidently alluding to this customary aspect of legal rules. But is custom a source of law? This problem has been a live issue for a long time, although no universally acceptable conclusion has yet been reached.

The solution depends largely on the definition of law and source of law.[2] If law means rules of conduct which are socially binding and effectively sanctioned, and source of law means the point at which law has, by analogy with a spring of water, its origin, then custom, which is the collective will of a social group, is, as Levy-Bruhl affirms, the sole source of law.[3] This theory of the historical school of law has doubtless some truth in it, but for present purposes more technical definitions of law and of sources of law will be adopted for reasons of precision and clarity. Law will be defined as the mass of social rules upon which a judge can rely to justify his decision—what German lawyers call *Entscheidungsnorm* (rules for judgment). Following this definition

---

[1] Jean Etienne Marie Portalis, *Discours, rapports et travaux inédits de J.E.M. Portalis* (Paris: Librairie de la Cour de Cassation, 1844), p. 1f.

[2] The penetrating criticism of theories on custom by Paul Amselek merits attention: *Methode phénoménologique et théorie du droit*, p. 150f.

[3] H. Levy-Bruhl, *Sociologie du droit*, p. 41.

of law, a source of law is anything that can be a persuasive basis for a judgment.[4]

Nowadays it is generally believed that a judge's duty is to apply preexisting rules in his decision. He judges, in effect, because there exist rules that have previously been formulated and declared to be law. But beyond that, the duty of the judge is to give a reasonable solution, a decision capable of persuading the parties to the conflict. The preexistence of applicable rules is not an essential condition of jurisdiction. The preexistence of well-structured rules applicable to a problem set out ahead of the need avoids the danger of subjectivism or arbitrariness on the judge's part, but such rules form only one of the possible bases for judgment. As article 4 of the French Civil Code states, a judge cannot refuse to decide a case that he is hearing on the ground that no pre-established rules exists. In cases where the judge finds no pre-established rule, he has to seek a basis for his judgment in some other reasonable source. The extreme position of the school of exegesis gave an almost absolute character to the requirement of existing legislation. As a reaction against this school, the free law school sought to affirm what the true role of judgment was. If this last point is emphasized, the logical conclusion is that when a judge decides a case on the basis of a reasonable line of argumentation, he does not do so because that was the law, but every legal basis of the judgment becomes law because it was used as such by the judge. Thus conceived, custom can be used by a judge to support his judgment, but it becomes law only when so used.

In Japanese law, custom is considered a source of law within the meaning of the law of 1875.[5] According to another law, the *horei* of 21 June, 1898, which contains rules relating to the general application of law and to private international law, custom that is not contrary to public order or to morality has the value of law, provided that it is not excluded by legislation and

---

[4] This definition corresponds closely to the Roman law *fons iuris*, a source of judgment. Cf. Max Kaser, *Das altrömische Ius* (Göttingen: Vandenhoek & Ruprecht, 1949), p. 27.

[5] Cf. the in-depth study by Taniguchi, "La loi et la coutume au Japon," in *Etudes juridiques offertes à Julliot de La Morandière* (Paris: Librairie Dalloz, 1964), p. 571f.

that it deals with matters that have not been provided for by statute or regulation (article 2). The result is that custom is usually a subsidiary source of law that a judge can apply, only in the absence of legislation.

For civil matters the Civil Code provides a rule that is slightly different. Article 92 says, "If there are customs contrary to the legislation which do not deal with matters of public policy, judgment can be given according to the customs if the parties wish that to be done." In this case legislation which does not deal with matters of public policy⁶ can be avoided by the parties and replaced by customary rules with a contrary meaning. Imperative law, therefore, overrides custom, but custom can in civil matters have a value superior to that of supplementary law.

There is of course some difficulty in matching this provision of the Civil Code with that of the *horei*, which excludes all custom where there exists applicable legislation. On this matter a theory has been advanced, according to which the custom referred to by the *horei* concerns only customary rules that are accepted as binding by the collective conscience of the people, while article 92 of the Civil Code deals with custom as simple fact—as the practice generally followed whether conceived of as binding or not. This distinction relates to that of Levy-Bruhl which differentiates between legal and extra-legal customs⁷ and provides an interpretation that seems to be artificial and ill-founded. The very distinction between legal and extra-legal custom is in practice extremely hard to make, and it is difficult to understand why non-obligatory custom could have a greater value as a source of law than binding custom. A rational interpretation of these two articles has been sought, but lawyers have not yet found one. One thing is beyond doubt: both rules exclude custom that is contrary to imperative laws.

Unfortunately this assertion, which is theoretically correct, does not express the social reality. Judgments often refer to customary rules which are incompatible with imperative rules of

---

⁶ I.e., non-imperative law.
⁷ H. Levy-Bruhl, *Aspects sociologiques du droit* (Paris: Librairie Marcel Rivière et Cie, 1955), p. 73.

law in order to reach an appropriate solution. In civil matters two striking examples can be mentioned.

The first concerns the law on *naien* marriage. In Japanese law a marriage is not valid until it has been declared to the civil status officer (article 739 of the Civil Code). However, in the national conscience, marriage is completed by the simple fact of a man and a woman living together with social recognition. It is customary to neglect to declare the marriage for some long time, particularly in the country areas, and so it would be rather inequitable to refuse all legal effects to this type of conjugal link. The courts have, following a famous decision of the Court of Cassation of 26 January, 1915, tended to treat this union, if not as real marriage, at least as a quasi-marriage. At present then, a conjugal bond which is approved by society enjoys some of the legal effects that legislation has reserved for legal marriages. Since article 739 of the Civil Code is an imperative rule of law, custom contrary to it should have been refused any effect by the courts, and though the cases could not go so far as to assimilate customary marriage to legal marriage, the matrimonial custom has nevertheless to some extent derogated from the law of marriage.[8]

The second example is found in decisions relating to the legal validity of a contract by which a debtor gives his creditor property in a thing by way of security either with or without dispossession. The Civil Code does not admit this practice, but in business circles it is in demand because of its great economic use. The most frequent variant, and the one that is most useful, is that realized by the transfer of title to moveable property by the debtor to his creditor without any dispossession of the property in the debtor.[9] This is a pledge without dispossession so far as the debtor is concerned and is contrary to article 348 of the Civil Code, which explicitly prohibits a creditor leaving possession of the pledged object in his debtor's hands. Article 345 of the Civil Code is an imperative law, so cases which have ad-

---

[8]   Cf. Taniguchi, "La loi et la coutume," p. 575–578.
[9]   By this means a small- or medium-sized enterprise can get credit from a bank without losing its means of production. The procedure serves almost the same purpose as the *nantissement de fonds de commerce* in French law.

mitted this type of pledge according to customary usage have admitted a custom *contra legem*.[10]

A further example is found in commercial law in those cases which have declared valid the transferral of registered shares by means of open proxy forms. Article 150 of the Commercial Code had, until the reform of 1938, forbidden the transferring of registered shares by way of endorsement. By virtue of this article a purchaser would have to have his name registered on the list of shareholders. But a share is both a title document which incorporates the shareholder's rights and a negotiable instrument. Most purchasers do not want to remain shareholders for long. They buy shares in order to resell them. For these people the transfer formalities were too cumbersome, and so an expedient was struck upon to avoid them. The first transferor of a share gave the first transferee, along with the share sold, a proxy form enabling him to proceed with the transfer formality with the name of the agent in blank. The holder of the share then sold it along with the blank proxy form to a second person, and so the chain continued until someone who wanted to remain a shareholder acquired the share. This last person then had his name written on the proxy form as agent and completed the transfer formalities. In this way registered shares were negotiated as if they were bearer shares. This custom, demanded by economic needs, was contrary to the imperative rule of article 150 of the Commercial Code, but the courts came to consider it as legally valid, and the reform of 1938 confirmed the validity of the practice by legislation.[11]

It is quite natural that the courts have often to accept customs *contra legem*, notwithstanding the prohibition on doing so, because a judge is not so much required to apply existing rules of law at any cost as to give a reasonable solution to the parties before him. Of course the law is presumed to be reasonable, but that is until, and only until, the contrary is proved. If, therefore, the judge is convinced that there is a more reasonable basis for the judgment he is to deliver than that provided by the law, he must use that other basis subject to his having to justify his opinion by well-

[10] Cf. Taniguchi, "La loi et la coutume," p. 575.
[11] Article 206, II, Commercial Code.

established methods of interpretation. Any such objectively valid justification would constitute the proof for him of the contrary, as regards the presumption of the reasonableness of the law. It is accepted that the maxim *stulta sapientia quae vult lege sapientior esse* is very useful for avoiding subjectivism in judges, but it must not be forgotten that *summum ius summa iniuria est*.

The body of rules of conduct which guide the social life of the Japanese people is in large part foreign to judicial practice, and whether these rules are called law or not a knowledge of them is indispensable to anyone who wishes to study the normative aspect of Japanese social life, for state law has a very limited role in Japan. Social relations are established and maintained outside of the law.[12] The rules which govern them are assimilated to physiological laws. Even in the case of a dispute, which could be said to be a pathological social phenomenon, recourse is rarely had to the protection of state law in Japan. The result is that much time must be spent on a sociological study of rules of conduct and the solution of disputes in Japanese social life outside the state law before the reality of what is normally called law can be appreciated.

JORI

Jori corresponds in broad terms to what the French know as the general principles of law. In all but criminal cases judges decide cases according to *jori* when there is no other source of law to follow. However, it is very rare that a judge relies on *jori* alone,[13] because nowadays the problems that are likely to come to court are usually those for which legislation or precedent exists. This was not the case before the promulgation of the present codes. Earlier the system of legislation was defective, and the customary rules which governed the life of the people were archaic, and their field of application was significantly limited. The judge was often unable to resort either to legislation

or to custom to reach a decision. That is why the decree permitting judges to resort to *jori* to fill gaps in legislation and
custom was promulgated, and as a result many of the decisions
of that early period were made on the basis of *jori*. Most of the
judges of the period were traditionally educated and incapable
of identifying the rules applicable to the dispute of which they
were seised, so they simply resorted to common sense. They could
only operate on the basis of concretely formulated rules and, in
the absence of such rules, their minds, which were unaccustomed
to modern legal reasoning, operated in a void. It can therefore be
assumed that the Japanese translations of the five Napoleonic
codes and the newly drawn-up codes of Boissonade were the
basis of *jori* which was used by the courts in their decisions.
"French law, the Civil Code in particular, became the *raison
écrite* for Japan which the courts began to apply, not as positive
law, but as natural law, and even today while the Japanese Civil
Code and Japanese Code of Commerce are being prepared, it
is nearly always the two French private law codes which provide
the courts with solutions to their cases."[14] The terms natural law
and "written reason" used here by Boissonade could well be
replaced by the Japanese term *jori*.

A judge may decide a case according to *jori*, even though it
is not a rule of law. Under the Meiji Constitution, when the judge
had to exercise his powers according to legislation, there was a
need to harmonize that requirement with the notion of *jori*.
Today, however, the constitutionality of a judgment given in
accordance with *jori* is accepted by everyone, and whether or
not *jori* is a source of law is a purely theoretical question, the
answer to which depends on the definition given to the term
"source of law." If it is accepted that all reasonable bases for
judgment are sources of law, *jori* is a source of law. The definitive
basis for a judgment rests in the rationality of the solution given
by the judge, and legislation and other rules set out in advance
are only rebuttable guarantees of this rationality. Since the
rationality of legislation cannot be guaranteed forever in changing social conditions, must a judge refuse to test the rationality

[14] Gustave Boissonade, *Projet de Code Civil de l'Empire du Japon*, Vol. I, Preface,
p. 5.

of legislation? Everyone agrees that a judge may set up a rational rule in the absence of legislation. Why should he be prohibited from setting up more rational rules than those of the existing legislation? Should it be, as Hegel says, that what is reasonable is what exists and that what exists is reasonable? And if so, what of justice or equity? If the mere existence of a thing can be its raison d'être, have we to resign ourselves to the existence of many ills and afflictions? Implicitly it has been admitted for a long time that a judge can examine the rationality of law, as witness the many judgments that have substituted for the rationality of legislation their own rationality under the pretext of interpretation.[15]

The law only functions well when it gives satisfaction to the two basic postulates of legal certainty and equitable solution. The first postulate demands that the legal solution be alike for like matters, and this means that well-structured rules are required in advance and that those rules be strictly applied. The second postulate demands, by contrast, that judges give the solution which best corresponds to the particular needs of each case, even if existing law requires them to give a solution which is less equitable to one of the parties. These postulates are therefore in conflict. The polarization of the first postulate would result in an inhuman legalism, and the polarization of the second in archaic sentimentalism. Excess in either sense is unacceptable, but both postulates must be satisfied to a reasonable extent in every case; they must be harmonized. The mission of legal science is to find the rules for the harmonization of social interests, just as musical theory has sought rules for the harmonization of sounds. Lawyers therefore must not be sparing in the use of their knowledge and full exercise of their capacities when they are confronted with legal problems, for social harmony, along with justice, equity, and peace, is also one of the ideals of law.

---

[15]   This approach does of course bring with it the danger of subjective judgment.

CHAPTER XII

CASES AND LEGAL THEORY

CASES

1. General

The number of court cases in Japan is much lower than in Western countries because social conflicts, for the most part, find their solutions outside courts. This does not mean, however, that case decisions have little importance in a study of the state law of Japan. Indeed, laws and regulations are formulated in general and abstract terms and are only molded to correspond to the reality of social life by their application by judges in specific cases. Further, the interpretation of a law given by the court is likely to be followed by other courts involved in deciding similar cases. The rules applied by the courts are, as in other countries, often quite different from the content of the law which the court claims to be applying in its pure form. Japanese law follows the common practice in this. Anyone, therefore, who knows only the rules as formulated in the legislative texts has a rather imprecise knowledge of Japanese law.

The body of rules built up by judicial practice around a legislative text is called *hanrei ho* (*han* means legal decision, and *rei* former). No formal text states whether or not *hanrei ho* is a source of law. Article 4 of the law on courts declares that the decision of a court of higher rank in one case binds a lower court to which the case is referred; however, there is nothing of the notion of binding precedent or *stare decisis* in this text.[1]

---

[1] This provision expresses a rule which is similar to that of article 16 of the French law of 3 July, 1967, although the Japanese rule is not limited to cases of cassation.

In strict theory no judge is bound by any judicial precedent. The Constitution declares that every judge must fulfill his duties independently and according to his conscience, and he is only bound by the Constitution and by the law (article 76). However, as already pointed out, judges can indirectly, by interpretation, change the meaning of legal texts or create new rules where legislation does not provide. The binding force of legislation is thus more theoretical than real for a judge. On the other hand, a judge cannot refuse to follow a line of cases that has been well established, particularly if the cases are Supreme Court decisions. His interpretation, however faithful to the exact words of the law, would undoubtedly be reversed on appeal if it were not in conformity with the case law of the Supreme Court. It can quite properly be asked whether case law has not in practice been substituted for legislation. Doubtless the judge has a degree of freedom, but it is, as Maury says,[2] freedom to do wrong—the freedom to hand down a judgment that is sure to be reversed.

In these circumstances it is natural that a theory has developed which recognizes case law as having the character of a formal source of law. But reasonable justification for the theory has yet to be shown. The customary nature of case law has usually been relied upon for support, but in fact case law does not have characteristic traits of custom. It may be said, as Geny did, that case law creates custom but is not itself custom.

Case law is a true source of law, in the sense used here,[3] when its content is rational. Legislation is the general criterion of rationality that the judge must always take account of first, but if he follows it blindly, without seeking further, it could hardly be said that he had judged according to his conscience. The judge must, without losing sight of the fact that legal certainty is one of the basic postulates of social life, test the rationality of

[2] J. Maury, "Observations sur la jurisprudence en tant que source de droit," in Le droit privé français au milieu du XXᵉ siècle: Etudes offertes à G. Ripert (Paris: Librairie Générale de Droit et de Jurisprudence, 1950), Vol. I, p. 28f., and p. 49. "But when the Court of Cassation intervenes either by 'inventing' a rule itself or by consolidating or destroying one of precarious authority established by the lower courts, and when a rule is born of this intervention, there is no longer any freedom for the lower court judges 'except to do wrong.'"
[3] I.e., an argument that justifies a solution that can be used to convince litigants of average intelligence.

every possible route to a decision, even that of the decisions of
the Supreme Court.[4]

In Japanese law the importance of cases varies according to
the branch of law under consideration. In the field of private
law, cases have enjoyed an important position for a long time,
and it was in fact in civil and commercial case law that Japanese
lawyers first showed special interest. From the time of the promulgation of the civil and commercial codes lawyers have been
publishing notes on judgments,[5] with the purpose, in the early
days, of providing practical examples for commentaries on the
codes.

An important date for the study of cases was that of the foundation of a learned association for the study of civil case law in
1921. One of the most noted civil laywers of Japan, Suehiro
Itsutaro, whose studies in the United States had left a lasting
impression on him of the value of the case method, advocated
the use of this method for a more scientific study of the law. An
association was created on Suehiro's initiative, under the name of
Mimpo Hanrei Kenkyu-kai (Society for the Study of Decisions in
the Civil Law Field). It was made up for the most part of professors and staff of the Law Faculty of the Imperial University
of Tokyo. In 1922 it changed its name to *Minjiho Hanrei Kenkyu-
kai*,[6] with the object of extending the field of investigation. This
society held regular weekly meetings to study all the civil law
judgments of the Court of Cassation that were published in the
reports. The study method adopted was that of appointing a rapporteur for each case to examine the case and make a report on
it at a later meeting when all the members would express their
opinion on the report. After the discussion the rapporteur would
draw up a written report, taking into account the discussion that
had taken place, which would express the view of the society on
the case. The report was the responsibility of the rapporteur and

[4] From this point of view the French system of cassation, which allows lower courts
to express their views against that of the Supreme Court twice in the same case, seems
better than the Japanese, which allows for only one such expression. It is to be
hoped that the Supreme Court will always be willing to accept a more reasonable
opinion than its own.
[5] No systematic study of the cases has yet been made.
[6] *Minjiho* means civil law matters and covers not only civil law proper, but
private law in general.

signed by him. These reports were published in a law journal published by the faculty, and at the end of each year they were reproduced with changes or additions in a separate annual volume. The society has done a great deal for the systematic study of case law in Japan, and is still very active and regularly publishes the results of its discussions. The society's merit is not only in the development of scientific studies of law, but also in the way it has helped educate young lawyers.[7]

Inspired by the activities of this group the study of civil case law became widespread, and no private law text now fails to devote a good number of its pages to an explanation of the main cases in the field of study.[8] Besides these texts, many monographs have been devoted solely to the topic of the analysis of case law, sometimes in a limited field, such as that of civil responsibility, and sometimes in a more extensive field, such as real rights.

In the field of penal law cases also enjoy an important position, and there is also a society that studies criminal case law. However, because of the principle of legality they play a role of a slightly different kind. The creative force of case law is more limited here than elsewhere. The cases serve rather to give precision to the legislative texts than to modify them.

In the field of labor law the situation is again a little different. As has been already observed, Japanese workers have only since the end of World War II obtained any legal guarantee for their rights, and the abrupt change in their social situation has engendered a rather peculiar outlook among workers. In their zeal to improve their social position, they have often made excessive use of legal methods. By way of response, employers who have not been able to adapt fully to the new work conditions, have reacted violently. The result has been countless disputes between the employers and the work force. The courts had a very important piece of work to do in this field, and their decisions

---

[7] By being present at the sessions and following the discussions of the session young lawyers receive a very good training in collective research methods.

[8] In the legal training given in law faculties the study of the cases is very important, and many case books have been edited for students' use.

created a body of case law in the field in a relatively short period of time. Disputes between workers and employers are, however, frequently less of a legal than of an ideological nature. Rights are claimed without any real justification for them being given, as is shown by the large number of cases in the labor law field aimed at obtaining injunctions to maintain the status quo, both parties seeking to retain their position of power until the court decides the matter definitively.

In the field of public law the role of case law has been rather striking since the reform of the judiciary in 1947. Before this time the administrative court was competent in all cases concerning public law, and the class of case that a person could bring to the court was also strictly limited. The individual was almost completely deprived of protection against abuse of power. The judicial reform of 1947 greatly changed this. From 1947 onward there was no administrative court, but all the ordinary courts had jurisdiction in public law matters. Public authorities have since then had to concern themselves with the decision that a court might give in cases that arose between individuals and them and have ceased to enjoy the privilege of being able to impose their "administrative" interpretation of the laws on the people. They have had to fall in line with the judicial interpretation of the law in order not to end up in court. The result has been a remarkable strengthening of the rule of law.

A court, when seised of a matter relating to the constitutionality of a law, must give a true interpretation of the Constitution, and this too serves to create a body of decisions in the constitutional law field which could not have existed under the former regime. The decisions of the Supreme Court are of special importance. Under the Meiji Constitution it was considered sufficient to give a purely political or ideological interpretation of this sacred document, but today the interpretation of the Constitution has to be a legal one. Controlling the constitutionality of law does mean that the court runs the risk of getting involved in politics, but when a truly political issue is involved this can be avoided by invoking what French jurists call "la théorie de l'acte de gouvernement."

2. Nature of Judgments

Every judgment must be given in open court (article 70 of the law on the courts). In civil cases the Code of Civil Procedure provides that judgment must be pronounced by the judge who presided at the hearing, and he must read the decision contained in the original of the judgment (article 189). The position is almost the same for criminal judgments (article 35 of the rules of criminal procedure). Judgments are written before they are delivered.

In civil cases the reading of the reasons is optional, and depending on circumstances the judge may read none of the reasoning, read it all, or give a brief oral résumé of the reasoning (article 189, II, Code of Civil Procedure). In criminal cases the reasoning must be read, or an oral résumé of it given, at the time the decision is read (article 35 of the rules of criminal procedure).

The written judgment is called *hanketsu-sho* and has three basic parts. The first part is the decision called *shubun* (literally, the principle sentence), and it comes at the beginning of the judgment. The content of the decision varies according to the cases. It may, for instance, include a proposition such as, "The defendant is obliged to pay the plaintiff 100,000 yen," or "The accused is committed to five years imprisonment with hard labor." In the case of a purely declarative or constitutive judgment the formula is a little different; for example, "[The court][9] declares that the building in question belongs to the plaintiff," or "[The court] declares the separation of the plaintiff and defendant by divorce."[10] The name of the court must be mentioned in the decision (article 191 of the Code of Civil Procedure).

The second part gives the legal and factual basis of the judg-

[9] The Japanese language usually omits the grammatical subject except when it is necessary to avoid apparent ambiguity in meaning. This practice is usually followed in judgments, but recently there has been a tendency even among judges to express the subject more frequently both in speaking and in writing.

[10] This is not a faithful translation of the formulae of a Japanese divorce decree. The Japanese word corresponding to divorce can be used both transitively and intransitively. The Japanese court says that it divorces the petitioner from the respondent as if this verb could be used in a transitive sense. It is the judgment itself which creates the divorce. All the former has to do is to pronounce the divorce; it neither declares the result of the act of divorce between the parties nor orders them to divorce.

ment. It describes the claims of the parties and the facts on which they are based. On this basis the court reaches its conclusion. The noting of these elements is not specifically required by the Code of Criminal Procedure, but the Code of Civil Procedure enumerates them among the obligatory parts of a judgment (article 191).

In the third part the court sets out the line of reasoning (*riyu*) by which it reached its decision. The court shows how it has dealt with the matters of fact and law presented by the parties and how it has chosen material facts in order to arrive at the conclusion required by the law. The reasoning must be given in every judgment (article 191 of the Code of Civil Procedure; article 44 of the Code of Criminal Procedure).

Every judge who has taken part in deciding a case must sign the original of the judgment and place his *in* or *han* on it (article 191 of the Code of Civil Procedure; article 55 of the rules of Criminal Procedure). The *in* or *han* is a small seal which serves to identify the person whose name is written beside it.[11]

The style of judgment is distinctive, and in Japan as in France the court speaks in a language that is rather distant from the everyday language of the people. Though judges are now trying to bring their usage into line with daily speech, there is still a court jargon. Judges are in no way obliged to follow the standard style, and there are some judges who try to improve the court style of language and make it more colloquial, but most cases are heard by a bench of judges and this acts as a leveling factor on the mode of expression.

By way of illustration of what has been said in the last paragraphs a typical example is given here from among actual judgments. The text is taken from a collection of judgments used by

[11] This means of identification is generally used throughout the country. It corresponds to a signature in Europe. In Japan a signature alone is not considered as in any way guaranteeing the authenticity of a document. The writing of a name does not need to be an autograph for a written document to be authoritative provided that the writing of the name is accompanied by the placing of the legalized seal beside it. For this reason a document marked with the legal seal is considered valid until the contrary is proved. The placing of the seal has such importance that article 82 of the law on bills of exchange assimilates the writing of the name accompanied by the imprint of the seal to the signature that is required by this law according to international usage.

students in civil procedure classes in a book edited by Professor Mikazuki of the Faculty of Law at the University of Tokyo. The whole text is reproduced without any modification except for the names of the parties. The decision was handed down by a judge sitting alone, but there would be no great difference if the decision had been that of a bench of judges.

No. 100 (*wa*) 1960[12]

Handed down on 1 October, 1960. The original of the judgment received the same day by Registrar Iwamura Masaru. (Signature and seal)[13]

Judgment
53, Hiyoshi-honcho, Kohoku-ku, Yokohama,
Plaintiff Koda Ichiro.
Represented by attorney, Oumi Hiroshi.

3, 2-chome, Misono, Ota-ku, Tokyo.
Defendant Otoyama Jiro.
Represented by attorney, Koike Kiyoshi.

The court decides as follows in case No. 100 (*wa*) 1960 between the above-mentioned parties in a matter concerning the payment of promissory notes.

Decision
The defendant shall pay the sum of 260,000 yen, plus interest

[12] The sign *wa* is used to indicate the type of judgment. *Wa* is written in *kana* (phonetic symbols). Every judgment is classified according to a category each of which has its own symbol. The symbol *wa* means that this judgment was given by a district court in ordinary contentious proceedings. Judgments in civil cases are marked by *katakana*, e.g., the judgment of the Supreme Court in a civil appeal is marked by the *katakana o*. Decisions in criminal cases are designated by *hiragana*. To determine the type of judgment a particular sign represents, cf. regulations of 23 February, 1947, for civil cases, and the regulations of 20 December, 1949, for criminal cases.
[13] This part appears in the margin of the judgment.

from 12 March 1960 until full payment at the rate of 6 percent because of tardy payment.

The defendant is to pay costs.

This judgment can be provisionally executed by giving 60,000 yen security.

Facts

The plaintiff's attorney asked the court to give a judgment which would admit the claims made in the first and second parts of the judgment and to make a declaration for the provisional execution of judgment. To justify these claims the following allegations were made:

1. The plaintiff acquired on 11 March, 1960, from the Nippon Kogyo Co. Ltd., which is not a party to the present action, two promissory notes signed by the defendant on 27 July, 1959, and delivered to the said company the space for the date being left blank. These two notes had the following purport:

(a) The first note: sum payable, 110,000 yen; date of maturity, 15 October, 1959; place of payment and signature, Ota-ku, Tokyo; place of actual execution, Kamata branch of Daito Bank.

(b) The second note: the sum payable, 150,000 yen; date of maturity, 15 November 1959; and the place of signature, payment, and actual execution, the same as for the first note. The plaintiff is still the holder of the note.

2. The plaintiff filled in the blank portions indicating the date as 27 July, 1959, which is identical with the date of signature, at the first hearing which took place on 11 March, 1960.

3. Founding his case on these facts the plaintiff claimed that the defendant should pay him a total of 260,000 yen plus interest running from 12 March, 1960, the day following that on which the date of issue was filled in, until payment was complete, calculated at the commercial rate of 6 percent.

As far as the defendant's case is concerned the plaintiff's attorney said: "The plaintiff denies the facts alleged by the defendant, that is, that he was a purchaser in bad faith of the notes in question and that he knew the other facts."

By way of proof he presented two documents in evidence—A-1 and A-2—and he has relied on the result of the questioning of the plaintiff by the court.

The defendant's attorney sought dismissal of the plaintiff's action. His defense was as follows:

1. Among the facts alleged by the plaintiff, the defendant accepts the fact he signed, as the plaintiff claims, two promissory notes addressed to the Nippon Kogyo Co. Ltd., which is not a party to this dispute, but he denies all the other facts.

2. The defendant signed these two notes in order to pay by way of advance part of the price that he owed the Nippon Kogyo Co. Ltd. for gravel, sand, and other materials that he bought from said company. The defendant had asked the company to return the two notes to him because it had delayed the execution of the obligations that it had assumed vis-à-vis the defendant to deliver the objects of sale within 15 days. The company endorsed the two notes to the plaintiff's order, and the plaintiff then opened a credit for it against this security. The plaintiff acquired the notes knowing these circumstances and that the company had to return them to the defendant for the above-mentioned reasons. Therefore, the plaintiff had no authority to seek payment of the notes from the defendant.

By way of proof the deposition of the witness Yamada Sampei and the result of the questioning of the defendant by the court were relied on. The authenticity of the documents A-1 and A-2 was admitted.

Reasoning

1. The fact that the defendant signed the two promissory notes in question addressed to the Nippon Kogyo Co. Ltd., which is not a party to the present case, and that said company endorsed them for the benefit of the plaintiff is contested by no one. It is evident to the court that the plaintiff filled in the blanks relating to the date and dated them 27 July, 1959, at the first hearing on 11 March, 1960.

2. Let us then consider the defense presented by the defendant.

Given the deposition of witness Yamada Sampei (except the part mentioned below) and as a result of the questioning of the defendant it is obvious that in about July, 1959, a contract of sale was made between the defendant as purchaser and the Nippon Kogyo Co. Ltd. as seller, and that the object of the sale was gravel for a total sum of 1,500,000 yen; that the promissory notes in question were signed in order to pay a part of this price by way of advance; and that the said company soon found itself in financial difficulties and was unable to execute its obligations under the contract. On the question of the delivery of the gravel up to the amount of the above-mentioned price there is the deposition of Yamada Sampei to the fact that the Nippon Kogyo Co. Ltd. did deliver, but his evidence is not credible although he claims it to be so. No other proof is available of the fact.

There is, however, no proof that the plaintiff was in bad faith when he acquired the notes from the Nippon Kogyo Co. Ltd., in spite of the claims of the defendant. On the contrary, given the evidence of Yamada Sampei and the result of the questioning of the plaintiff, it can be stated that the plaintiff received the notes by way of security for a credit that he had opened for the Nippon Kogyo Co. Ltd. at its request, and that he knew that the notes had been signed by the defendant to pay the price under a sale contract concluded between the Nippon Kogyo Co. Ltd. and him. The plaintiff did not, however, know how the contracting parties were proceeding with the execution of the obligations under the contract: he checked the solvency of the drawer at the bank designated on the note as the place for execution.

For these reasons the defense of the defendant is ill-founded.

3. For the following reasons the claim must be admitted as well-founded: the defendant is bound to pay to the plaintiff the total sum of 260,000 yen, which represents the total of the sums of the two notes as well as interest for tardy payment at the commercial rate of 6 percent from 12 March, 1960 (the day following the day on which the date was entered on the notes), until the completion of said payment. It is for these reasons that the court gives judgment as the decision sets out: the question of costs is governed by article 89 of the Code of Civil Procedure and as far as a declaration of provisional execution is concerned article 196 of the same code is applicable.

The . . .th civil chamber of the Tokyo District Court.

Judge Yoshikawa Tadasuke
(signature and seal)

3. Law Reports

There are a great number of official and private law reports in Japan. The main official collections will be dealt with first.

(1) *Reports Edited by the Supreme Court since 1947.* There are several collections of judgments of the courts of every rank, but in almost every case it is the Supreme Court which edits them. The Supreme Court orders all the subordinate courts to choose their important judgments according to general criteria laid down by the Supreme Court, and to send them to the Supreme Court.

Judgments are usually chosen by case law committees set up within the Supreme Court and in each of the superior courts by a Supreme Court subregulation of 15 December, 1947. Each committee has to determine whether a decision of the court to which it belongs should be published in the collection (article 2). The committee of the Supreme Court consists of not more than seven members, and that of the superior courts of not more than ten members (article 3). Each committee has an office and secretarial staff (articles 6 and 7). The case law committee of the Supreme Court at present consists of six judges, two appointed by each division of the court. The president is elected by cooptation. The secretariat is made up of all the assistants and two chief executive officers. The assistants specialize in either civil or criminal matters and attend only the meetings concerned with cases in their field of speciality. Only the first secretary is a permanent member. Judgments which are to be discussed at a given meeting are chosen beforehand by the assistants, in accordance with the views of members from the bench.

(a) *Collection of Decisions of the Supreme Court (Saiko saibansho saibanshu).* This collection is for use by judges. It is printed, but only for the purpose of distribution to persons on a list drawn up by the court. Not all Supreme Court decisions are included in this collection. The decision on which cases to include is taken by the Supreme Court judges' assistants. The way in which the cases are chosen depends on whether the matters involved are civil or criminal.

(b) *Collection of Supreme Court Cases (Saiko saibansho hanreishu).*

This collection contains all the judgments of the Supreme Court that are considered to have value as precedents, is available to the public, and is published every month. The collection is published in two separate series, civil and penal, and is the one that the societies for the study of case law use as the source of judgments they study.

(c) *Collection of Superior Courts Cases* (*Koto saibansho hanreishu*). This collection contains all the important judgments of the eight superior courts, chosen by the case law committee of each superior court. The committees are of a varied nature, reflecting the different composition of each of the courts. The superior court of Tokyo has a committee of twenty-eight members, which includes ten judges, five representing the civil chambers and five the criminal chambers. The president of the court sits in on each session as an observer. The chairing of the committee alternates every year between the judges of the civil and criminal chambers. The sessions are held separately for civil and criminal matters, and the president of the session is therefore not always the president of the committee. It is said that each committee has a tendency to choose judgments which express the general opinion of the court without worrying very much about their precedent value. The selection of judgments is often therefore, a means of propaganda for the court.

(d) *Collection of Administrative Law Decisions* (*Gyoseijike saiban-reishu*). In terms of a Supreme Court circular to subordinate courts, every subordinate court must send important decisions given in administrative affairs to the Supreme Court for consideration. The criteria for choosing important decisions are set down in the circular, and from the decisions sent to the Supreme Court in this way and those given by the Supreme Court itself in administrative matters are selected the judgments for publication in this collection. Judgments which have already been included in the *Collection of Supreme Court Cases* and those which apply well-established principles are not included. The collection is published monthly, includes about forty percent of the total number of decisions sent to the Supreme Court for consideration, and is available to the public.

(e)   *Collection of Decisions on Civil Matters in the Field of Labor Law* (*Rodokankei minji hanreishu*).   As an aid to judges, a Supreme Court circular like that for administrative matters has been addressed to subordinate courts for the collection of labor law cases. The collection appears every two months and contains about half the judgments referred to the Supreme Court for consideration by the subordinate courts. It is available to the public.

(f)   *Collection of Decisions in Civil Matters Given by Subordinate Courts* (*Kakyu saibansho saibanreishu*).   This collection, too, is compiled by the Supreme Court from those decisions sent to it in response to a circular and includes those that appear important from the point of view of judicial practice. The judgments are chosen in an interesting way. Each assessor evaluates a case by allotting it a figure on a 1 to 5 scale. A decision getting an average of 4 must be included, a decision getting 3+ is considered as desirable, one getting 3 as average is less desirable, a decision coming out with a 3 — average need not be included, and so on. Once a first selection is worked out on this basis, the cases are reviewed a second time. About twenty-five decisions are published each month, and the collection is available to the public.

(g)   *Collection of Decisions in Criminal Matters Given by the Subordinate Courts* (*Kakyu saibansho keiji hanreishu*).   This collection is similar in nature to the preceding one and follows a like collection with a different title that was published until 1959. One assistant judge handles decisions with basic rules, and another one decisions with procedural rules. The collection is published monthly but is available only to a limited number of persons.

(h)   *Monthly Bulletin of Decisions of the Family Courts* (*Katei saibansho hanketsu geppo*).   The decisions in this collection are chosen from those that are sent by each family court to the Supreme Court as required by a circular which states the importance of the decision for judicial practice as the criterion for choice. The bulletin is very useful for the study of family law because most of the family law cases are to be found in it.

(2)   *Other Official Reports since 1947.*   Alongside the eight collec-

tions edited by the Supreme Court there is the *Bulletin of the Judgments of the Superior Court of Tokyo*, published by the information services of the court, and *Quick Facts on Criminal Law Cases of the Superior Courts*, published by the ministère public to facilitate the prosecution of cases by the parquet. The bulletin originally included only criminal cases, but since 1953 it has also included civil decisions. It is available for distribution to the public. The collection of the ministère public includes judgments which may go on appeal, those of the Supreme Court, those in which the decision on matters of fact has been particularly difficult, and those which are so unusual that they will be of especial value in the work of the ministère public. The idea is to give quick facts, and only a résumé of the decisions is published. This publication is not available to the public.

(3) *Law Reports before 1947.* The Court of Cassation (*Daishinin*), the predecessor of the Supreme Court, was created in 1875. The judgments given by this court from 1875 to 1894 have been collected in the *Collection of Judgments of the Court of Cassation (Daishin hanketsuroku)*. The compilation is in two series, one civil and one criminal. Each series is of twenty-two volumes, and each volume contains judgments of one year.[14] In 1895 the editing methods changed, and a new series for both criminal and civil cases was started under the same title; in 1922 the manner of editing was changed again, and the annual volumes of each series were published under the title *Collection of Judgments of the Court of Cassation (Daishinin hanreishu)*. The last volume of the civil series was published in 1946 and of the criminal series in 1947.

The judgments of the administrative court can be found in an official collection called *Collection of the Judgments of the Administrative Court (Gyosei saibansho hanketsuroku)*. It contains judgments given by the court between 1890 and 1947, that is, from its creation to its abolition.

There is only one source for reference to the judgments of the lower courts before 1947, and it is less satisfactory than the official series for the decisions of the Court of Cassation. This is the journal *Horitsu shimbun* (law journal), which from 1900 to

---

[14] All the volumes of the civil series have been reproduced recently.

1942 contained, besides a chronicle of contemporary legal problems, the main judgments of the Court of Cassation and of the lower courts.

The main private systems of law reporting are the following:

(1)   The *Hanrei taikei* (systematic collection of case law) and the *Shin hanrei taikei* (big new collection of case law) gather together all the important judgments of all courts in a systematic manner. They are regularly brought up to date by a system of loose leaves and are reasonably complete. The judgments themselves are not reported in toto, and it is necessary to consult the official collections for details.

The *Hanrei taikei* is published by the law publishers, Daiichi Hoki Shuppan Kabushiki-kaisha. The editing is in the hands of a committee made up of about ten specialists in various fields of law. The collection is divided into three parts, public law, civil law, and criminal law, and contains about fifty volumes. The judgments are classified in a methodical way and grouped under accepted legal headings.

The *Shin hanrei taikei* is a similar publication brought out by Shin Nippon Hoki Shuppan Kabushiki-kaisha. Under the direction of three of the leading contemporary jurists, an editorial committee deals with the methodical classification of the cases. This collection is also divided into three parts, of which the structure is almost the same as that of the *Hanrei taikei*.

(2)   In spite of its title, the monthly *Hanrei Times*, (case law times) which has been published since 1948, does not contain only cases, but it is worth consulting for the most recent judgments because the main public and private law reports appear a considerable time after judgment.

(3)   The *Hanrei jiho* (case law periodical), published every ten days, is truly specialized in that it contains only cases. From its appearance in 1953, it has provided a very quick and ready source of information on the important judgments given in all fields.

(4)   *Case notes*. All law journals devote some pages to the study of cases. Among the many, the publications of the Association for the Study of Case Law of the University of Tokyo are the most important. This association has, since the war, succeeded

the two societies that were mentioned earlier. The association is at present divided into three sections, private law, criminal law, and public law. Each section holds separate sessions to deal with the judgments in its particular field, but for discussions on judgments in the constitutional law field a plenary session is held. All the judgments published in the *Collection of Supreme Court Cases* are studied by the association.

The studies made by the association of the civil law cases are published in *Civil Case Law*, and the new series includes notes on judgments in administrative law cases.

The work of the society for the study of criminal law cases is found in fourteen volumes covering the period 1938–1952 and published under the title *Collection of Critical Studies on Case Law in the Criminal Field*.

Cases are also studied by three other societies[15]—the Commercial Law Study Group at the University of Tokyo, the Labor Law Study Group at the University of Tokyo, and the Interstate Business Law Study Group, which studies judgments in the field of private international law. The collective work of the three groups is published periodically in the review *Jurisuto*.

LEGAL THEORY

Unlike Roman law of the classical period when certain jurisconsults had the *ius respondendi* and legal theory had the force of law, Japanese law, like other modern laws, does not recognize legal theory as a source of law. The research of jurists is, of course, very important to the formation of positive law, but only in an indirect manner. It prepares the theoretical basis for the formation of legal rules, excites legislative activity, and inspires judicial thinking. In modern society the control of legal relationships can be guaranteed only by resort to scientific knowledge. Neither the legislator nor the courts can fulfill their role without reference to theory, and so both legislation and cases have their origin in relevant theory. In this sense theory is basic to law and is a source of law.

[15] Membership in these groups is not limited to those at the University of Tokyo.

SOURCES OF LAW

In Japanese law the role played by theory in the development of legal rules is recognized by the judiciary. Judges are much closer in outlook to law professors than to public officials, and they are proud of being theoreticians and not simply practitioners. The courts are dominated by an outlook very close to that of the law faculty, and courts and faculties are closely linked by feelings of solidarity.[16]

Government and Parliament, on the other hand, do not like theory. Even when they have to resort to it, they try to use only technical information, because they find the critical spirit of scientific thinking unbearable. This attitude was particularly strong in the era of the Meiji Constitution. Then, every progressive theory was violently repressed, and in the field of public law no truly scientific theory was allowed to exist other than in a disguised form. Professor Minobe, when he explicitly affirmed that the tenno was only an organ of the state, was deprived of his status as a member of the House of Lords on the pretext that his doctrine attacked the sacred character of the tenno, and he was later also the victim of an attack by an individual of extreme right-wing beliefs. Truly unhampered research in the social science field has only become possible since World War II.

Before the war all theorizing had a strongly exegetical tendency. The theoretical activities of lawyers consisted mainly in clarifying legislative texts and cases and in explaining the inherent logic in legislation or case law; there was no discussion of law in relation to social, economic, political, or philosophical factors. The studies only justified or rationalized what the state had done. This approach suited lawyers trained to be faithful to the power hierarchy, and the complaint that the Imperial University served as a nursery of loyal bureaucrats is not unfounded. Though the predominant trend was clear, some truly

---

[16] The Japanese judge resembles the French judge whom David describes for us in *Le droit français*, Vol. I, p. 52. This is as one would expect because at the beginning of the Meiji era almost all the judges were trained in French law by French professors. The tradition was strengthened by the influence of German law, which succeeded French law in this role. In spite of strong Anglo-American legal influences since the end of the Second World War, the Japanese judge usually stays within the framework of the Romano-Germanic tradition.

scientific work was nevertheless done during the Meiji era, as Professor Minobe's work alone proves.[17]

Since the war the situation has changed completely. All theory aims at being scientific. By way of reaction against the repression of earlier scientific efforts, theory now runs the risk of going to the other extreme. As soon as the yoke of the absolutist military regime was lifted, theory showed a strong tendency to denigrate everything from the past without inquiring whether there had been anything that was good. Generally, however, the current approach is healthy, and fruitful theoretical discussions are now frequent in all scientific fields.

In current legal thinking three main tendencies can be seen. The first is a sociological rather than a legal one. An attempt is being made to build a truly scientific theory of law to distinguish the science of law, properly so called, from the study of law at a practical level. The latter serves to interpret positive law, while the theory of law seeks to study legal phenomena objectively in their role as social facts. Within this current there are two main streams: one is based fairly directly on Marxist methodology, the other tends to be influenced by American sociology. The sociological school has already rendered great service to the rejuvenation of Japanese jurisprudence. In particular its research into social facts and traditional life, which resulted in the observance of rules of conduct in society independent of state regulation,[18] has been very valuable in establishing the correlation between the state law and the life of the people. The accent that this school places on the urgent need for further sociological studies is related to the historical peculiarities of Japanese law.

A second tendency is toward giving legal terms greater clarity and precision. Under the influence of analytical philosophy an attempt is being made to define legal concepts more scientifically, and to exclude from the field of law any metaphysical ideas

[17] Cf. Saburo Ienaga, *Minobe Tatsukichi no shisoshiteki kenkyu* [Minobe Tatsukichi: Study in the History of Ideas] (Tokyo: Iwanami Shoten, 1964). This book is in Japanese and is the best work from the point of view of a general presentation of Minobe's ideas. Cf. also Frank O. Miller, *Minobe Tatsukichi: Interpreter of Constitutionalism in Japan* (Berkeley: University of California Press, 1965).

[18] The results of this type of research have been used throughout this book.

which, so the followers of this line of thought say, breed theoretical confusion and sterile controversy. It does not appear that the aims of this school of thought can be quickly achieved, but its efforts are nevertheless useful. In Japan very vague words are generally used even in scientific fields, and this school can do a great deal to expose the fact that Japanese language and thought are in general shrouded in irrationality. The reason analytical philosophy is not as popular in France as in Japan doubtless reflects the precision and clarity of the French language.

The third tendency has had greater practical importance than the other two. Under the influence of Anglo-American law, which replaced European law in its role as advisor to Japanese law, all legal problems are looked at from a procedural point of view. This school tries above all to see what the courts have done in solving this and that problem. Following the American realist method, law is seen in the final analysis only in judges' decisions. The analysis of case law becomes the central object of study, not for the purpose of giving precision to the logic inherent in the cases generally, but to note the general tendency of legal decisions on a given point so that the solution that the court will give on that same point can be predicted in the future. The basis of this approach is the same as that of the natural sciences, in that science must study the natural laws within the framework of life in order to be able to control these laws effectively. Thus this tendency is akin to the first in the emphasis that it places on sociological, or more precisely psycho-sociological, method.

As can be seen from this summary of the principal currents of legal theory, the allure of Western ideas is still dominant. Without in any way denying the value and necessity of resorting to the use of the methods of other human cultures to deepen scientific knowledge of law, it must be recognized that scientific method must be built up and continually reworked in order to apply better to the objects under investigation and to provide for better analysis of them. Pure mechanical application of a method imported from a quite different environment, however excellent it may be in itself, does not always help in the scientific study of local social factors which have been determined geographically and historically by forces peculiar to themselves.

Apart from those truly universal elements which are found without exception in all human cultures, there is a need, if there is to be objective communication with others, to establish a clear picture of Japanese law, omitting no point which brings out the individuality of the Japanese legal culture. To date, the efforts in this particular line of research have not been very satisfactory.

BIBLIOGRAPHICAL NOTES

Apart from references to be found in the standard law bibliographies and periodicals, indexes, lists of books on or relating to Japanese law can be found in the following:

International Encyclopedia of Comparative Law, Vol. I, p. J22–J25 (Japan).

Japanese Law: Legal and Related Materials in English, University of Illinois Law Library (1974).

Japanese Law: A Selective Bibliographical Guide, Law Library Journal, Vol. 63 (1970), pp. 189–230.

Juris-Classeur: Droit Comparé, beginning of the section on Japanese law.

Noda, Yosiyuki. *Introduction au droit japonais*. Paris: Librairie Dalloz, 1966. Appendices 4 and 5, pp. 269–280. This bibliography has a short list of materials in European languages and a very full list of texts in Japanese.

INDEX

A

administrative commissions, in the United States, 102
administrative law, 23, 29, 57, 112–118, 125, 127–132, 207, 211, 229, 237, 239
amnesty, 67
appeals, 129, 205, 211
arbitration, 206
association, right of, 17
attitude toward law, Japanese, 159–174. *See also* conception of law, Japanese
attorneys, 135, 142–150, 152, 153
Ausschliessung, 205
Ausschlussurteil, 206

B

Bakufu, 27–32, 34–36, 41–43
bankruptcy law, 53
beneficium, 28
bengoshi, 144–145
bills, legislative, 45, 100, 188
bills of exchange, 53, 204, 231
board of audit, 88, 100
Boissonade, Gustave, 37, 44–48, 50, 51–54, 125, 149, 207, 209, 223
Bousquet, Georges, 45, 53
Buddhism, 31, 32, 160, 170, 172
budget, 56, 87, 88, 97, 188
bugyo, 36
buke, 26, 30, 32
buke-ho, 29–31
bungen, 33, 34, 177
bushi, 26, 27, 29–34, 42, 48, 50
bushido, 30, 31

C

Cabinet. *See* Naikaku
Cabinet Legislation Bureau, 100
capitalism, 8, 13, 14, 42, 48, 59–61
case law, 188, 225–229, 242. *See also* judgments
cheques, 53, 203, 204
Chinese characters, 9–11, 159
chonin, 33
chozenshugi, 98
Civil Code
    Argentinian, 187
    Austrian, 187
    French, 43–47, 51, 52, 59, 177, 180, 189, 197–201, 218, 223
    German, 51, 52, 199, 206
    Japanese, 44–46, 48, 50–53, 55, 81, 177, 180, 187, 197–202, 204, 206, 219, 220, 223
    Spanish, 187
    Swiss, 187
civil law, 23, 35, 36, 54, 227, 230
civil procedure, 35, 53–55, 113, 114, 116–118, 125, 230
Civil Procedure Code
    French, 55, 207
    Japanese, 189, 204–207, 230–231. *See also* civil procedure
clergy, 32
code of chivalry, 30
Commercial Code
    French, 53, 100, 204
    Japanese, 52, 53, 188, 202–204
Commission for Constitutional Research, 66, 190, 192
Commission for Constitutional Studies, 191